PRAISE FOR *BOYS*

'A damning look at toxic masculinity. It's the most important thing you'll read this year.' ***Elle* Australia**

'*Boys Will Be Boys* is a timely contribution to feminist literature. Her central point is clear and confronting, and it represents something of a challenge... Ferocious, incisive, an effective treatise.' ***Australian Book Review***

'A piercing gaze at contemporary patriarchy, gendered oppression and toxic masculinity.' ***Sydney Morning Herald***

'A truly vital piece of social commentary from Australia's fiercest feminist, *Boys Will Be Boys* should be shoved into the hands of every person you know. Clementine Ford has done her research—despite what her angry detractors would have you believe—and spits truths about toxic masculinity and the dangers of the patriarchy with passion and a wonderfully wry sense of humour. Read it, learn from it, and share it—this book is absolute GOLD!' ***AU Review*, 16 Best Books of 2018**

'*Boys Will Be Boys* is an impassioned call for societal change from a writer who has become a stand-out voice of her generation (and has the trolls to prove it) and an act of devotion from a mother to her son.' ***Readings***

'With pithy jokes and witty commentary, this is an engrossing read, and Ford's spirited tone evokes passion for change.' ***Foreword Reviews***

'Clementine Ford reveals the fragility behind "toxic masculinity" in *Boys Will Be Boys*.' ***The Conversation***

'*Boys Will Be Boys* highlights the need to refocus on how we're raising our boys to be better men. The ingrained toxic masculinity within society does just as much damage to our boys as it does to our girls, and this book highlights how to change that.' ***Fernwood Magazine***

PRAISE FOR *FIGHT LIKE A GIRL*

'Her brilliant book could light a fire with its fury. It gets my synapses crackling and popping; I find I can't sit down while reading it, so instead I pace the sitting room.' ***Sunday Times***

'There's a wonderful book by Clementine Ford that I advise every woman, and especially young women, to read called *Fight Like a Girl*.' **Kate Beckinsale**

'It's the wit and searing honesty of her own personal life laid bare where *Fight Like a Girl* truly shines.' ***Irish Independent***

'Changed my life. I have never read a book like this.' **Pandora Sykes**

'Clementine Ford was put on this earth to give courage to the young girl inside all of us. This is an exciting, essential book from Australia's most fearless feminist writer.' **Laurie Penny, author of *Unspeakable Things***

'Yes, *Fight Like A Girl* will make you angry. It will make you feel uncomfortable. But, ultimately, it will inspire you to create change.' ***Marie Claire***

'Required reading for every young man and woman, a brave manifesto for gender equality, harm minimisation and self-care.' ***The Australian***

'Clementine is furious and scathing . . . yet compassionate and encouraging every moment she can be. This book is both a confirmation of sisterhood and a call to arms.' **Bri Lee, author of *Eggshell Skull* and co-founder of Hot Chicks with Big Brains**

'An intimate, though universal, call to arms . . . Ford's book is a galvanizing tour de force, begging women to never give up on the most radical act of all: loving themselves wholly and completely in a world that doesn't love them back.' ***Booklist***

'A potent mix of memoir and manifesto, equal parts fierce and friendly; an intimate, witty self-portrait and a rousing call to arms for women everywhere to know their rage, own it, wear it and channel it into fighting for change.' ***Sydney Morning Herald***

'*Fight Like A Girl* is fuelled by Ford's clear-eyed defiance and refusal to compromise, and by her powerful combination of personal testimony and political polemic. In the vein of Caitlin Moran's *How to be a Woman* or Roxane Gay's *Bad Feminist*.' ***Books + Publishing***

'It's a call to action but, more importantly, it's a call to reason. A must-read for all women.' ***Fashion Journal***

'Brutally honest and unapologetic . . . Ford tackles society's double standards and contradictions, tackling these head-on like a fearless heroine . . . *Fight Like A Girl* is a feisty call to arms for modern women . . . Keep on fighting the good fight, Clem, so that one day we may all enter the ring with you.' ***The AU Review***

'Clementine Ford was one of my very first formative feminist influences, initiating me into the world of feminism. She is someone whose tenacity and fearlessness I admire greatly, and she helped me along the path to becoming the humourless, bitter, lesbian feminist I am today.' **Rebecca Shaw, writer, SBS and WomanAgainstFeminism@NoToFeminism**

'Though casual in tone, *Fight Like A Girl* is persuasive and confronting . . . you finish the book angry—and rightly so . . . It reminds readers to be angry, because there is a lot to be angry about. It is a launching pad into a world of intersectional reading, and more specific advice on how to rock the status quo.' ***Lip Mag***

'Never did I realise I held so much rage against the devaluement of women until reading *Fight Like A Girl* . . . Confronting, immersive and influential.' **Diva Book Nerd**

Clementine Ford is a freelance writer, broadcaster and public speaker based in Naarm/Melbourne.

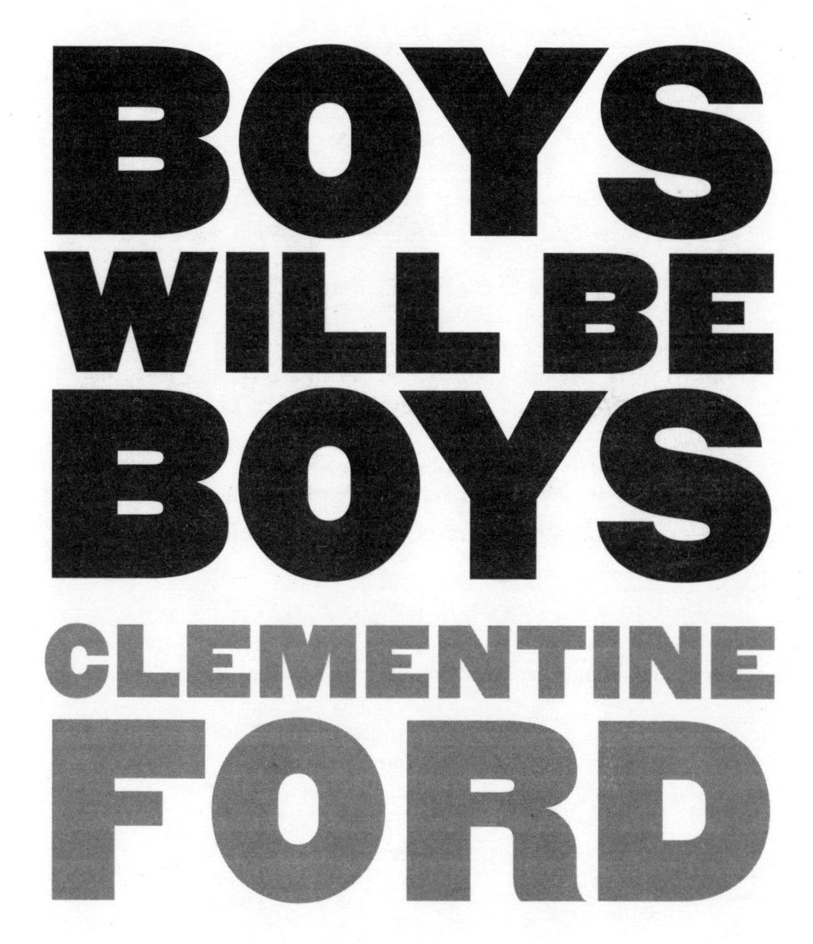
BOYS
WILL BE
BOYS
CLEMENTINE
FORD

ONEWORLD

A Oneworld Book

First published in Great Britain and North America
by Oneworld Publications, 2019

A CIP record for this title is available from the British Library

ISBN 978-1-78607-663-2
eISBN 978-1-78607-664-9

Printed and bound in Great Britain by Clays Ltd, Elcograf S.p.A.

Oneworld Publications
10 Bloomsbury Street
London
WC1B 3 SR
United Kingdom

For my boy

CONTENTS

Author's note xi
Introduction 1

1 It's a boy 13
2 A woman's place 39
3 Girls on film 70
4 Not all men 101
5 We know what boys are like 123
6 Mass debate 151
7 The manosphere 177
8 Your Honour, I object 204
9 The king of the hill 230
10 It's just a joke 257
11 Asking for it 284
12 Witch hunt 324

Epilogue 352
Acknowledgments 359

AUTHOR'S NOTE

Readers should be advised that this book contains detailed references to homophobia, transphobia, men's violence against women, online abuse and misogynist harassment. There are detailed descriptions of rape and assault. Please go gently if you are likely to be triggered by these things.

There is a much larger discussion to be had about the impact of the gender binary in regard to our understanding of 'masculinity' and 'femininity'. I encourage readers to seek out the work of trans and gender diverse writers with lived experience of this, and to continue to seek out the voices of trans and gender diverse people within feminism and social justice. Please note that this book is largely about the harm wielded by cissexist, heteronormative ideals of masculinity and, as such, much of the broader discussion of 'men' in this context is referring to cisgender men who are for the most part white and heterosexual.

A brief note for readers unfamiliar with some of the terms found within:

Transgender: The word applied to people whose assigned sex at birth differs from their gender identity. Please note that gender non-binary trans people may not identify as male or female at all, or as one or the other only some of the time.

Cisgender: The word applied to people whose assigned sex at birth accords with their gender identity. For example, I am a cisgender woman who was assigned female at birth and who identifies as a woman.

Cissexist/Cisnormative: The presumption that cisgender experiences are superior or standard, and the discrimination directed towards trans people and issues because of this.

Heteronormativity: The presumption that heterosexual experiences are superior or standard, and the discrimination directed towards queer people and issues because of this.

Cis-het: Shorthand for someone who is cisgender and heterosexual.

Disabled person (as opposed to **person with a disability**): I follow the lead of the disability activists I know who subscribe to the social model of disability. The social model dictates that people are disabled not by their bodies or conditions, but by the reluctance or outright refusal of a broader ableist society to adapt itself to their needs.

■

This book is not meant to be a definitive guide to toxic masculinity or how feminism responds to it; it would be impossible to cover everything. Trust me, I have had numerous anxiety spirals about this! It's better to consider this book as just one contribution to a larger conversation. I hope very much this is a conversation that you will keep having not just with me but with your friends, family and community.

In solidarity,
Clementine Ford

INTRODUCTION

In 1996's *The Craft* (an epic ride of a movie about four teenage witches who join together to form a coven—shit goes down, people get hurt, don't mess with the gifts you're given etc.), Manon is the spiritual deity who can be invoked to bestow power on his devotees. In describing Manon to newcomer Sarah, coven leader Nancy (played to gothic perfection by Fairuza Balk) says, 'If God and the Devil were playing football, Manon would be the stadium that they played on; He would be the sun that shone down on them.'

The fabricated deity of Manon wasn't intended to represent patriarchy (although you have to question why the spiritual being created as a figure of worship for teenage witches is written as a male figure—something something male scriptwriters, something something don't understand women), but I'm going to steal the analogy to explore how a system that oppresses everybody by, in part, reinforcing regressive stereotypes of binary gender can be continuously unseen even by those oppressed by it.

Like Nancy's explanation of Manon to Sarah, the concept of patriarchy is hard to explain. It is especially hard to explain to those people who have either never heard of it or whose only experience of it is in laughing sarcastically at feminists and all our LOL TRIGGERED paranoia. Patriarchy isn't a visible building that we can walk in and out of. It isn't a wardrobe of clothing we can run our hands through, whose fabric we can feel and count the fibres of. It's in the air we breathe, the gravity that keeps us weighted to the earth. It is a language we learn to speak from the moment we're born, but it has no pattern of speech, no formal sentence structure and no written alphabet.

It's the stadium that the game of life as we know it is played in, the sun that shines down on it and the grass that carpets the ground.

I knew there was a reason I hated football.

Some people are resistant to discussing patriarchy or its impact, because they understand it, not as a form of structural power that is woven through every facet of our lives, but rather as something hysterical women whinge about in order to make men feel bad. But it isn't feminism or the challenges it throws down to patriarchy that creates the cultural expectations placed on men that lead to their self-doubt, to their increased levels of poor mental health (and the subsequent refusal to talk about such things) or to the shame many of them feel for 'failing' to measure up to the so-called rules of manhood inflicted on them from birth. Although the system of patriarchy is designed to privilege masculinity (with an emphasis on cis-het masculinity), it also demands of men a conformity to rigid constraints that, depending on their ability to move freely within these constraints, carries a degree of harm and oppression.

In her no-holds-barred TED talk on patriarchy and how to dismantle it, Professor Ananya Roy, a scholar in urban planning and global development, says, 'Patriarchy also defines the identity of men. It is as much the enforced script of proper masculinity—how to be a real man—as it is that of proper femininity.'

Roy's thinking echoes that of the great feminist and civil rights scholar, bell hooks. In *The Will to Change: Men, Masculinity and Love*, hooks writes:

> The first act of violence that patriarchy demands of males is not violence toward women. Instead patriarchy demands of all males that they engage in acts of psychic self-mutilation, that they kill off the emotional parts of themselves. If an individual is not successful in emotionally crippling himself, he can count on patriarchal men to enact rituals of power that will assault his self-esteem.

I think of this quote often when trying to wrap my head around the ways in which some boys and men are able not only to cause catastrophic harm to girls and women as individuals, but also to collude with each other to perpetrate pack attacks that range from the mildest forms of sexual harassment (if such a thing can ever really be dismissed as 'mild') to the kind of orchestrated, ritualistic gang rapes and assaults that have become more visible now (if not necessarily more common), because of the sickening trend of filming them and sharing them so that even those men who weren't able to join in physically can at least vicariously consume the humiliation of a woman or women and thus deepen their connection to the Brotherhood of Man.

It needs to be understood that we are not talking about outliers here, or people who are inherently evil. Some of them perhaps are; most of them are just easily led. They may be drunk on the thrill of being part of a pack or too afraid to speak out and risk the pack turning on them. And if our sons and brothers and friends and partners and nephews and cousins and fathers and husbands are all susceptible to a bit of 'follow the leader', to 'getting carried away', to not speaking up, to laughing along, to putting themselves and their preservation first in a patriarchal system that rewards complicity among men—if they are all at risk of surrendering to weakness and supported to do so by a culture that refuses to understand the gravity of the problem, none of us can ever really be safe.

■

Two weeks before I sat down to write the introduction to this book, a string of things happened that confirmed to me just how far we had travelled into the fog of toxic masculinity.

The first was the disappearance and presumed murder in early June of a twenty-eight-year-old woman named Qi Yu. Less than a week after she went missing, a nineteen-year-old man—her housemate—was arrested and charged with her murder. At the time of writing, her body had still not been recovered.

That same week, a twenty-two-year-old comedian named Eurydice Dixon was raped and murdered as she walked home after work. Her body was found in the early hours of the morning on the soccer pitch of a popular inner-city Melbourne park, less than 900 metres from her home. A nineteen-year-old man surrendered himself to police a day or so later, after CCTV images of his face had been released to the public. Between the discovery of Eurydice's body and the arrest of the man charged with her murder, a detective from Victoria Police gave a press conference in which he advised people to practise 'situational awareness', as if being hyper aware of our surroundings isn't something women especially have been practising since childhood.

A makeshift memorial site was established at the place where Eurydice was found, and an evening vigil was planned to remember her. That morning we woke to the news that in the dead of night, someone had desecrated the site with a twenty-five-metre-long cock and balls drawn in sticky white paint. Emergency service workers tried to remove it in time for the vigil, but it proved so resistant to their efforts that, in the end, they had to cover it with a tarpaulin.

Just let that sink in for a moment. A woman was raped, murdered and dumped on a sports field. And in response, someone chose to draw a giant dick pointing at the flowers that had been laid to honour her. The actions of a child, surely? Unfortunately not. The man ultimately arrested and charged was Andy Nolch, a thirty-one-year-old man from within the comedy community who had railed against what he saw as the media's demonisation of men in the wake of Eurydice's murder. He later told Fairfax he had done it as 'an attack on feminism'.

The same week of Qi and Eurydice's murders, an eleven-year-old girl was abducted in Newcastle and sexually assaulted for several hours by a man in his late forties. When he was finished, he dumped her by a train line and she walked nearly one kilometre to get home. That little girl worked bravely with police to identify her attacker, and a man was arrested less than a week later and charged. When his name and photograph was released to the public, I watched as online comment sections overflowed with astonishment at how *normal* he looked—as if feminists haven't been arguing for all of eternity that predators don't carry badges that formally identify them as such. Five days after the rape and murder of Eurydice Dixon, a woman was dragged into a car on Lygon Street, a busy strip in Carlton, less than two kilometres from where Eurydice's body had been found. She was raped and then dumped at her home. A few days later, two men handed themselves in to police. They were cricket teammates.

This was one week of high-profile cases in Australia, and I haven't even raised the fact that every week approximately two women are murdered in this country by a current or former intimate partner. (Indeed, less than a month after this, three separate women were murdered on the same day. In a terrible case of syncronicity, the same week I made updated changes to this book for its international release, a young Palestinian woman living in Melbourne was also raped and murdered as she made her way home from seeing a comedy show one night. There was no desecration of her memorial, but it came at the same time as a global outrage towards Gillette for daring to use an advertising campaign to address the topic of toxic masculinity.) In the aftermath of all of these gendered homicides, men everywhere fall over themselves to insist that 'not all men' are responsible for crimes such as these; that, in fact, *most* men are good, decent, wonderful people who would *never* tolerate gendered violence and would always, always, always stand up to intervene when they saw it happen.

The truth is very different. Most men struggle to speak out against sexism and abuse, not necessarily because they're bad people, but because patriarchy impacts us all and the pressure to conform to it is intense. That doesn't mean they aren't very good at pretending. Entire organisations are built on the appeal of rewarding men for just showing up, festooning them with white ribbons and bending over backwards to call them champions, ambassadors, heroes and any other celebratory title you can think of that effectively heralds men for being basically okay humans *some of the time*. Only a few days ago, I read an article in which a quite famous male parenting 'expert' crowed about how *wonderful* it was that men had now increased the time they spent with their children to up to forty minutes a day! Well, hell, let's have a fucking parade.

This is a book about what lies beneath all of this. It's a book about patriarchy, gendered oppression and toxic masculinity. It's a book about how gender inequality and the specific kind of violence meted out to women is maintained because all three of these things work together to keep structures in place that are harmful to everyone, but more superficially beneficial than not to men.

It's not a book about how men are shit. It's a book about how the systems we live in allow men to get away with doing deeply shitty things.

■

A month before I published my first book, *Fight Like A Girl*, I faced one of my toughest challenges yet as a feminist: I became the mother of a boy.

I often hear from parents that they're frightened of having girls in this world. We know what violence can be done to our daughters, and people on the whole seem desperate to find a solution to this. (Practise situational awareness!) Curiously, this search for solutions has yet to include looking at ways to change the behaviour of boys. Instead, we see general pleas to recognise the humanity of girls and women by positioning them in relation to men: she's somebody's daughter/sister/mother/wife, so you must treat her with the reverence with which you treat your own daughters/sisters/mothers/wives.

But who is 'he', the Shadow Man thought to be responsible for all this harm? Is he a mythical creature who hides in the cracks of alley walls, emerging only to wreak havoc on the women who will later be considered naive and foolish for failing to take their own safety seriously? Is he a monster? A loner? A basement dweller getting his kicks out of harassing women on the internet because he's never talked to one in his entire life? A sexual deviant, a criminal, a sadist?

In some cases, yes. (Okay, except for the bit about living in the wall.) But in the vast majority of cases, no. These Shadow Men live very much in the daylight. And just like the women they victimise, hurt, belittle, betray and wield power over, they also have familial connections. They are probably somebody's brother/father/husband. They are more likely than not somebody's colleague, teammate, friend.

In every single case, they are somebody's son.

And yet, we never hear anyone say that they're afraid of having a son in the way that they fear having a daughter. Why? Why are they not afraid of how the world conditions boys to ignore sexism? To dismiss emotions that are considered 'too feminine'? To become macho, to express entitlement, to believe themselves worthy of privilege and praise just because they have grown up hearing how special they are? To hurt women, either alone but sometimes together, because it makes them feel powerful?

Our culture is geared towards privileging boys. They are supported to be our leaders, our bosses, our CEOs, heads of households and legislators. Indeed, the world we live in has been designed by men with the purpose of elevating them to (and keeping them in) power. The patriarchal system under which we all labour is designed to uphold this power while punishing those who challenge its existence in any way. Within this structure, boys are given the space to unfurl and grow, to creep further and further outwards, while girls are forced to retreat ever more inwards.

Every excuse is made for boys to allow them to continue on this path to greatness, even as it creates a rigid blueprint for what masculinity and its inscribed power is supposed to look like. Because everyone knows what boys are like. They're rambunctious. They like to roughhouse and fool around. Boys are drawn to adventure. As children, they like dinosaurs and toy guns and clothes emblazoned with cars. They have no such thing as an inside voice, preferring instead to roar wherever they go. Boys are messy and boisterous, barrelling through the world with an admirable lack of restraint. Here comes trouble! Trouble is their middle name!

Boys are instructed from a very early age to pledge their allegiance to each other. They take care of each other. They have each other's backs. They look after their mates. Mateship is very important to boys. Boys don't cut each other's lunches. You don't go after your mate's missus and you aren't allowed to date their sister unless you get permission. Boys respect each other's property, especially when they're married to it or share the same DNA. Boys respect each other most of all, and close ranks against anyone else who threatens that. *Don't dog the boys.*

Boys like girls too though. They tease and hit girls because they like them so much, pulling their hair and pushing them around in accordance with the strength of their crushes. Boys are red-blooded. They go after what they want. They can't help themselves. Girls have to be on their guard around boys. If girls fail to take the proper precautions to keep themselves out of harm's way, they only have themselves to blame. Boys don't mean to hurt girls. They just lose control. They make mistakes. Hasn't everyone made a mistake at some point in their life? They don't deserve to have their lives ruined over it. Boys have promising futures. They shouldn't be punished for a lapse in judgment, an action that was entirely out of character. Where was the girl in all this? Doesn't it take two to tango? Shouldn't she have been more careful? She should have known what she was getting into, dealing with a boy. It's not as if we don't know what boys are like.

Boys will be boys, after all.

The kind of boyhood that's codified by mainstream cis-normative western society is not an innate state of being. Boys can and will be many things, but what the boys in our world are currently conditioned to be *as a rule* is entitled, domineering, sexist, privileged and, in all too many cases, violent.

We have the power to change that.

In *Fight Like A Girl,* I took a phrase that's commonly used to denigrate girls and repurposed it as something more powerful. My intention with this book is to do the same but in reverse—to take hold of a common sentiment that's bandied about without thought and expose just how damaging it is for everyone, boys included.

Boys Will Be Boys takes aim at toxic male spaces and behaviours that are used to codify male power and dominance, but that also secure protection from the consequences of them. I've looked at how gender inequality is first learned in the home and then filtered down through pop culture, and how this provides the perfect launching pad into even more damaging practices later on—the embrace of online abuse, rape culture, men's rights baloney and even the freezing out of women from governance and leadership.

Of course, there are people who are reluctant to unpack this reality. There's a prevailing belief that toxic masculinity is little more than *laddishness*. That it's part and parcel of what it means to be a man. But I think we should all be deeply concerned about allowing masculinity to be constructed in such a dangerous and, above all, *lazy* way.

As the mother of a boy, I don't believe that he's incapable of controlling his impulses or distinguishing between right and wrong. And as a citizen of the world, I don't accept that this is the best we can offer to boys and men. Why is the perceived freedom of boys to exert their power over space, bodies and society considered so much more important than the dignity and humanity of those harmed in this process, including the boys and men unable or unwilling to collude in this power?

One of the many benefits that will come from dismantling patriarchy is the liberation of boys and men from its grip. Boys are not born with a disdain for girls or for the parts of themselves that are coded as feminine. The unapologetic, unselfconscious desire for affection and tenderness that pours out of little boys is not a gift given to them by nature to be enjoyed briefly before receding against the grain of their growing limbs. Society forces this tenderness out of boys in the same way it punishes forthrightness in girls, rebranding them as 'sissy' and 'bossy' respectively. As hooks says, patriarchy and its insidious messaging teaches boys to kill off the emotional parts of themselves, but if we as their protectors do nothing to stop this then we might as well be handing them the knives.

Very few people seem to worry about boyhood, because it's far easier to frame the real concern as lying with their counterparts (who are always seen as the reflection of boys, rather than individuals in their own right). Fathers of girls joke about erecting force fields around them, sitting on porches with shotguns to scare off any boys who come sniffing around. 'She can date when she's thirty-five!' they holler, because of course they know 'what boys are like'. When stories of sexual harassment or assault hit the news or even arise in conversation, the same men who once upon a time turned away as they saw it happening or perhaps even participated in it themselves now respond with declaration: 'As the father of daughters . . .'—because of course his ownership of a young girl has enabled him to see her as a human being instead of a conquest.

Everyone's afraid that their daughters might be hurt. No one seems to be scared that their sons might be the ones to do it.

This book took me a year to write, but it is the culmination of many years of writing about power, abuse, privilege, male entitlement and rape culture. After all that, here's what I've learned: we shouldn't just be scared. We should be fucking terrified.

—1—

IT'S A BOY

Roughly halfway through my pregnancy, I turned up to a clinic in Melbourne for my second trimester morphology ultrasound. It's a fairly standard procedure, the purpose of which is to determine that the foetus is growing and developing as expected. Among other things, your sonographer will examine the foetus's head and brain, heart, kidneys, bladder, stomach, spine and limbs, including their hands and feet.

Oh yeah, and whether they have a ding or a dong.

As I very quickly discovered once my pregnancy became obvious, one of the first questions asked of expectant parents is whether or not they know the sex of their baby. While there's nothing consciously nefarious about this enquiry, the subtle motivations for it are worthy of critique. Forming an idea of something or someone may well be a natural part of connection, but one of the first ways we're socially conditioned to imagine the outline of a person is by assigning them a gender.

As such, 'gender reveal parties' have been growing steadily more popular alongside the rise of social media. Expectant parents can now use Pinterest to source inspiration, Instagram and Snapchat to upload photographs, Facebook to share the results with friends and YouTube to try to land themselves some sweet advertising coin and a spot on *Ellen*. Why do they do it? Well, it seems that no matter how many conversations are being had around the complexities of identity (not least of which is that no test can determine gender, only biological sex characteristics—and even that has some wiggle room), the rush to assign babies to a rigid category of blue or pink persists. On arrival, guests may be asked to cast a vote for either of those colours, because nothing says welcome to the world like having a roomful of Saturday-drunk strangers take a punt on your junk. After the bets have been cast, typical reveals include things like cutting into a cake to discover a pink or blue interior, smashing piñatas to be showered in pink or blue bonbons or opening a box to release a bunch of balloons in—you guessed it!—either pink or blue.

If the idea of gathering your closest friends and family to celebrate your child's genitalia isn't disconcerting enough, the dominant themes of such parties should flip your nausea switch. A cursory search on Pinterest (the go-to site for DIY party planning, interior decorating and basically anything else that is guaranteed to look worse when mere mortals try to copy it) highlights such grotesque hits as 'Wheels or Heels', 'Touchdowns or Tutus', ''Staches or Lashes' and, sickeningly, 'Rifles or Ruffles' (with 'Guns or Glitter' being a variation on that theme). Personally, I cannot fathom what kind of strange vortex you'd need to live in to think it was appropriate to enthusiastically connect an innocent little baby with a fucking gun, but I'm wacky that way.

Let's just get something out of the way, because I'm aware that critiquing cultural practices like this can sometimes feel like a criticism of an individual and their worth. Some of you reading this may have hosted your own version of these parties or may be planning one for when the times comes. You might feel a little defensive about the fact I'm deriding something you consider to be just a bit of light-hearted fun. It's okay. I'm not calling you a terrible person or questioning your taste (I listen exclusively to musical theatre and used the opportunity of turning thirty-five to freely embrace wearing socks with sandals, so I am in no position to judge). What I'm suggesting is that your impulse to assign meaning to something as arbitrary and functional as genitalia is born out of a cultural imperative to affix labels where none are necessary, and that individual participation in these rituals enforces a larger pattern of collective gender stereotyping that ultimately proves harmful for everyone. You are not a bad person (probably), but you are doing a bad thing.

But why are gender reveal parties bad? you might be wondering. Isn't this just a case of feminism going too far (again!) and ruining everything for everyone in the entire world?

First, let's talk about the concept itself. Gender is neither fixed nor tangible. It cannot be seen and categorised as easily as genitalia, though the two are so often assumed to be one and the same. The characteristics we associate with biological sex—a chromosomic make up of XX or XY, for example—might be indicators of certain hormonal probabilities within the body, but they no more define gender than wearing pink skirts or blue ties do. Assigning gender based on what we assume to be the visible indicators of chromosomal sex characteristics (vaginas with XX chromosomes = girl; penises with XY chromosomes = boy) is therefore not just a guess at best, it also perpetuates the trauma experienced by trans and gender non-conforming people born into a cis-normative world.

Then there are the multitude of biological possibilities that contradict the idea of biological sex itself being the ultimate arbiter of whether or not your child will be declared a 'touchdown' or a 'tutu' and gifted either guns or glitter. An intersex child may present with biological and anatomical sex characteristics traditionally considered both male and female, but still identify as a single gender. Is their chosen gender any less authentic because their biology is more colourful than it is straightforward?

That's before we take into account the fact that even when sex characteristics and genitalia present in a way considered biologically common, there's still little we can determine about gender identity from either. If we can understand that biological discrepancies may create circumstances that complicate how society might traditionally assign sex, why is it so difficult to understand that gender may equally be felt and understood as something separate to the way our down-theres look?

So back to the concept of the gender reveal party. Aside from being a manifestation of capitalist ideals and the showcasing of a certain kind of individual affluence (seriously, how many parties are people entitled to throw to celebrate something that basically only impacts their own life?), the whole premise of a 'gender reveal' is flawed, cis-normative and, if you consider how dodgy it would be to sit around with our friends and discuss the junk of born children, also kind of unethical. Parties like this should really be called 'genitalia reveals', because they invite a community to assign an entire identity to an unborn child on the extremely basic and arguably deceptive premise of what those children are *still in the process of growing between their legs*!

Personally, I like my friend Dev's idea. Invite your friends around for a big bash and have them place bets on the following themes: 'books or books', 'balloons or balloons', 'ice cream or ice cream', 'shoes or socks', 'yellow or green', 'Angel or Spike'. Bake a cake and dye the inside of it neon green. Make a piñata in the shape of the renowned philosopher and gender theorist Judith Butler and fill it with birdseed. Open a box to release a flock of parrots all trained to squawk, 'GENDER IS A SOCIAL CONSTRUCT!'

You might be laughing, but I'm 100 percent serious. Especially about the Judith Butler piñata.

These kinds of ceremonies might seem harmless to you, and maybe on a superficial level they are. After all, the baby chilling out in the human hot tub doesn't know or care about the effort being put into deciding what kind of clothes they're going to be gifted for the next three years. But that's not really the point. The unborn baby doesn't have an opinion about these things because they aren't yet aware of social conditioning, nor have they been exposed to it. It's all the people around them who'll be responsible for policing that in their formative years, and gender reveal parties are an open invitation to let them begin straight away. It might seem like a cute joke to compare hair bows (a girl!) to bows and arrows (a boy!), but line all those choices up against each other and you'll see just what kind of picture it paints about how we collectively view girlhood and boyhood. Girls are heels and lashes and bows and tutus. Boys are cars and touchdowns and arrows and rifles and guns. Girls are expected to be pretty and delicate, boys are supposed to dominate and destroy shit. This isn't just a totally fucked-up way to define humans—it's also deeply unimaginative.

An unexamined view of gender that perpetuates stereotypes such as these isn't harmless, nor is it passive. Rather, it underpins the very structure of gender inequality. It's impossible to examine the conditioning that leads boys and men to exhibit some of the more harmful aspects of the 'boys will be boys' mentality later on in life without critiquing the mindset and practice from which this evolves. If we weren't so invested collectively in policing a binary vision of gender and the limited ways those who sit on either side are encouraged (and in some cases forced) to express themselves, we wouldn't need to ostentatiously announce to anyone—let alone an entire backyard full of people—what category of child we were preparing to welcome into our lives.

If genitals and chromosomes and gender identity are essentially non-reliant on each other (even if they still often work in tandem), how in the heck can they be used as a blithe explanation when boys behave badly? It isn't the state of being a boy that prompts aggressive or sometimes criminal behaviour, because there's no such thing as a universal boy. When people chuckle and dismiss bullying or aggression as a simple case of 'boys being boys', they're not only maintaining a particularly one-dimensional idea of laddish masculinity, they're also diminishing the authenticity of boys who cannot or will not perform this version of boyhood.

After all, what happens to the boy who prefers glitter to guns?

■

Somewhere around the thirtieth week of my pregnancy, I found myself sitting in a throng of people at the Royal Melbourne Hospital, all of us waiting to be seen by a midwife for a routine check-up. My phone's battery was about to die (a common theme in my life, as anyone who knows me will confirm), so I sat on the floor against one of the walls and plugged it in to charge. In front of me, a heavily pregnant woman perched on one of the hard chairs and chatted with her mother while a young toddler played at her feet. As people in waiting rooms sometimes tend to do, we started making small talk. The pregnant woman told me when her baby was due, her daughter's name and age—the usual kind of pleasant chitchat. The child's hair had evidently only established any kind of presence recently, but her mother had grabbed what she could of it and fashioned it into a spout at the top of her head, secured in place with a glittery band. I made a polite comment about how her follicles seemed to be doing well and her mother winced.

'I hate it!' she moaned. 'I can't wait for it to grow longer!'

'Why?' I asked, genuinely bemused.

'Because everyone always calls her a boy!'

'Oh, well that's alright. Who cares what everyone else thinks?' I replied.

The woman murmured something non-committal and turned her attention back to her mother. At her feet, her daughter spun in circles and stuck a finger up her nose. Clearly the conversation was over.

Since becoming a parent myself, the paranoia some people feel about how others perceive their child's gender has become even more obvious—and perplexing—to me. The old hair-spout trick seems a fairly common one, and although there are bound to be some children rocking the geyser because it's the most convenient way to keep hair out of their eyes, there are surely others wrestled into it because it seems less humiliating than wearing a t-shirt that screams, I'M A GIRL, DAMN IT.

I've never understood the need to make sure the world approves of how your children are dressed or what gender they appear to be 'correctly' inhabiting. As a child, I was inexorably drawn to what people would consider stereotypical expressions of femininity (pink is still my favourite colour), but as a stocky, gap-toothed, freckle-faced nerd, I also felt deeply isolated from the kind of girlhood I aspired to. Did 'correctly' dressing as a girl make childhood any easier for me? I wouldn't say so.

As an adult, my sensibilities are ever changing. Although I'm a cis woman, my self-expression isn't dictated by any arbitrary rules related to what that's 'supposed' to look like or be. Some days I feel like dressing androgynously. Other days I feel more explicitly masculine. I delight in femininity. Being able to freely explore my identity through aesthetic and expressive play is a joy. Why on earth would we seek to deny that to children, the very people for whom play was not only invented but who are its most ingenious architects?

More particularly, as our awareness of trans and gender non-conforming identities grows, it seems less plausible or forgivable to adhere to such doctrinal faith about what girls and boys (and everyone in between and on the outsides of those basic definitions) 'should' and 'shouldn't' look like. If exploring different aesthetic expressions and behaviours is difficult for cis people, imagine how much more of a challenge it is for trans and gender-diverse people whose lives and safety are quite often on the line?

Until such time as I discover otherwise, I have a son. I have always tried to be conscious of not restricting him to the accepted uniform of boyhood, which is to say his wardrobe features lots of different clothes and colours as well as sparkles and glitter and other things that capture the attention of babies with a fondness for shiny things. And yet I've found that even when he's wearing clothes considered traditionally masculine, people are still liable to act confused over 'what' he is. Often they apologise if they hear me refer to him as a he, but a woman once became mildly cross with me over it. 'But he's wearing pink!' she exclaimed. 'So he is,' I replied.

Shortly after my son turned one, I asked a man on the street to take a photo of us together. FJ was swathed in a yellow parka and tucked into his stroller underneath a yellow blanket. Our street photographer fretted that he couldn't see the baby's face properly, and came closer to check if it was a 'he or a she'.

'Ah!' he announced. 'It's a she!'

I didn't try to correct him, because what does it matter? In some ways, I think I'm even trying to make the negative gender stereotyping that might come from being read as a girl work in his and my favour. By being coded this way, I hope that he'll be exposed to a kind of soft and gentle nurturing that might otherwise be withheld from him by people eager to bounce him on their knee or tell him to stop crying and act like a big boy. Still, I found this incident especially curious because the only thing visible was my son's face amid a literal sea of functional yellow fabric. I can only surmise the assumption was made because he has long eyelashes and quite soft features, and our general stereotypes of femininity are so deeply ingrained that these things automatically denote 'female' in our minds.

I guess this is why some people become so irate about the need to put children in clothes that make it easy to identify their gender. But this anxiety about dressing our kids 'appropriately' to reflect their respective genitals isn't just totally bonkers, it's also extremely recent in terms of historical practice. From about midway through the sixteenth century to the early 1900s, children pretty much all wore the same thing: dresses. The long gowns of infancy gave way to smocks for both sexes, with the boys only transitioning to breeches or trousers at the age of six or seven. Remarkably, the world wasn't knocked off its axis by the sight of a boy child in a dress, because it turns out the integrity of the earth's gravitational pull isn't as fragile as twenty-first-century masculinity.

Even more fascinating is the discovery that the colour themes modern society traditionally associates with masculinity and femininity are completely sideways. That is to say, when children's fashion ditched generic white for pink and blue, it wasn't to establish girls as the former and boys as the latter—it was the other way around. Pink, being a lighter shade of red, was associated with Mars, the god of war, so it was thought to be an appropriate colour for boys. (Guns!) Blue was more commonly associated with Venus and the Madonna (you'll notice historic works of art always depict Our Lady's veil as being a light blue), so it was assigned to girls. (Glitter!) The trade publication *Infants' and Children's Wear Review* even reiterated in 1916, 'The generally accepted rule is pink for the boy and blue for the girl.' In 1918, the *Women's Journal* confirmed, 'That pink being a more decided and stronger color, is more suitable for the boy, while blue, which is more delicate and dainty, is prettier for the girl.'

The delegation of pink for boys and blue for girls began to change gradually around the mid-twentieth century. A popular (if unproven) theory holds that the reversal solidified in Nazi Germany when Adolph Hitler ordered that gay prisoners sent to concentration camps be forced to wear a pink triangle. Whether or not this caused the gender associations we have today or merely hurtled them along is unclear. Regardless, by the 1950s the new order was understood: pink for girls and blue for boys. In 1959, the *New York Times* reported one department store buyer for the infant wear section as saying, 'A mother will allow her girl to wear blue, but daddy will never permit his son to wear pink.' Because LOL #nohomo!

We've moved on a lot from the post-war period of petticoats and undershirts, but mass cultural anxiety about the clothes we dress our children in seems to persist. It's hard to say which one makes parents more fearful—their son being confused for a girl, or their daughter being confused for a boy. Society might have its own insecurity and inherent misogyny, femmephobia and queerphobia to answer to for that, but it's definitely an insecurity that has been happily seized on by capitalist forces.

One of the most common observations made by parents who choose not to find out or divulge what their unborn child's genitalia looks like is that some of their friends and family get frustrated—even angry—because it makes it difficult to know what to buy for gifts. Leaving aside for a moment the absurdity of how society's devotion to gendering children is defended as a means of knowing how to appropriately spend money, the idea that our options become limited without proper signposting is just silly.

At least, it should be considered silly. But to wander through the children's clothes aisles in any high street shop or department store is to learn a swift lesson in both gender stereotyping and anger management. The most noticeable thing is the distinction of gender according to colour. The 'girl' section bursts with pinks, yellows, purples and glitter (tutus! ruffles! heels!), while the 'boy' section wades through a more muted palette of dark blues, black, red, khaki and beige beige beige. What the boys' section lacks in vibrancy, though, it more than makes up for in affirmations and positive reinforcement. T-shirts and jumpers scream words and slogans like AWESOME, COOL, FUTURE SUPERHERO and LITTLE BUT LOUD. Conversely, girls' clothes are emblazoned with descriptions like CUTE, STAY HAPPY and GORGEOUS. Because never forget that boys are defined by how impressive they are while girls are defined by how impressive they look. That's before we even get into the weirdness of onesies and rompers declaring I'M A BOOB MAN and DADDY'S LITTLE PRINCESS.

One of the (many) reasons my partner and I chose not to reveal whether our unborn baby had an innie or an outie was because I couldn't stand the thought of being gifted the very rompers and t-shirts and toys from which I recoil whenever I head to the children's department of any store. I figured it was going to be tricky enough to raise a boy in an environment that prized masculinity and whiteness above all else—it was my job to disrupt that dynamic, not facilitate it.

It seems like such a small form of protest to make, but it's incredible how irate it makes people. In 2017, I posted a photograph to Instagram to capture an ongoing small act of resistance in my local Kmart. Ever since my son was born, I've been making it my mission to swap the t-shirts that yell BRAVE & STRONG from the boys' aisle into the girls' one, and doing the reverse with shirts emblazoned with HAPPY and PEACE. When I shared an image of one of these disruptions on my Facebook page, some people grew angry. These things are just clothes, they yelled. They don't mean anything! The kids don't even know they're wearing them, so what's the bloody big deal?

That's true. Babies and children can't read the slogans on the clothes we dress them in. But the people meeting, playing with or handling those babies can. And clothes that reinforce stereotypes of brilliance in boys and aesthetics in girls contribute insidiously to the general conditioning to which we've all been subjected that not only teaches us certain traits are innate to gender, but instructs us to treat people differently based on how we code them.

Most people probably believe they don't modify their behaviour when it comes to the specifically gendered treatment of children. (We can only guess whether they believe they modify their behaviour when it comes to the specifically gendered treatment of adults, but I'd wager they consider themselves fault-free in that area too. The wage gap would like to register its disagreement.) Despite what we may all believe about our unique perspectives and approach to child rearing, most people respond without question to the social conditioning that codifies gender as a binary expression of distinct traits. One of the first experiments to assess the treatment of gender was conducted in 1975, when three neuroscientists, Carol A. Seavey, Phyllis A. Katz and Sue Rosenberg Zalk, tested the responses of forty-two men and women (all of them non-parents) when presented with a three-month-old baby. The paper was titled 'Baby X: The effect of gender labels on adult responses to infants', and it's widely recognised as being the precursor to a series of similar studies exploring gender and socialisation.

In Seavey et al.'s study, Baby X was dressed in yellow and accompanied by three toys: a football, a doll and a teething ring. Participants were split into three groups and were observed interacting with the baby and the toys. Those who were told the baby was a boy were more likely to offer it the football or teething ring. Those who were told it was a girl overwhelmingly interacted using the doll. Where there was no gender descriptor alongside a now-neutral baby, men favoured the teething ring while women favoured the doll.

The responses to Girl Baby and Boy Baby are fairly expected and yield few insights that would astonish us today. But those presented with Neutral Baby (or 'Baby X') proved to be the most interesting. When presented with no gender label at all, the majority of participants decided the baby was a boy. Curiously, women were even more likely than men to make this judgment, which perhaps speaks to how successfully patriarchy has conditioned women to assume a narrative backseat (but is vaguely reassuring at the same time, given that they mostly reached for the doll). It's easy for us to imagine that something important (like a science experiment) would involve a boy, because (as I look at later in 'Girls on film') the most important stories always involve boys. At least, that's what we learn from a very young age. If the default version of 'human' is 'white male', a prodigal sun with peripheral planets of Other orbiting around it from now until eternity, of course we assume the default identity of characters or heroes or small humans dressed in anything other than pink would be 'boy'.

Not all the adults assessing Baby X identified the child as a boy, but regardless of how they assessed the baby's gender, the participants all said they 'could tell by the strength of the grip, by the lack of hair, or by how round and soft [the baby] was, whether it was a boy or a girl'.

Fascinating, isn't it? That we are so attuned to the lessons of social and gender conditioning that we could (and frequently do) assign sex based on arbitrary indicators. A fuller head of hair, a pretty smile, strong limbs, a penchant for rough and tumble playtime—all these things and more are unconsciously absorbed as messages that enable us to code gender in children, and in turn teach them to code it in themselves. Less fascinating and more worrying is how infants respond. As Jo B. Paoletti wrote in *Pink and Blue: Telling the Boys from the Girls in America*, 'Multiple studies between 1975 and the mid-80s established that children understand and can apply gender stereotypes well before they reach their third birthday.'

As it turned out, there was only one baby used in the Baby X experiment. She had a hell of a grip, though.

Yeah, but those are forty-year-old studies! I hear you shout. *Find something recent!*

OKAY, I WILL.

In mid-2017, the BBC *Stories* program replicated elements of the Baby X experiment when it invited participants to spend some time in a toy room with two babies—a girl and a boy—who had been secretly dressed in clothes typically associated with each other's gender. Adults were invited to spend some time playing with one baby then the other while a camera recorded their responses. Overwhelmingly, subjects not only took a gender cue from the colour of the baby's clothes, they also adapted their playing style to match. When the baby was perceived to be a girl, participants were more likely to explore gentle activities focused on nurture and care. They selected dolls and soft animals and minimised their physical movements with the baby. Where they coded the baby as a boy, they were more rambunctious and jocular. They selected 'active' toys that would stimulate the child's motor functions and coordination. Afterwards, many of the participants expressed dismay and disappointment that they had conformed so willingly, with at least one participant talking about how they pride themselves on taking a consciously non-gendered approach to children.

I guess you could consider this nature versus nurture as well. As an animal species, we are naturally very good at doing what we're told; it takes a lot of work to overcome a conditioning that began before we even left the uterus. But we should never grow so comfortable with our conscious brains that we start to assume our unconscious ones have ceased to exist.

As to the consequences of the British experiment, I'm sure it comes as no surprise to learn that neither baby seemed particularly perturbed by the things they were being given to explore, primarily because babies are essentially advanced computer programs sent here from outer space to download everything they can about Earth and its people, and they haven't yet learned to be extremely fragile and pathetic about whether or not wearing skinny jeans makes them gay.

I'm not saying that inflicting gender stereotypes on babies is bad. I'm saying that inflicting gender stereotypes on babies is one of the worst things we can do to inhibit their natural development; it carries potentially devastating consequences that are wholly avoidable; and it is, above all, extremely fucking lazy and gross.

But why are you being so mean and parent-shamey, you ugly feminazi? I'll tell you why. Because a recent study showed that, from the age of six onwards, children were more likely to assume natural intelligence and superiority in men rather than in women. Meanwhile, separate studies confirm that more pre-pubescent girls than ever are developing insecurities about their bodies and the way they look. A 2009 study from the University of Central Florida found that half of American girls aged between three and six think they're fat—and trust me, these girls haven't yet discovered the body positivity movement. A BBC Two documentary staged an experiment with a primary school on the Isle of Wight in which a class of twenty-three seven-year-olds and their teachers were challenged to go 'gender neutral' for a term. Testing at the start of the experiment revealed worrying results, according to an article written by Antonia Hoyle for the *Telegraph* ('What happened when a primary school went gender-neutral', 15 August 2017):

> The boys are less able to express their emotions but more confident in their abilities, while the girls have lower self-esteem and a lesser ability to process numbers and shapes. All but one girl believe boys are 'better' than them and their self-perception is largely limited to their appearance. One pupil, Kara, says 'girls are better at being pretty' while another, Tiffany, declares 'men are better at being in charge.' The boys are similarly old-fashioned: little Louis says 'girls look after the child and boys do lots of cool stuff,' while Bradley declares, 'men are more successful because they could have harder jobs.'

But as detrimental as the effect of gender stereotyping is on cis kids, it's even more damaging on trans and gender-diverse children. A 2017 survey conducted by the Telethon Kids Institute and the University of Western Australia found that transgender youths are roughly ten times more likely than other young Australians to experience severe depression and anxiety. The Trans Pathways' anonymous online survey had 859 trans and gender-diverse respondents between the ages of fourteen and twenty-five as well as nearly 200 parents and guardians of trans and gender-diverse youths. One-fifth of trans kids reported having an eating disorder, four-fifths reported self-harming behaviour and three out of four had been professionally diagnosed with depression or anxiety. But the worst statistic of all was this: almost half had attempted suicide, which is a rate six times higher than that of the general population.

These are our *children*, for fuck's sake.

I'll tell you another reason why I have a dogmatic approach to this: because even when we think we are Super Right On about these issues, the chances are that we're much weaker than we perceive ourselves to be. In her ground-breaking (and hysterically funny) work, *Delusions of Gender: The Real Science Behind Sex Differences*, the cognitive neuroscientist Cordelia Fine discusses the implicit associations of the mind, which, as she puts it, is an otherwise 'tangled but highly organized network of connections [containing] representations of objects, people, concepts, feelings, your own self, goals, motives and behaviours with one another'. Dr Fine points to Anthony Greenwald, Mahzarin Banaji and Brian Nosek's Implicit Association Test (IAT), in which participants are asked to rapidly pair categories of words or pictures. Participants worked more quickly when asked to pair names commonly recognised as female with communal words ('like connected and supported') and names commonly recognised as male with more agentic words ('like individualistic and competitive') than when female names were paired with agentic words and male with communal. Fine writes, 'The small but significant difference in reaction time this creates is taken as a measure of the stronger automatic and unintended associations between women and communality, and men and agency.'

It's easy to dismiss the impact of gender stereotyping as 'meaningless' or even 'harmless' (it's not), but it's worth reminding ourselves that humans are intensely impressionable. We are subject to a wide range of influences across every aspect of our lives and it's foolish for us to think that childhood is immune to that. I mean, if we didn't respond so enthusiastically to marketing then we wouldn't be living in a destructive capitalist nightmare.

Resisting social conditioning for children—even for people who count themselves as progressive—has so far only seemed to focus on how we can protect little girls from the evils of loving princesses, fairies and pink. Girls gravitating towards trucks and 'gender-neutral clothing' (which usually just means clothes that are coded as masculine) is often seen as cause for subtle boasting, because most people are still conditioned to think girls liking 'boy' stuff represents some kind of promotion. It's not as common for people to celebrate the opposite—sons loving pink, tutus, fairies and anything more typically associated with 'girliness'. This is partly because of sexism (because things girls like are inherently rubbish, of course) and partly out of a combination of homophobia, transphobia and fear of the feminine (yikes, our son likes girl stuff, WHAT ARE WE GOING TO DO?!). Both motivations are utterly shit.

But the tragedy of gender stereotyping existing at all (let alone starting so early) is that it doesn't just limit our collective understanding and acceptance of what it means to be a girl (and the wonderful leadership, ferocity and strength that can be embodied by girls in a decidedly determined way). It also reduces our idea of boyhood to one in which softness and tenderness are considered 'unmanly'. Why do people think baby boys shouldn't be allowed to enjoy flowers, sparkles and butterflies while baby girls are required to have those same things glued onto their heads to offset their 'unfeminine' baldness?

In 2017, a face painter named Sandra wrote a micro essay on Twitter that quickly went viral. In it, she outlined what she saw as a contributing cause of male violence in America. A four-year-old boy had asked for a butterfly to be painted on his face. His mother denied his request, insisting instead that he get something 'for boys'. She then turned to his father, 'a big guy in a jersey', and had him confirm that he didn't want his son having a *big, ole GAY* butterfly on his face [my emphasis].

This boy's parents taught him that day to associate shame with anything considered feminine and to apply that shame to himself for wanting it. And what did he walk away with? A skull and crossbones on his cheek. 'Sorry,' the face painter said to him as his mother walked him away.

'And I am,' she wrote. 'I'm sorry that he is not allowed to love something as miraculous and beautiful as a butterfly.'

When I read stories about little boys who have their softness and love shamed out of them by parents who are in thrall to their own fear, my heart breaks. This is why it's so important to break down rigid learning around what gender is and isn't supposed to be. It's why it's so important to advocate for the removal of gender labels in clothing and toy aisles, because these things exist more to shape behaviours rather than respond to them. It's why we all have to be keenly aware of how we treat the children we interact with in our own lives, and question how much space for expression we're providing them. We must be prepared to question the reductive, harmful stereotypes that limit the growth of our children into the perfect, wonderful people they are meant to be and not just the ones that we're comfortable being around. Little girls can be brave and strong, and little boys might want to be a princess every now and again. Some children might want to be both or neither, and that goes for being girls or boys at all. As adults, all we have to be is supportive. As parents, all we have to do is love them.

Trust me, there are enough people out there willing to hate children for threatening their own sense of what it means to be a 'boy' or a 'girl'. We certainly don't need to make it any easier for them. To understand that, we only need to look as far as the response to Australia's postal survey on marriage equality and the campaign against sartorial choices led by one man in particular.

■

In 2017, the Australian government announced it would be conducting a frivolously expensive, totally unnecessary and blatantly homophobic postal survey to assess the public's views on same-sex marriage. That numerous studies and polls had consistently shown the majority of Australians to be in favour of same-sex marriage was irrelevant. Prime Minister Malcolm Turnbull may have spent some years wooing otherwise left-leaning citizens into thinking he'd be an *okay* bet to lead the Liberal Party (for any foreign readers, to be a Liberal in Australia means to be conservative; it's the upside-down land, after all), but once he wrestled the leadership from Tony Abbott, he became devoted to appeasing the right of his party in order to maintain his tenuous grip on power.

Putting the issue of Turnbull's stale legacy aside, one of the many repulsive things the plebiscite did was to provide a platform for people's privately held and expressed homophobia to be broadcast to a much larger audience. The 'silent majority'—as conservative newspapers and commentators referred to them—were ready to don their Loud 'n' Proud t-shirts and take to the streets. (Sidenote: In my experience, the 'silent majority' is rarely either of those things.)

But this was no ordinary Straight Pride parade. See, campaigning against marriage equality was just the icing on the traditional three-tiered wedding cake for the Australian Christian Lobby and its army of sensibly dressed soldiers. The real target was the Safe Schools program, an initiative launched in Victoria in 2010 and then later rolled out nationally to voluntary participants. The Safe Schools Coalition Australia describes itself as 'a national network of organisations working with school communities to create safer and more inclusive environments for same sex attracted, intersex and gender diverse students, staff and families'. Scary stuff! That is, if you're a total dingleberry.

One of the most prominent critics of Safe Schools and same-sex marriage was the far-right politician Cory Bernardi. If you want to see a case study of the terror felt by some people when they even contemplate the thought of boys acting outside their strict ideas of gender, you need only look to how Bernardi directed his homophobic, transphobic ire at a fundraising campaign run by a South Australian primary school that just happened to coincide with run-time for the postal survey.

Every year, Craigburn Primary hosts a 'gold coin donation' casual day to raise money for a nominated charity. In 2017, they decided to nominate One Girl, an organisation that assists girls in Africa to receive an education. For One Girl's 'Do It In A Dress' campaign, the school administration invited students and staff to come to school wearing 'a dress or casual clothes', noting, 'The main thing of course is to focus on supporting the education of girls in Africa . . . so that girls can look forward to a positive future.' Craigburn set themselves a target of $900, an admirable goal for a small primary school and one that its students would no doubt have felt proud to achieve.

The story might have ended with Craigburn donating that sum or thereabouts were it not for Bernardi's attempts to conflate a simple fundraising activity with the broader marriage equality debate taking place at the same time. On 20 September, he tweeted, 'One school in SA now has "wear a dress day". This gender morphing is really getting absurd.' Despite the fact that the option to 'wear a dress (or casual clothes)' was open to everyone, it was clear Bernardi was solely concerned with the idea of schoolboys frocking up. He was later quoted in the Adelaide *Advertiser* as saying: 'In the midst of a debate about the safe school gender ideology program, the redefinition of marriage and attempts to de-genderise society it seems this school is playing into a political cause rather than an educational one.'

Although Bernadi's plan was clearly to exploit the philanthropic efforts of children in order to further stoke the flames of queerphobia in his bigoted supporters and thus help bolster the No campaign, it thankfully backfired. Josh Thomas, a popular actor and comedian with more than 470,000 Twitter followers, quickly exposed Bernardi's efforts when he tweeted, 'These kids are being bullied by Cory for trying to help underprivileged girls.' Thomas pledged $2000 towards the school's campaign and others eagerly followed suit. By midday the next day, less than twenty-four hours after Bernardi first sounded the Repressed Homophobic Terror Factory alarm, nearly $35,000 had been pledged by the public towards Craigburn Primary's Do It In A Dress fundraiser.

If this were the tale's end, it would be heart-warming enough. But I guess there's something about an adult man with significant political power choosing to bully morally conscious primary school-aged children that just doesn't sit right with the public. The money kept pouring in, and not just from locals. Even people as far away as the Yukon, in Canada, heard about Bernardi's attempts to misrepresent and shame kids, and they started donating too. Thanks in large part to Thomas's signal boosting, by the campaign's end more than $300,000 had been raised for Do It In A Dress, courtesy of Craigburn Primary. And although negative comments around the so-called 'brainwashing' of children persisted, public feedback was overwhelmingly positive.

When I think of those enthusiastic boys targeted by Bernardi and his poison, it's hard not to think of my son. He is all chubby thighs and waddling body now, squawking garbled words and obsessed with Emma Wiggle. But one day he'll be moving through a schoolyard himself, absorbing cultural messages at lightning speed and learning just what kind of boy it is the world will allow him to be. It didn't surprise me to be confronted (again) by Bernardi's melange of bigotry. But I still feel viscerally angry about the toxic way he tried to sabotage a group of young children and their community-minded project and to do it in such a way that it might deter them from participating in such public acts of decency in the future. Despite Bernardi's claims, no one was forcing boys to wear dresses. They were invited to, and many of them embraced the opportunity with delight and excitement. How horrendous, how cruel, how abusive to take that excitement and try to turn it into something dirty and shameful; to invite the entire country to point fingers at the 'weird' and 'disgusting' behaviour being taught to children who, up until that point, almost certainly didn't realise there were people out there who would link their actions to perversion. How fucking dare he?!

This is bigger than one politician's campaign against a group of primary school children in an effort to oppress the queer community. These are the foundational lessons being taught to and about boys all over Australia, the same lessons that codify masculinity as one particular, immutable thing so that it becomes both a prison and a weapon. Boys don't cry. Boys don't like rainbows. Boys don't dance. Boys don't wear pink. Boys don't like dresses. Boys will be boys, but not if they like any of those things. *Not on my watch.*

We have a clear choice. We can choose to participate in the teaching of that shame, and bear responsibility for the damage it causes later on (and believe you me, it causes untold harm to place boys in emotional straitjackets and teach them that their masculinity is defined by their defeat of the feminine). Or we can do what so many did in response to Bernardi's fear-mongering and not just embrace the creative expression of our children without censure or fear, but actively celebrate it—and always, not just when there's a fundraiser involved. It is only by choosing the latter course that we can hope to breed the kind of children—boys, girls and anyone outside those two states of being—who daily exercise compassion, kindness and love for all people. This is the first step in disrupting the damage done by patriarchy.

It takes a lot of insecurity to believe something as simple as an item of clothing, a colour, a hobby, or a love for a particular toy can wield enough power to destroy heterosexual, patriarchal civilisation as we know it. Who knew that all it takes to dismantle the systems of power that oppress us all is to wave a dress in its general direction? If only it were that easy!

The truth is there's no such thing as 'boys' clothes' or 'girls' clothes', nor are there toys that are 'for boys' versus toys that are 'for girls'. There are no jobs that belong to boys, just as there are no jobs that belong to girls. You can't learn anything about unborn children by finding out what's between their legs, nor can you tell just by looking at them later what their gender is. The notion is as absurd as suggesting there's air that only boys can breathe or heat that only girls can feel. A thing is a thing is a thing, no more and no less.

There is no gender licence required to use things. A truck is for a girl as long as a girl is playing with it. A baby stroller is for a boy as long as a boy has fun pushing it around. And, hell yes, a fucking dress belongs to a boy if he chooses to wear it.

Personally, I look forward to a future in which my son will be supported to wear what he likes without fear of being bullied, degraded or made to feel subhuman. Where the concept of boys wearing clothes commonly deemed feminine won't even be a source of amusement or embarrassment anymore because society will have grown up enough to recognise that there is nothing embarrassing about being a girl.

This is the future I want for my son. This is what I'm working towards for all boys. And hey—if more boys start wearing dresses, perhaps more dressmakers will start designing them all with pockets.

Now *that's* liberation.

—2—

A WOMAN'S PLACE

'Dear Jess,' the letter began, addressed to Jessica Rowe in her role as agony aunt for *Sunday Life* magazine:

> We've recently employed a cleaner but my husband says it's an indulgence. Not for me! I work full time and I'm tired of being the one responsible for keeping our house tidy, doing all the cooking and getting the kids to bed. How can I deal with his snide comments about having help with cleaning?

Rowe answered with the characteristic impartiality of a seasoned journalist, telling the anonymous writer that her investment was 'money well spent as it means you can focus on what you enjoy doing when you're home instead of feeling resentful'. She then advised the harried woman to 'have a calm chat' with her husband and tell him 'you'd like him to help more'.

It's not unreasonable advice, I suppose, although mine would have probably been a bit more blunt: divorce him.

Before you start tweeting at me, demanding my man-hating reptilian self be forced to apologise to all the men in the world who are *totally* happy for their wives to hire a cleaner to 'help' them with the housework, relax—that little thing I did just there is what we call a joke. I'm not really advocating the dissolution of a marriage and a family because one party is too lazy to do any of the work himself.

No, I'm advocating the dissolution of a marriage and a family because this woman's husband is clearly a selfish cockjangle who views his wife's job as secondary to her larger role as an unpaid domestic labourer, and whom he's charged with the primary responsibility of facilitating his life, ambitions and home comforts because he secretly wanted to marry his mommy. I bet he expects her to do his laundry too. (Just FYI: the revolution won't be won if we continue to wash men's clothes, ladies. Tell him to buy a hamper and start cleaning his own dirty jocks. While we're at it, stop marrying men and taking their names as a matter of course. It isn't 'choice' when it's mostly going one way. Before you argue that 'it's just your father's name anyway', stop for a moment. It's *your* name. You were born with it, just as men were born with theirs. The difference is that our patriarchal society still treats women as if our names are on loan from one man until we find another to claim us and gift us with our new and true identity, while men get to own their names from the start and claim their destinies for themselves. I'm not saying you're wrong for doing it, I'm just saying think a bit more deeply about the fact that women are expected to do it at all. And if you say it's because you wanted to have the same last name as your children, just ask yourself why women for the most part do all the work of growing and birthing children only to turn around and give naming rights to men who did barely anything at all.)

To be fair, these domestic dynamics are all relatively new territory for me. Prior to my current relationship, I had never lived with a romantic partner. As much as I love the bloke who rattles around the house beside me, I've also often said that if our romantic relationship ends then I would never live with a man again. Why? Simple. The gendered conditions of domestic labour are still too deeply entrenched to be anything but a burden for most women living in hetero partnerships, and managing those conditions (whether you're challenging them or conforming to them) takes a fuckton of work. Until we can confidently say the patriarchy has been destroyed, women who enjoy sex with men are much better off living alone and inviting them into our houses as guests occasionally. #truefact

While the problem of shared domesticity as an adult is something I'm still navigating, it's not like its existence has come as a surprise to me. For most of us, the impact and witnessing of gender inequality in the home begins when we're children. I may have been raised by parents who instilled feminist values of independence and ambition in my sister and me (even if they didn't call it feminism explicitly), but there was also a marked difference between what was expected of us and what was expected of our brother. He was never told to wash dishes, sort and fold laundry or—heaven forbid!—iron the shirts my father wore to work. Instead, he was given the wholly undemanding task of sweeping the footpath outside and taking out the bins, both of which he seemed to do only sporadically. Whenever I raged about the unfairness of it all (which was often), my mother would try to placate me. 'It's just that I know I can trust you and Charlotte to do a good job,' she'd say. 'If I let Toby do the dishes, I'd just have to do them again.'

Because you make it so easy for him to get away with it. I'd scream inside.

The gender split in my childhood home is still typical of most families. Girls are assigned chores that accord to a homemaking role (like washing dishes, sorting laundry and ironing clothes) while boys are generally given 'dirtier', more physical tasks (like taking out the rubbish and sweeping outdoor steps). The inequality here isn't only reflected in the types of task considered appropriate for girls and boys, but also in the length of time required to complete them. Washing dishes and ironing clothes takes a lot longer than ducking outside to throw some rubbish in the bin.

But the problem is even bigger than that. In 2016, a UNICEF report titled *Harnessing the Power of Data for Girls* found that girls worldwide spend 40 percent more time on household chores than boys. Taking into account the global population of girls, that equates to 160 million more hours a day. That's 900 years' worth of hours. *A day.*

According to Anju Malhotra, UNICEF's principal adviser on gender equality, 'the overburden of unpaid household work begins in early childhood and intensifies as girls reach adolescence'. This work begins from the time girls are five years old and increases dramatically as they enter adolescence. On average, by the time they're fourteen, girls are expected to perform more than half of the housework.

This disparity in labour has a massive impact on the wellbeing and security of girls, particularly those in countries considered part of the Global South (sometimes referred to as 'the developing world'). As Malhotra says:

> Girls sacrifice important opportunities to learn, grow and just enjoy their childhood. This unequal distribution of labour among children also perpetuates gender stereotypes and the double burden on women and girls across generations.

In some cases, the work expected of girls—collecting firewood and well water, for example—puts them at direct risk of sexual violence. These demands can lead to girls prematurely leaving school, which in turn sets them on a path towards early marriage and motherhood—neither of which are necessarily chosen consensually.

Perhaps the biggest slap in the face is how this inequality is compounded by its invisibility. It isn't just that it's easy to ignore; it's also that the importance of it is dismissed entirely. Despite the lip service paid to how the work of caring, child rearing and domestic management is 'the most important job in the world', mainstream society largely treats it and the women who do it as bullshit.

But it's women's work, right? This is what we're naturally drawn to, what we're good at, what we *like* doing. It's not a conspiracy, it's biology! Women have the babies and take care of the homes, and men go out and earn the money. Different, but still equal!

First, who the *fuck* decided that keeping house for men was something women can't hold ourselves back from doing? When I was asked as a little girl what I wanted to be when I grew up, I always answered the same thing: a secretary. It wasn't just that it was one of the few jobs I saw women doing on TV—it was also that these women were always young, single and didn't have to pick up after anyone else when they got home at night. It's a pop culture staple to assume that women all grew up indulging fantasies of their wedding day, but I can't ever remember daydreaming about what mine would look like. I assumed I would be married at some point, but only because this was what was supposed to happen to women once they passed a certain age. First comes love, then comes marriage, then comes the baby in the baby carriage. If these things didn't happen to you, it could never be because you were off doing something more interesting; it was always because you had failed somehow. Women can only become fully realised human beings if they find a man to put a ring on their finger and a baby in their jukebox. Without these essential ingredients to happiness, women are just purposeless atoms bumping our way through the noiseless vacuum of space. (See exhibit A: Jennifer Aniston.)

Second, let's just put to bed right now the lie that 'women's work' is truly considered 'different but equal'. It isn't considered equal at all, not by a long shot. It's considered convenient and necessary to men's more valuable and important success, which is hardly the same thing. And be assured that any opportunity that *can* be taken to discredit it *will* be.

In 1988, Marilyn Waring published her seminal feminist text, *Counting for Nothing: What Men Value and What Women Are Worth*. This was Waring's response to the fact that women's unpaid work, from domestic labour to child rearing to care of the elderly and sick, had historically been excluded from the United Nations System of National Accounts (SNA). Her research uncovered the infuriating little tidbit (included in the original 1953 edition of the SNA standard) that women's unpaid labour was 'of little or no importance', and this was the reason for its exclusion. Profiling Waring recently for *The Monthly* magazine, Anne Manne asked the formidable writer and activist how she'd felt on reading those words for the first time. 'Oh, terrible,' Waring replied. 'I wept.'

Even today, the System of National Accounts doesn't include the cost of unpaid labour alongside its measure of gross domestic product. Instead, there's a provision for satellite accounts that allow it to be measured alongside GDP—an improvement, sure, but still a reflection on how the work of women is made peripheral to global economic outlooks rather than essential to them. As Manne writes in the Waring profile, 'An Australian Bureau of Statistics study in 2014 revealed that unpaid work in Australia was worth $434 billion, equivalent to 43.5 percent of GDP.'

But women do it for the love, we're told, as if love will pay our bills and feed our children and take care of us in our old age. In fact, one of the most significant impacts of gender inequality and what 'counts' as value is the poverty faced by ageing women whose lifetime of unpaid work has earned them no superannuation or similar retirement funds. The fastest growing group of homeless people in Australia are women over the age of sixty-five—the same women who supported men as they established their careers, gave birth to their children and devoted their time to caring for them, and who were then frozen out of the workforce by a perceived lack of suitable skills. Even now, decades after Waring first started reading the System of National Accounts, unpaid labour is still framed as 'women's work' and it's still dismissed as 'of little or no importance'.

The fact is, there are overwhelming numbers of heterosexual partnerships in which this kind of labour is enforced daily in both subtle and not so subtle ways. The problem encountered by

Jessica Rowe's advice seeker—her need to outsource some of the work around her shared home to a professional, yet encountering opposition from the partner who is demographically far less likely to ever do it himself—is not uncommon, whether one or both are working outside the home. The idea that it is a luxury to spend money on work women are 'supposed' to do for free is widespread.

Fighting over household chores might not seem like that big a deal in the grand scheme of things, but the consequences of this go well beyond personal feelings of frustration and indignation. What we are exposed to in our homes is fundamental to the values and behaviours we grow up viewing as normal. It doesn't matter how politically progressive your household is when it comes to aspirations *outside* the home and the limitless capabilities of women; if it's made clear within those four walls that it is the responsibility of women to perform the unpaid labour of domesticity, this is the value system that children will internalise: boys are born to rule the world, and girls to clean up after them.

■

Here's another #truefact; no matter how much love there might be in the relationship, women who choose to live romantically with men are acting against their own economic interests.

I know, I know. 'More man-hating from the irrelevant Chlamydia Ford!' screams the cohort of angry men who follow my every move on Facebook. Because why would something as meaningless and petty as the unpaid labour performed by women to the detriment of themselves and the endless benefit of the men in their lives possibly be a topic worth discussing?

Except it's not irrelevant. A 2016 study titled 'Making money, doing gender, or being essentialist? Partner characteristics and

Americans' attitudes toward housework', presented to the American Sociological Association's 111th Annual Meeting, found that 'most Americans still believe that women should be responsible for the majority of the cleaning, cooking, grocery shopping and child-rearing—even if the woman has a full-time job or makes more money than her partner.'

That same year, the Australian Census data showed the average Australian woman spends between five and fourteen hours a week doing unpaid housework. Compare that to the average Australian man, who spends fewer than five hours on the same tasks. To put that another way, the typical Aussie bloke's greatest output of domestic labour is still less than the typical Australian woman at her 'laziest'—which is, as a plethora of posts on various mums' forums tell me, a word that gets hurled at women all too often when their male partners come home at the end of the day and seem surprised they aren't living in the boy heaven of the 1950s.

Women aren't born with a particular talent for scrubbing floors and washing clothes. We don't instinctively know when to buy more toilet paper because the peculiar genetic condition we've been saddled with known as 'womanhood' makes us extra sensitive to the smell of pulped woodchips. The expectation that we not only service these needs but that we do so enthusiastically is part of the social and domestic conditioning most of us grow up with, and it absolutely quadruples in intensity for women who later choose to partner romantically (and domestically) with men.

In a 2017 article for *The Conversation*, the academic Leah Ruppanner observed that 'it's during singlehood that housework time is most equal by gender' ('Census 2016: Women are still disadvantaged by the amount of unpaid housework they do'). But 'most' in this scenario still isn't the same as 'completely'.

Ruppanner pointed to the findings of Australia's 2016 Census to show that even when women are single or in full-time employment, they still perform more unpaid domestic labour on average than men. Worse, though, is this: 'When women start to cohabit, their housework time goes up while men's goes down, regardless of their employment status.'

And they say we can't have it all.

Listen, I didn't spend the self-esteem wasteland of my twenties sleeping with men whose chronically unwashed bedsheets had spawned entirely new ecosystems just to move in with them in my upwardly mobile thirties and become their long-suffering mother. Unfortunately, challenging this dynamic sometimes feels like being stuck in your own personal Groundhog Day, except you never get past the bit in the middle where Bill Murray keeps trying to electrocute himself. If having repetitive conversations about labour load feels exhausting to those of us who know how to use the phrase 'fucking heteropatriarchal bullshit' in a sentence, how much more frustrating do you think it is for women who aren't in the habit of questioning sexism and gender inequality?

But as annoying as these conversations are, we have to keep having them and demanding real follow-through, because it tends to get a lot worse once children enter the picture. I hate to be the bearer of bad news, but the tears and fractures that appear once you've delivered kids over the threshold of your humble abode won't improve by themselves.

Kind of like your traumatised pelvic floor, really.

■

When I was still pregnant and blissfully naive about everything to do with children, I mentioned to a friend who'd already crossed the divide from clueless ingenue to harried mum that I planned to breastfeed because 'breastmilk is free!'.

'Yes and no,' Ilaria replied. 'Technically, you don't have to pay for breastmilk. But it's only "free" if you consider the mother's labour worthless.'

Theoretically, I understood what she was saying, but it didn't fully hit me until my son arrived and became permanently attached to my nipples. I've been called a cow by trolls almost every week for the last decade, but I finally knew what they meant when I found myself acting as a never-ending milk supply to a baby whose appetite never seemed to wane.

It's an inescapable fact that the work of feeding a newborn baby can be labour intensive, particularly if the birth parent chooses to breastfeed (and is able to). In fact, as feminist economist Julie Smith wrote in her article '"Lost milk?": Counting the economic value of breast milk in gross domestic product', published in *Journal of Human Lactation* in July 2013, breastfeeding has an annual value of approximately $3 billion in Australia.

In their first few weeks, a baby feeds for approximately eight hours of every day. Even if you were *only* doing the job of breastfeeding a three-week-old baby, you'd still be working a full-time job. When you consider the fact that there are no weekends, your work as a food producer actually outstrips the average Australian's working week. Oh, except in addition to having to work seven days a week, you also get no sick leave, no lunch breaks, no formalised training and substandard pay. Who negotiated the enterprise bargaining scheme on that?

But in your average heterosexual relationship, lactating mothers don't *just* do the breastfeeding. They also do the majority (if not the entirety) of work involved in rocking babies to sleep, massaging painful wind out of their bellies, dangling colourful objects over their heads to entertain them, supervising tummy time, keeping track of medical appointments, reading about and tracking milestones, not to mention all the other general housework—though apparently all that extra baby-related work is hardly real (and definitely not really hard). By the time you factor all of this in, you're looking at a workload that spans *at least* twelve to fourteen hours a day and often a lot more. Don't even mention the time spent trying to get the smell of dirty nappies out of your hair (my friend calls this the 'shit shadow'). The slap in the face of it all is that, aside from the breastfeeding, none of this work needs to be done solely by the birth parent (who in almost all cases will be a woman). And yet, it's amazing how the responsibility for it almost always seems to fall under her new job description, which could accurately be laid out as follows:

> An exciting new opportunity to join the organisation of Motherhood has arrived. Duties include being screamed at, vomited on, shat on, slept on, washing clothes, washing clothes again, washing clothes a third time, folding clothes, dying in a mountain of clothes, learning to tune out the repetitive sounds of The Wiggles, sweeping floors, resweeping the floors after your child uses their toy broom to 'help' you sweep them, stopping your child from eating the pile of dust and debris collected from the newly swept floor, putting on nappies, changing nappies, nappies again, poo, being woken up with a kick in the throat by a nineteen-month-old who's spent most of the night sleeping with their butt on your face, negotiating tantrums, dishes, more dishes, booking appointments with the doctor, using Facebook to research childhood diseases, planning

nutritious dinners that end up thrown on the floor, buying nappies, buying toilet paper, washing towels, wiping benches, memorising a catalogue of nursery rhymes, wiping crayon off the walls, more nappies, cleaning out the fridge, cleaning out the pantry moths, scrubbing the bath, cleaning poo out of the bath, scrubbing the bath again, remembering to wash cot sheets, more clothes to fold, being screamed at again.

Hours vary, but may include some short sleep breaks.

Please note: This is an unpaid position.

Speak to any first-time mother and she'll generally tell you that her expectations of parenthood (gentle scheduling, easy nap times, a sweetly decorated nursery and a swift return to sexual intimacy—and function—with her partner) were vastly different to the reality (in which a tornado tears through her home daily, the nursery has become a storeroom because the baby only wants to sleep attached to her breasts, and hearing her partner say 'I'm tired too' in response to her 'I'm fucking exhausted' becomes the world's most foolproof contraceptive because the thought of having sex with such a clueless *wanker* makes her want to eat her own face and, besides, who wants to bone when you're worried about pissing yourself?).

If you'd asked me about the gender politics in my relationship before I'd fallen pregnant, I would have told you that we had that shit *locked down*. We managed to live reasonably independent lives while still maintaining emotional intimacy and connection. Neither of us ever asked for 'permission' to do anything. I would sometimes plan a week or two away for work here or there with barely any warning, and the thought of having to explain myself or my absence was a completely foreign concept. We did fight about the distribution of domestic chores (I wanted him to stop leaving his cereal bowl by the sink as if it were my job to clean it), but we also fought about security (he wanted me to stop leaving doors unlocked so our home insurance wouldn't be rendered invalid if we were broken into). These arguments were more like the ones you might have with a housemate, though—one whose domestic footprint hasn't yet been magically erased by the fact they poke their junk at (or in) you every so often.

(Sidenote: Isn't it incredible how many cis men think sleeping with a woman earns them special She Can Do My Washing privileges? My dudes, your dicks ain't made of diamonds.)

Like an ignorant fool, I assumed little would change once our communist bloc of two became a picket-fenced trio. But the funny thing about babies is that they can't actually do anything. They haven't even figured out that they have opposable thumbs yet, so the days of picking up after themselves are still a long way off. So if the introduction of a baby brings with it a whole new level of workload to a house, who takes responsibility for that?

For example, I always considered it non-negotiable that I would never wash a man's clothes, and my partner certainly never expected me to do it. But what did it say about the dynamic of a feminist partnership that the responsibility for laundering our baby's clothes always seemed to fall to me? In that first year after becoming parents, some of our biggest barnstormers started because I found myself washing and folding yet another load of tiny leggings and singlets that my partner had just stepped over or walked past without even noticing.

'Why is this my job?!' I'd rage at him. 'This is your baby too! We need to be equally responsible for making sure he has clean clothes to wear!'

If laundering onesies challenged our relationship, then the issue of sleep-ins almost detonated it completely. Many a morning passed by with me insisting on having an ~~argument~~ discussion about the fact that I seemed to be expected to wake up with the baby every day. Fuelled by lack of sleep and feminist outrage, I reminded him that ours was supposed to be an equal partnership and that I shouldn't have to wheedle and bargain every time I wanted to sleep while he did the morning shift.

'You're not my boss!' I yelled at him. 'I shouldn't have to feel like I'm a nervous employee calling in sick to work!'

I want to stress that things are greatly improved now. My partner is a wonderful, loving father who splits childcare responsibilities with me roughly equally. Our son sees him washing and folding laundry, doing dishes, cooking food, wiping benches and changing more nappies than can possibly ever be counted. I have no doubts at all that the kind of masculinity he's modelling is of a gentle, supportive and nurturing kind. I feel extremely lucky to be raising a child with someone so patient and beautiful. But it took showdowns and arguments from both of us to get to this point, because the division of gendered labour is just so damn insidious and deeply conditioned. In the first two years of my son's life, I was probably tempted to walk out of my relationship (or kick my partner out of it) at least once every couple of weeks. It was hard work trying to inject equality into a circumstance in which inequality is so consistently represented by society as the happy norm. Navigating these new boundaries put a huge amount of stress on our relationship, so I shudder to think what inequality is being accepted in relationships where these conversations aren't a regular occurrence. If I learned anything at all after becoming a parent, it's that resentment is a well that can always hold more liquid but can never be fully drained.

I'm far from the only woman who feels this way, nor is this inequality only present during the breastfeeding and nappy years. As I prepared to write this chapter, I issued a call-out for testimonies on one of the online mothers' groups that saved my life after my son was born. This is a group mainly populated by progressive women aware of the damage done by gender stereotypes and their impact on our children. I'd be willing to bet that most of the group's members consider themselves feminists. Yet not only did my questions about domestic frustrations and gender inequality yield a huge response, almost all of them featured one chief complaint: the expectations placed on them by their male partners to carry the mental load.

In 2017, a French cartoonist who goes only by the name of Emma depicted this form of domestic labour brilliantly in *You Should've Asked*. This essay-length comic lays bare the expectation that women become the 'household managers' for men who may be happy to perform household tasks, but who require delegation from their wives or girlfriends to be prompted into action. These are the same men who genuinely love and adore their children, but who still ask their partners what they should feed them for lunch. The men who know when their favourite football team will play, but not when their child's next vaccinations are due. Who understand that growing children frequently need larger shoes and clothes, but never take the initiative to buy them.

These men aren't bad people, and they're probably unaware of how uneven the workload is in their family. If you were to ask them, they'd almost certainly say the balance was more or less equal, 'give or take'. But this is because they haven't been conditioned from the outset to absorb the kind of boring, repetitive mental labour that is considered not just the domain of women but our area of special expertise. It spawns from the same conditioning that sees women acting as 'the glue in men's conversations', as journalist Tracey Spicer calls it. In this framework, women don't lead—we facilitate. So it is that we facilitate the smooth running of a household, whether or not we want to or are even particularly good at it. If a household is a living organism, women's work is the fascia that connects all those muscles together.

There are other influences at play here, and they touch on what one mother reminded me was the tendency for us to sometimes assume, even to our own detriment, that we're superior at these tasks. Not long after Emma's *You Should've Asked* was published, the writer Cerys Howell criticised what she (and others) have referred to as the 'cult of motherhood'. Howell was writing in *The Guardian* about her postnatal depression, in an article titled 'I deleted my baby apps when I realised how much they fetishise motherhood'. She observed that the vast majority of these online motherhood communities 'assume mum-exclusive care', noting that fathers were often only mentioned 'as a subsection, like a type of buggy'.

I don't share Howell's disdain of these groups, but I agree that women in Anglo, often middle-class communities seem determined to prove our competency as highly skilled Professional Mothers, the modern, 'empowered' version of the 1950s housewife who can suddenly do and have it all but with less easy access to gin and Bex. My theory is that 'instinctive' child rearing and domestic management live in the miniscule realm of things women are allowed to boast about being good at, because it suits the patriarchal order for us to aspire to greatness within this unpaid and grossly underappreciated skill set. Men may be best at running the world, but women are best at running the house—or at least this is what we are supposed to satisfy ourselves with.

When you combine this with the element of competition—that is, the endless competition women are constantly forced into with one another, the one that plays out in the Mummy Wars, the media critiques and the irritating persistence of querying whether or not we can really 'have it all'—the situation just gets worse.

Around the same time that Emma's comic was published, *Harper's Bazaar* published an article by Gemma Hartley about women's emotional labour in the domestic sphere, poignantly titled, 'Women aren't nags—we're just fed up'. In reflecting on the example she and her husband were setting for their children (one girl and two boys), Hartley wrote:

> I find myself worrying about how the mental load bore [sic] almost exclusively by women translates into a deep gender inequality that is hard to shake on the personal level. It is difficult to model an egalitarian household for my children when it is clear that I am the household manager, tasked with delegating any and all household responsibilities, or taking on the full load myself. I can feel my sons and daughter watching our dynamic all the time, gleaning the roles for themselves as they grow older.

Hartley's just one of many women in heterosexual partnerships who feel obliged to 'manage' not just the workload of the home she shares with at least one other adult, but also the way her home is perceived by other people. I'm speaking generally here, but I've rarely, if ever, encountered the same level of domestic embarrassment in my male friends in hetero partnerships as I have in my female ones. They don't give the toilet a quick once-over to check for rogue floaters, nor do they apologise for presiding over a living room that actually looks lived-in. As the women trained to pick up after them exclaim in exasperation, 'It's as if they don't even *see* the mess!' A convenient form of myopia, you'll agree.

To be extremely clear, I'm talking about families and partnerships which are *not that bad*. No wonder women feel compelled to host award ceremonies when their partners occasionally 'help'.

Lucky us.

■

It's difficult to get analytical data on the nitty gritty of what's happening in homes across Australia, but I feel confident saying that they're built on some deeply sexist fault lines. Not surprisingly, it all starts with how much involvement we expect men to have with their kids from the very beginning.

Anecdotally, it seems there are a lot of men who consider a nine-hour day spent at work plus a bit of playtime with the kids afterwards to be the extent of their contribution to family life. They leave the kid-wrangling in the mornings to their partners, get home as dinner's being prepared (when they might also complain a bit about how messy the house is because, 'What do you *do* all day?') and then relax in front of the TV or computer while Mum does bath-and-bedtime. The weekends are for sleep-ins (his) because—as their exhausted wives or partners rage to networks of similarly disenchanted women around the country—'he says he's tired'. Afternoons are for sport, and evenings are for winding down after sport. On the rare occasions that he parents solo, it's called 'babysitting'. When he empties the dishwasher or vacuums the floor, this is referred to as 'helping'.

In case you weren't already full to the eyeballs with annoyance about those two particular depictions of fatherhood and male domesticity, let me remind you that:

1. Men who look after their children aren't 'babysitting'. They aren't doing a job that's been outsourced to them. They aren't being paid the pitiful salary given to the mostly female workers oppressed by the feminisation of their industry. These are *their* children. What they're doing is called 'parenting'.
2. It isn't 'helping' to do a handful of chores in a house *you live in*. 'Helping' is when you go around to your mate's place for a working bee or provide the answer to a hard crossword clue. It isn't 'doing less than your equal share and patting yourself on the back for being such a Good Guy'. Everyone, no matter what their gender, needs to stop framing men's contributions to the domestic workload as 'helping'. All this does is position that workload as belonging to women, with anything done by men an unexpected act of generosity that deserves acknowledgment and praise.

In another essay for *The Monthly*, titled 'The wife and times', Anne Manne recalls a recent period during which her husband assumed primary domestic care responsibilities while she finished writing her book. She was annoyed to discover that some people found this arrangement 'amazing'. As she wrote:

> My husband taking over the care role seemed a reversal of the proper order of things, like a waterfall suddenly flowing

> upwards. In earlier times, when I took on that role, under more exacting circumstances with small children to care for, reactions ranged from condescending to dismissive. I cannot recall a single instance of tears shed in sentimental gratitude.

When we say men 'babysit' their kids and 'help out' around the house and heap praise on them for doing so, we're perpetuating the mindset that these things are outside the scope of the job description of Father and Husband/Partner. The flipside of this is that child-rearing and domestic work are maintained as the responsibility of women—obligations for which we can occasionally (but not too often!) seek assistance from men, whose paltry contributions inevitably end up being hailed as worthy of a ticker-tape parade.

Gosh, isn't it nice to be with someone who gives you some time off every once in a while? And you're just so *lucky* that he helps you around the house without complaint!

Baaaaaaaaaaaarf. Christ, the bar is set low for men.

But domestic and parental gender inequality is even more insidious than the bugbears of 'babysitting' and 'helping'. In a lot of partnerships, it isn't uncommon to find women who feel obligated to trade privileges or services with their partners in order to nab some 'time off'. He 'babysits' his kid for a few hours so she can go to a cafe or get a pedicure or a massage or some other form of pampering (it's always pampering, because this dynamic relies on women feeling that 'time off' is a reward and not actually something they deserve) and in exchange he gets to go out on an all-night bender with his mates.

Very, very rarely does this negotiation happen in reverse. Of course, there are exceptions, but generally speaking men don't feel pressured to make sure their home and parenting duties are suitably covered in order to blag a few hours by themselves.

When a friend of mine was struggling with a child who wouldn't sleep, she and her partner spent a weekend at a sleep school. Aside from my friend's partner, there were no other men there. As she told it, some of the other mums adopted a teasing tone and asked what she'd had to do to 'drag' him along.

'Uh . . . nothing?' she replied. 'It's his kid too.'

The thought that a man might take active responsibility for participating in the tedium of sleep school seemed shocking to these women. In response, another mum described how she'd had to agree to let her husband have a weekend away playing golf in exchange for her entering the program.

'But that makes no sense!' I shrieked at my friend when she recounted this later. 'She's not getting a weekend at a spa! She's taken her baby *with her* to try to teach them how to fucking sleep! He's getting *two freaking free weekends*, and he's had to do nothing!'

While it seemed unbelievable to me, I also recognised how frighteningly true this situation is for a lot of women in Australia who are charged with taking care of men and children. The comedic trope of the woman rewarding her partner with sex because he slightly reduced her domestic workload (by 'helping', naturally) is popular for a reason.

One of the most revolting things I've ever seen was a photograph labelled 'Daddy's Sticker Chart'. After being posted by Karen Alpert—who writes the parenting blog *Baby Sideburns* and whose Facebook page has over 300,000 followers—it quickly went viral and has been popping up around the place ever since. The chart lists seven different household chores, and it's important that I list them all to properly demonstrate how very little is being asked of the husband in this joke.

1. Wash dishes
2. Put toilet seat down
3. Change blowout diaper
4. Bathe the rug rats
5. Pack the kids' lunches
6. Vacuum car seats
7. Clean up throw up [vomit]

After each chore listed, the chart has six spaces for stickers. Six stickers earns Daddy a reward, and here's where things get extra gross. These rewards range from receiving 'a 12 pack of his favorite beer' to 'no nagging for a week' to '1 get out of the dog house free card' and 'don't have to go to some annoying kid's bday party'. But the reward that's shown with all the stickers already filled is the lucky last, 'Clean up throw up'. This is the one where Daddy's 'help' nets him, wait for it, a BJ!!!!!!!!

Yes, I'm aware that this chart was almost certainly posted as a cheeky joke. But the system of chore-for-reward actually does play out in loads of heterosexual homes. This isn't just bad for the women who almost always end up with the short end of the stick when it comes to the domestic workload (and, evidently, bedroom duties), it's also really destructive to the expectations being formed by the children looking on. It's bad enough that children are conditioned to see women as the providers of unpaid domestic labour. It's even worse that part of this socialisation involves learning that sex is just another job women are required to do.

One of the cornerstones of patriarchy is its oppression of women via the enforcement of reproductive and domestic labour, and that includes the provision of sex. We need to note again here that women are not the only ones who can birth a child. Trans men and non-binary people can and do get pregnant, and their capabilities in this area should be respected and recognised. But it's also important to acknowledge that patriarchy is invested in maintaining reproduction as a matter *only* for cisgender women. That is to say, the 'traditional values' of patriarchy and its adherents aren't interested in accommodating the spectrum of gender. Assaults on reproductive healthcare (which includes limiting or entirely removing access to uterine birth control and abortion) aren't rooted in concern for unborn children but in the desire to maintain a strict gender binary that keeps cis women in reproductive servitude and thus subservient to the cis men who appoint themselves captains of the domestic vessel. Marriage and childbirth are sold to women as essential components for our happiness, but the reality is that both contribute to the structural inequalities that severely impact our lives—and all too often, this includes the belief that every part of our body belongs to the men who claim access to it.

When I was pregnant, I signed up to an online group of women who were due in the same month as me. Through the months and months (and months) of pregnancy into the terrifying beyond of parenting, I looked on as women shared not only queries about Braxton Hicks and teething, but also intimate, vulnerable stories detailing the extensive emotional and domestic labour they performed in order to keep the tenuous balance of their families in check. I've been privy to testimonies of domestic violence, family abandonment and, frighteningly, what I would call comprehensive sexual abuse. There have been more stories than I can count of women whose partners cajoled them into sex either in the late stages of their pregnancies or early postpartum weeks, with many of the women tentatively asking each other how they could help these unweaned sulks to understand that they just didn't feel physically or emotionally up for it—because the management of men's feelings and entitlement around sex is just another job required of us, even when we are in physical and mental recovery from pregnancy and childbirth.

Make no mistake, servicing men's sexual needs is still considered a wifely duty. They used to call this conjugal rights, which was just a fancy legal way of saying, 'Rape is okay if you're married to her.' But, like so many things, changing the law hasn't necessarily changed the practice.

In 2017, Ginger Gorman wrote a harrowing article for News.com about the numbers of women who either feel pressured to have penetrative sex shortly after childbirth or whose partners actually rape them ('Women are being pressured into sex too soon after giving birth'). Through anecdotal research, Gorman identified three main causes for this:

1. Succumbing to verbal 'nagging' or pressure
2. Overt and physically violent sexual assault
3. A sense of obligation to 'service their man'

These stories aren't uncommon. I've heard women joke flippantly about how they've 'never given so many blow jobs' as they have in the weeks after their baby was born, because God forbid Him Upstairs goes without having his cock worshipped for a few months. One particularly horrendous story involved a woman recovering from a physically traumatic birth. After three months of what he called 'being understanding', her husband insisted that it was time to take care of him now. She refused, so he took to watching porn and angrily masturbating in the living room whenever she was in there breastfeeding their child.

They're divorced now.

Unfortunately, not every woman has the power to up and leave an abusive or coercive relationship, particularly not when there are children. What does the woman who relies on her husband or partner for financial support do when sex is treated as one of her many domestic obligations? 'Sacrifice' is an unavoidable part of having children, but the demands it places on women are very different to those it places on men.

Which leads us here: looking at one of the most oppressive inequalities shouldered by women partnered with overgrown oafs cleverly disguised as human males.

Money.

■

'She was going to go back to work, but her salary barely covered the childcare!'

You're probably familiar with this classic argument about how heterosexual couples choose to wrestle with the challenge of childcare, employment and financial burdens following the birth of a baby. My favourite is when it's offered by the man in the relationship, because it means that, while listening, I get to indulge my secret internal fantasy of scooping him and all the men like him up into a giant net and dropping them into the middle of the sea.

Oh, *her* salary barely covers the childcare that you apparently have nothing to do with? Thanks for that, Brian, you smarmy git.

Repeat after me: *The cost of childcare isn't the fucking responsibility of the mother.*

Now, I know how maths works (and I'm a girl!). I know that when you add two salaries together and take away childcare fees and repayments on a car he mostly gets to drive, you end up with the same figure no matter which column you subtract it from. But there's a subtle difference between assuming that the partnership ends up with only, say, twenty dollars more overall and assuming that, after childcare fees are paid, the *mother* ends up with only twenty dollars more overall.

Making childcare the emotional and financial responsibility of the partnered mother alone doesn't just further distance men from the responsibility of raising children, it fundamentally disadvantages women by keeping them out of the workforce, threatening their superannuation payments later on and denying them the ability to live a life beyond their identity as a mother. It disadvantages children, because it helps to reinforce a society in which those things are the automatic domain of women, thus repeating the cycle ad infinitum. Women who are kept out of the workforce are more likely to suffer later on, particularly if their relationships dissolve.

But, like all issues, this is one made comprehensively worse when class and racial oppression are introduced. Women from low-income backgrounds and/or women of colour (especially Aboriginal women) face enormous oppression in Australia, not to mention the very real threat that their children will be taken away from them. It's just an extra layer of shit on a thick shit sandwich.

As long as women are considered the 'natural' caregivers for children, we'll be expected to sacrifice more in order to have them and to be grateful for that sacrifice. This is what allows unequal domestic and economic arrangements to persist, fundamentally challenging women's right to individual autonomy and freedom. As if there are no benefits to a woman working other than financial ones, as if she needs to justify her desire to work in the sense of cost versus gain, as if it would be something she would only *want* to do in order to benefit financially, and as if it's her responsibility alone to cover those costs. The rates of Australian women working part time are among the highest in the world, with more than one child destabilising paid employment even further, to the point where many women feel obliged to opt out altogether. And here's a sobering fact for you: average Australian women with super retire with around 42 percent of the superannuation of men, and one-third of us retire with no super at all.

In the toxic dumpster fire that is our patriarchal world, women are still expected to be the best at, and most capable of assuming, caregiving roles, like being teachers, childcare workers, nurses and wives. It's surely just a very interesting *coincidence* that these roles are often underpaid, undermined and underappreciated. When social conditioning also instructs us to believe women do these jobs because a) we're just better at them and b) we love them so much we would do them for free, it becomes even easier to ignore the huge responsibility they actually represent (not to mention to dismiss the massive favour women do society in general by relieving it of the responsibility of that burden).

So, what's the solution?

In my own home, having open lines of communication has been hugely rewarding. My partner and I have ongoing conversations about how we can model equality to our son, from having set weekdays in which one or the other of us acts as primary parent to making sure he sees both of us doing things like vacuuming, washing clothes and cleaning the kitchen. I'm not afraid to have endless discussions about our domestic dynamic, even though I find it boring and frustrating most of the time. Unfortunately, this seems to be largely why women in hetero partnerships just throw their hands up and conform to gendered domestic expectations—it's too tiring and dull to keep having the same arguments over and over.

But we have to keep pushing for these things. Look at Sweden, where parents are entitled to 480 days of paid parental leave after the arrival of a child. For just over a year, parents are paid nearly 80 percent of their wage, with the remaining ninety days paid at a flat rate. Parents are also allowed to reduce their working hours by up to 25 percent until the child turns eight. Notice I said 'parents' and not just 'mother'. In Sweden, each parent is entitled to 240 days of the 480 days of paid leave, with ninety days reserved exclusively for each parent. A parent can give 150 days of their 240-day entitlement to the other parent, but the ninety-day reserve is non-transferable. So in your basic heterosexual relationship, men are supported to take three months off work to be the primary carer for their kid or kids while the mum goes back to work. And in Sweden, the men *do*. Imagine if we had a similar model of care here in Australia. It would go a long way towards dismantling archaic ideas around what women's true purpose is.

Paid paternity leave is just as important as paid maternity leave, not just because men who are thrust into the responsibility of being primary parents gain firsthand insight into what's actually required in the day-to-day care of children but also because it models empathetic masculinity from day dot. I cannot stress to you enough how important building empathy is in the fight against gender inequality. Men are just as capable of caring for children as women, and it's imperative that children see men in this role if we are to disrupt the sexist lessons that take root in childhood and can morph into full-blown misogyny later on.

I want my child to see value in extending empathy and care to people beyond himself. I want him to consider the gentle care of children to be as much a masculine trait as a feminine one, and for him to value the work that women do both in and out of the home. I want him to reject the bullshit, dangerous notion that women exist to amplify the greatness of his own life. We exist in our own right, and our potential for success isn't conditional on helping to give men like him a free ride.

The lessons taught to boys and girls about who does what in the home are inextricably linked to the roles they feel entitled to assume later in life. What is made easy for boys to 'get away with' might not seem like that big a deal when you're talking about a five-year-old, but it becomes a much larger deal when that five-year-old becomes a grown man with expectations of what the world either owes him or will allow him to escape punishment for. When there are teenage boys who still sleazily demand that girls and women 'get back in the kitchen' to 'make me a sandwich' as a means of putting those girls and women in their proper place, then we are still battling against a deeply embedded, learned culture of sexism.

No, these aren't just harmless jokes. Even if individual boys and men don't think they mean it this way, what they're buying into is the misogynist idea that women are subservient to them. It's a silencing tool meant to disempower the women being targeted. Most of these men will have been birthed and raised by women. Many of them will go on to marry women and possibly start families of their own. But when the world itself remains fundamentally unequal and sexist, and the essential economic work performed by women is rendered meaningless and therefore invisible, this is what it will always come back to whenever those men find themselves being challenged by mere girls.

Get back in the kitchen, bitch. Where you belong.

—3—

GIRLS ON FILM

I wasn't a particularly outdoorsy child. While other kids seemed to have energy to burn riding their bikes up and down the street or playing organised sports (Sidenote: Why?), I spent most of my free time reading *The Babysitters Club* and playing Barbies in my room (which really just involved making Barbie and Ken do sex). Occasionally, I would hang out in the living room and re-create scenes from the 1985 movie *Return to Oz*, a terrifying follow-up to L. Frank Baum's classic tale that begins with Dorothy being institutionalised and almost subjected to electric shock therapy and then goes on to feature talking chickens, a gang of crazed hybrid men called the Wheelers who rolled around on all fours, and an evil princess named Mombi with a cabinet full of women's heads that she wore interchangeably depending on who she wanted to be that day. It scared the shit out of me, so naturally I watched it whenever I had the opportunity. What can I say? My parents didn't keep a close eye.

Fairuza Balk's Dorothy Gale seemed more relatable to me than Judy Garland's turn as the ruby-slippered heroine back in 1939. It seemed conceivable to me that Balk's Dorothy and I could be friends or, you know, maybe even *the same person*. For years, I gazed hopefully into the mirror in my bedroom and told myself that, if I just believed harder, Ozma would appear to me just as she had to Balk's Dorothy at the movie's end.

Spoiler: she didn't.

I was a lonely girl with a big imagination, and I looked for heroes and adventure wherever I could find them. Every week, my mother would drive us to a video store packed with floor-to-ceiling racks of pirated movies. New movies came in all the time, but there were titles we went back to again and again. Our favourites included *The Goonies*, *Indiana Jones and the Last Crusade*, *Dream a Little Dream*, *The Princess Bride*, *The Lost Boys*, *Spaceballs*, *Bill & Ted's Excellent Adventure*, *White Water Summer*, *Back to the Future*, *Explorers*, *Stand By Me*, *Labyrinth*, *The NeverEnding Story*, *Terminator 2: Judgment Day*, *Teen Witch* and *Wayne's World*.

You might have noticed that most of these movies are stories about boys and treasure, or boys and aliens, or boys and computers, or boys and time travel, or boys saving the world or, in the case of *The NeverEnding Story*, boys and a giant flying dragon that looks like a dog. I didn't question this when I was a kid, because why would you question something that has formed the backdrop of your entire life? They were movies, I watched them, and I went to sleep at night pretending I was in them.

But as much as I loved slipping *The Goonies* into the VHS player and lying back in a beanbag with a packet of microwave popcorn on my lap (as children, we considered the advent of instant popcorn to be right up there with landing on the moon and air-conditioned cars), when I reflect on the experience now I realise something was missing. I could pretend I was Dorothy in *Return to Oz* or Sarah in *Labyrinth*. I could imagine myself as *Teen Witch*'s Louise. I was in awe of Sarah Connor, that total badass who, like the best heroines, liberates herself from the prison in which men have trapped her and goes on to save the world. But these four were really the only leading ladies I had on high rotation. There were girls living in the other worlds stacked in the video cabinet, but they were sidekicks or romantic rewards for the boys and men whose actions dominated the plot.

If I learned anything during the formative years of my childhood, it was that if a girl or woman *was* ever allowed to be the hero, it also meant that most of the time she could be literally the only woman in the film. I can't overstate how much this has impacted my cultural understanding as an adult of women's place in the world—so what has the flipside of that done for my male contemporaries who grew up watching an endless stream of men dominating stories, embarking on hero's quests and teaming up with other men as they plotted to either take over or save the world? Toxic masculinity exercises itself in multiple forms, not all of them obvious. Men can be ostensibly 'good', but the assumption that the world's stages exist to tell their stories first and foremost is just another way for them to help keep women in the wings.

Fun fact: I went through the IMDb entries for the films listed above, which represent a good cross-section of movies that kids all over the world grew up with in the 1980s and 1990s, and counted all the parts credited and uncredited to male and female actors, because that is the kind of super-cool and way-fun person I am. What I found was depressing, but completely unsurprising. Strap yourselves in, folks, because we're in for a stats party!

Across these sixteen movies, a total of 521 roles were assigned to male actors compared to 179 roles for female actors. Percentage-wise, that means that in the movies I watched on repeat as a child, women account for only one-third of the characters or bit parts.

I broke it down further to compare the gender balance of performers across each title. Women account for around a quarter of the characters in each movie—even in movies supposedly *about* a girl and her quest (a rarity in films of the 1980s and 1990s). For example, *Labyrinth* tells the story of a bookish girl named Sarah who wishes her annoying baby brother away then has to travel to the land of the Goblin King to retrieve him. It's an incredible movie, full of magical Jim Henson puppetry, literal twists and turns, and a healthy serving of David Bowie's nutsack in a pair of spandex pants. But the cast of this story about a girl's quest is still infuriatingly weighted in favour of men—sixty-two to twenty-eight to be exact.

You could argue that *Labyrinth* should be made an exception because so many of the characters are actually puppets. Does it really count if the majority of people operating them are dudes? Well, yeah, it does actually. Not only because it speaks to the gender gap that exists in terms of employment (as in who gets to count themselves in it) but also because workplaces dominated by any one demographic—be that gender, race or, I dunno, people who wear clown shoes to work—is not representative of the world we live in and/or the diverse range of folks who occupy it. And the entertainment industry seeks to tell stories *about the world we live in and its inhabitants.* That's impossible to do accurately when you have one demographic of people—white, straight, cisgender men—in charge of deciding what matters and what doesn't.

But besides that, the actual characters in *Labyrinth* count as well as the people pulling the strings. While 32 percent of the performers employed to run the animatronics might have been women, the characters portrayed on screen tell a different story to the audience watching. During her time in the labyrinth, Sarah encounters a number of characters who either help or hinder her on her quest. There's Hoggle, the crotchety gnome-like creature sent by the Goblin King to lead her astray (but who ends up an ally); Ludo, a giant beast Sarah rescues from a dicey trap; Sir Didymus the brave terrier, who rides around on his steed Ambrosius, a shaggy English sheepdog; Firey, the leader of the Firey monsters; the Helping Hands, the Four Guards, the Left and Right Door Knockers, all of whom stand in Sarah's way; the Junk Lady, a mean old behemoth of a scrap heap who tries to poison Sarah so she'll give up; Wormy, the worm who invites Sarah inside to 'meet the Missus 'n' have a cuppa tea!'; and aaaaaaaaalllllll the goblins who live with Jareth/Spandex Nutsack in the castle, and whom we can probably assume are formerly kidnapped babies-turned-stooges.

Whichever way you cut it, this is a story about an adolescent girl making her way through a land that is, like, *almost entirely* populated by dudes, one of whom is literally preceded by the outline of his enormous dick. Had an analysis been done on the ethnicities represented, a similarly bleak story would have emerged—it might seem churlish to expect a movie primarily populated by puppets to have a cast of racially diverse actors, but the sad truth is that you're still more likely to find mythical creatures than people of colour, especially women of colour, filling roles in Hollywood.

The same basic truth goes for *Terminator 2: Judgment Day.* It might seem like a movie that showcases raw female strength and skills, but like so many other films it does so through the portrayal of a lone woman fighting to survive in a world dominated by men. Sarah Connor doesn't exactly fit into the trope of the Strong Female Character (more on that later) because she's flawed and frequently unlikeable, and this elevates her into something greater. But her existence complicates attempts to have frank discussions about the representation (both literally and figuratively) of women on screen precisely *because* she's such a celebrated feminist icon. The men invested in shutting down conversations about sexism in entertainment think it's some kind of trump card to point to characters like Sarah Connor (along with Ripley in the *Alien* franchise), as if the two of them negate decades of marginalisation in favour of men's stories.

As I was writing the paragraph above, I asked my friend Karen if she could think of any other female roles as iconic as Sarah Connor and Ripley. She thought for a moment before saying, 'They're it, I think.' Then she exclaimed, 'No, wait! Uma Thurman in *Kill Bill* as The Bride.'

Always be prepared for your ideological opponent to produce a third example. Because if one extra example can be found to contradict your thesis then it stands to reason that there must be an *infinite* number of examples that can be used to prove you wrong.

Except that there isn't. *Kill Bill* wasn't released until 2003, twelve years after *Terminator 2*, which was in turn released twelve years after *Alien.* Compare this to the reams and reams of male counterparts churned out by Hollywood over the years: John McClane, Indiana Jones, Wolverine, Rambo, Rocky, Jason Bourne, James Bond, Neo, Clint Eastwood playing Clint Eastwood, John Wayne playing John Wayne, Tom Cruise playing Tom Cruise . . . you get the picture.

But the difference between someone like Sarah Connor and, say, Neo is that Neo still gets to live in a fictional world inhabited by a shit-ton of people who look like him. Sarah Connor is one of only a few women in *Terminator 2*; men don't just play her counterparts, they play most of the background humans as well.

On the one hand, there's a certain narrative sense to creating lonely space around female heroines and directing them to fight their way to freedom. It's a fairly good analogy for the frustration and isolation women feel in general. But don't be fooled into thinking this is why it's done; that this is why male screenwriters (who, like everyone else working in production and behind the scenes in Hollywood, outnumber their female counterparts) have traditionally chosen to fill the gaps around these women with as many men as they can. Nor is it accurate to say these writers always make a conscious choice to do so, to flood their story with as much testosterone as possible, to make sure that men's integral relevance isn't forgotten just because the camera is trained on a woman.

The answer lies somewhere in the middle. The uncritical man tells stories that he knows, the ones he grew up watching and learning from too. He knows the story of the princess in the tower, the one who is now allowed to fight her way out (but usually still requires the help and company of at least one man along the way). He can tell the story of that woman's liberation in a reasonably compelling manner. But this is the *only* story he seems to know. He doesn't know how to fill in the space around it with characters whose gender is incidental to the plot points. He doesn't know how to do that because he doesn't know how to write fully formed women beyond the trope of The Woman, around whom all the men orbit or work in conjunction to. And he doesn't know how to write women because he never bothered to take the time to actually understand women or listen to them or, I don't fucking know, employ a fucking woman to work with him in the writers' room.

Under this gaze, female characters are crafted not so much as afterthoughts but as understudies. They help out when the story calls for a mother or a fuckbuddy or a tired waitress or a sex worker who apparently needs saving, but when they've served their purpose they disappear backstage to wait for their next curtain call.

For example, *Terminator 2* features two other sort-of-prominent women in addition to Sarah Connor. One plays John Connor's foster mother. The other plays the wife of Miles Dyson, the man responsible for inventing the neural-net processor that leads to the development of Skynet, the artificial intelligence system that eventually becomes self-aware and tries to kill all of humanity (not a bad idea, tbh). Pretty much all the rest of the speaking roles are assigned to men. *The Lost Boys* has only two women of any importance: Lucy, mother to vampire hunter Sam and fledgling vampire Michael; and Star, a love interest who wears lots of floaty skirts. Everyone else with a speaking role? Dudes. *Indiana Jones and the Last Crusade* has ONE woman in the entire movie (aside from some giggling students with the horn for Professor Jones), and she gets to be the love interest *and* the smarty pants *and* the eye candy *and* the baddie all at the same time! Women are so good at multitasking.

These things are not meaningless. Sure, girls can consume plenty of stories about boy heroes, boy gangs, boy villains, boy inventors and sometimes even anthropomorphised boy objects, like a car or a plane or, I dunno, a talking hamburger. We can enjoy these movies for what they are, which is generally meant to be light-hearted entertainment or diversion. But what we can't do is view them as aspirational blueprints for life in the same way that the boys watching them can. We can't project ourselves into the stories because the stories are so rarely about us. We don't have enough of our own heroes to make it an irrelevant fact of life that boys get to have so very, very many. We didn't grow up with fucking George Lucas telling us that we could be a Jedi Master—instead, we learned we could be the only woman in the galaxy but we wouldn't be allowed to wear a bra in case it strangled us in the zero-gravity expanse of space.

(Interjection: Yes, I know there are technically other women in the original *Star Wars* trilogy, but their roles are so tiny as to be almost non-existent. Leia is arguably the only female character the trilogy bothers to feature or develop. Also, none of these women talk to each other. Consider this: the original trilogy runs at 386 minutes long. Women who aren't Leia speak for 1.03 of those minutes. In fact, in each movie only one woman who isn't Leia speaks in a language audience members can understand—Aunt Beru in *A New Hope*, an unnamed Rebel soldier in *The Empire Strikes Back* (she says four words) and Mon Mothma in *The Return of the Jedi*. Don't email me about it, you're wrong and I'm right.*)

---

* Thanks to Chris Wade from *Vulture* for compiling footage to demonstrate this. I trust you were as depressed by it as I was.

But there's the question again of relatability. Girls participate in mainstream pop culture because that's what we've been conditioned to do, which means we witness these stories about men and accept them as being reflective of a life that we can understand and in which we can find meaning.

Are boys conditioned to do the same with stories about girls? I think it's patently clear that they're not. Stories about girls are considered niche and peripheral, in the same way stories about people of colour or stories about disability or queerness are. They can be included by a sort of unspoken invitation (and are still most often told by men or white people or able bods or straighties etc.), but they don't ever get to be the standard. Right from the start of childhood, boys are not expected to *choose* to watch stories about women and they certainly aren't encouraged to do so by the mainstream, just as white people are not expected to *care* about stories featuring the lives of people of colour or to seek out content that champions them. Without anything to disrupt that insidious gender conditioning, these boys grow into men who think that stories about anything other than themselves are 'unrealistic' or 'boring' or, my fave, 'another example of political correctness infecting the entertainment industry'.

Women don't get a choice. We take what we can get and hold on tightly to even vaguely positive representations of people whose stories and lives are more like our own, because we have learned that if you gather enough crumbs you can sometimes put together a pretty good meal.

■

This stuff doesn't just hit in adulthood, nor is it only present in the distant past of the boombox era. It continues to be instilled almost from birth, delivered to our kids in a stream of children's books, movies and kids' shows. It isn't necessarily that there are *no* girls. That would be too obvious. It's just that girls are few and far between, and they're never allowed to overshadow the boys in case it starts to look like an 'agenda'.

In a 2013 article for Fairfax titled 'Girls on film', the author Emily Maguire recalled some of the attitudes she encountered from children in the writing workshops she facilitates. One of her eight-year-old students—a girl—had written a story about a fierce but heroic pirate called Jessica.

'Pirates aren't girls!' one of her classmates protested, and several others agreed.

'What about Anamaria in *Pirates of the Caribbean*?' the young writer shot back.

'She's not a main one,' came the reply. 'The main pirates are all boys.'

'The main pirates are all boys,' Emily noted. 'So are the main robots, monsters, bugs, soldiers, toys, cars, trains, rats and lions.'

This is the lesson that mainstream culture teaches to all its young dreamers: you're allowed to include a girl in your motley group of ragtag heroes, but she'll never be one of the main ones. And there will rarely be more than one of her and certainly never an equal number of hers to hims.

I'm not lying about this, or even exaggerating. It is quantifiably true that the experiences and presence of women are considered peripheral to storytelling. In 2015, the Geena Davis Institute on Gender in Media released *Gender Bias Without Borders*, an investigation into the depiction of female characters in popular movies across eleven different countries. The report found that women featured as protagonists only 23 percent of the time; that they accounted for only 21 percent of the dialogue; and that, on average, for every one visible woman there were 2.24 visible men. They were also twice as likely to be depicted in revealing clothes, with teen girl characters the *most likely* to be sexualised in this manner. You know, because if we gotta listen to women blathering on then they better give us something nice to look at while it's happening.

And again, let's remember that of the bare scrape of women allowed to appear on-screen, the overwhelming majority of them are still white, able-bodied and cisgender. A 2017 study of 900 films between 2007 and 2016 found that while women only occupy around 30 percent of screen time, a whopping 76 percent of them in the top 100 of those films were white ('Inequality in 900 popular films', Professor Stacy L. Smith with the Media, Diversity & Social Change Initiative). In American cinema at the same time, only 14 percent of all female characters were black, 6 percent were Asian American and a paltry 3 percent were Latina. When we protest the marginalisation of women, it's essential that we are also honest about how white supremacy elevates some of us over others, and work to dismantle that too. As the inimitable Audre Lorde once said, 'I am not free while any woman is unfree, even when her shackles are very different from my own.' The idea that liberation will somehow trickle down is bullshit, and working towards this goal only serves to reinforce the systems of oppression from which we benefit.

So what *are* girls allowed to be, if it isn't being allowed to wear practical clothes while driving a storyline?

How about a Strong Female Character!

Yeah, nah. The SFC is an easy way for storymakers to pretend they care about gender diversity, but it usually just acts as defence against any criticism about a story's lack of diversity. 'How can we be sexist?! We have such a *strong female character*!'

The problem with the SFC isn't just that she's a two-dimensional figure; it's that her 'strength' is all too often about hitting the right notes to make male viewers desire her and female viewers feel validated by her. She's described as being 'feisty' and 'quick-witted'. She wields a gun just as well as she does a wisecrack, and can use both to take a man down. It's clear that she can take care of herself . . . but at some point, she'll probably need the hero to rescue her to remind her that it's okay for other people (read: him) to take care of her too. Women are supposed to want to be her, men are supposed to want to fuck her.

This is a distraction, a ruse designed to stop us from realising that the women's liberation we're supposedly witnessing on screen is all smoke and mirrors. As author Sophia McDougall wrote in the 2013 *New Statesman* piece, 'Why I hate strong female characters':

> Nowadays the princesses all know kung fu, and yet they're still the same princesses. They're still love interests, still the one girl in a team of five boys, and they're all kind of the same. They march on screen, punch someone to show how they don't take no shit, throw around a couple of one-liners or forcibly kiss someone because getting consent is for wimps, and then with ladylike discretion they back out of the narrative's way . . . Their strength lets them, briefly, dominate bystanders but never dominate the plot. It's an anodyne, a sop, a Trojan

Horse—it's there to distract and confuse you, so you forget to ask for more.

When women do remember to ask for more, we're met with the same tedious, aggressive and occasionally frightening backlash that follows all of our 'Please, sir' moments. Reasons abound as to why we can't *have* more, many of them contradicting each other. We can't have more because nobody wants to watch women on screen, but also there are *too many* women dominating the movies now. Our shrill demands for more are the perfect example of why women are turning away from feminism in droves, and yet feminism has also taken over Hollywood with its politically correct, ball-breaking misandry. Your personal complaints about this imaginary issue show how easily triggered and sensitive you are, so here are a thousand completely rational men with a personalised rape threat for you. You're welcome.

Okay, so things are fucked up for women on-screen. Surely things are better for little girls? I mean, we're always telling girls they can be and do anything they want. We love little girls!

Yeah, sure we do. Right up until they hit puberty, then we slap 'em across the face and scream, 'Welcome to hell, sweetheart! WHO'S SPECIAL NOW?'

Sorry to burst your bubble, but it turns out that the entertainment industry thinks little girls are pointless too—so pointless, in fact, that little boys have to be tricked into caring about them.

In 2010, Disney Pixar released a movie about a girl trapped in a tower for eighteen years with only twenty metres of golden hair to keep her company. Everyone knows this story. Everyone knows that it's called Rapunzel. But Disney Pixar announced early on that it would be changing the widely recognised title of that story to the less female-centric *Tangled*. Why? Ed Catmull, president of Pixar and Walt Disney Animation Studios, said at the time, 'We did not want to be put in a box. Some people might assume it's a fairy tale for girls when it's not. We make movies to be appreciated and loved by everybody.'

Ah! I get it! If you make people think it's a movie *about* a girl, they'll think it's a movie *for* girls. A movie about a girl can't be for everyone, because why would boys be interested in watching a story that has nothing to do with them?

But Disney Pixar went a lot further than a simple re-brand, writing a love interest whose role was not only emphasised in the lead up to the film's release but featured so prominently you'd be forgiven for thinking he was the movie's sole protagonist. 'In our film,' wrote producer Roy Conli, 'the infamous bandit Flynn Rider meets his match in the girl with the 70 feet of magical golden hair. We're having a lot of fun pairing Flynn, who's seen it all, with Rapunzel, who's been locked away in a tower for 18 years.'

The first official trailer released for *Tangled* was two minutes and six seconds long and opens with an extended shot of Flynn Rider alongside the description, 'He's fearless'. As for Rapunzel, she doesn't even appear until over halfway through and says only three words just before it finishes.

In their research, the Geena Davis Institute found that films with more than one woman working as directors resulted in significantly more women in speaking roles than films with a heavy male production quota. Of the thirteen senior crew working on *Tangled*—the directors, the writers, the producers, the music composer and the film editor—only one was a woman: Aimee Scribner, an associate producer. And the impact of that is startingly clear. *Tangled*, one of the few films across any target bracket that featured a female protagonist (in 2010, women accounted for only 11 percent of lead protagonists in mainstream cinema—*down* 5 percent from a decade earlier), has a cast of thirty-six speaking characters. Only 30 percent of them are women. Of the ten speaking characters with names, 80 percent are men—the other two are Rapunzel (the princess) and Gothel (the evil witch).

And yet Disney was so concerned that this film not appear too fucking *girly* that they changed the title and repackaged the marketing to assure boys that there would be something in it for them. Because everyone knows that all the main pirates are boys.

Yeah, yeah—but what about *Frozen*, hmm?

It's true that *Frozen* marked a significant departure from Disney's previous princess vehicles. For a start, there were two women in it. Not only were neither of them evil, one of them didn't even have to end up with a man to be considered worthwhile (feminazis in Hollywood strike again). *Frozen* subverted numerous tropes associated with the princess tale, most notably that true love's kiss is unlikely to occur between two strangers who barely know each other and people probably shouldn't get engaged only a few hours after they've met. Kids bloody loved it—*Frozen* quickly became the highest grossing animated film in history, taking $1.2 billion in global box office sales. It's widely held up as an example of feminism making its way (finally) into Disney's headquarters. At last!

Oh, except that *Frozen* still only has two female characters of any importance in it (by which I mean they speak and they have names) compared with five prominent male characters, one of whom is a snowman and one of whom is a reindeer. This ground-breaking, trend-bucking, animated feminist celebration conforms exactly to the already known statistics of women's representation on-screen: in it, women account for a third of major characters and speak for less than half the time. (*Frozen* was also criticised following its release for the severe whitewashing of the Sami people, who are presented in the movie as blond and white—a far cry from the Asiatic, brown-skinned features of the real-life Indigenous group.)

The stats on *Frozen* were presented in 2016 by linguists Carmen Fought and Karen Eisenhauer, who conducted research analysing all the language used by male and female characters in Disney princess films, from *Snow White* (1937) to *Frozen* (2013). What they discovered contradicts a generally held view that 'feistiness' and a can-do attitude in our female heroes necessarily equates to social progress.

Few (if any) of Disney's early animated films could be said to have passed the Bechdel test, created by cartoonist Alison Bechdel in her comic strip *Dykes to Watch Out For*. (To pass the test a movie must have: 1) more than one woman in it, who 2) speak to each other 3) about something other than a man.) But despite this, they were still more likely than not to let women speak. In fact, women speak the same number of lines as men in *Snow White* and significantly more than men in both *Cinderella* (1950) and *Sleeping Beauty* (1959). While Disney's versions of these classic fairy tales could not reasonably be viewed as feminist, at least we were allowed to listen to the female characters we were being conditioned to propel into married drudgery. We must take our victories as we find them, I guess.

The arrival of *The Little Mermaid* in 1989 shifted things. Ariel, we were told, was an independent and adventurous heroine, meant to channel the values of the girl power movement that was already beginning to set down roots. Yet a major plot point in *The*

Little Mermaid has Ariel sacrificing her voice in order to grow legs and inspire Prince Eric, a walking jawline with a body attached, to fall in love with her. As a result, this supposedly female-centred story has women speaking for only 32 percent of the time.

Even if you set *The Little Mermaid* aside out of deference to its 'lost voice' narrative, Fought and Eisenhauer show the disparity still holds up across later titles. *Beauty and the Beast* (1991) has Belle, another Strong Female Character, trapped in the castle of a beast who refuses to let her leave. Naturally, she falls in love with him, because all girls love a bad boy and it's apparently our job to save him from himself. In *Beauty and the Beast*, men are responsible for 71 percent of the dialogue.

Aladdin (1992): 90 percent.

Mulan (1998)—is about a woman saving China from the motherfreaking HUNS, but men still get to speak 77 percent of the lines. If that doesn't stoke your rage, consider this: Mulan's helper dragon (voiced by Eddie Murphy) speaks *50 percent* more than the character for which the movie is named.

The findings were a touch better for the aforementioned *Tangled* (2010), with women slightly edging out men at 52 percent, and *Brave* (2012) blew out at a whopping 74 percent of dialogue spoken by women. Then along came *Frozen* in 2013 and we were right back to eating a smaller portion again. (I couldn't find any stats related to *Moana* (2016), but it's without a doubt the best princess movie offering Disney has put up yet.)

This issue of representation is insidious and industry-wide, and it absolutely has an effect on how people view the space women are allowed take up in the world, not to mention a weird insecurity about what that means for men's importance. Another comprehensive 2015 study from the Geena Davis Institute found that, much like the reasoning behind Flynn Rider's role being plumped up in *Tangled*, creators are just really fucking antsy about giving women or female characters too much airtime in general. In a study of the 200 top-grossing (non-animated) films of 2014 and 2015, they found that movies with a male lead featured male characters on-screen nearly three times more often than female characters, *and* they also spoke roughly three times as much. But the opposite was not true for movies with a female lead—then, men and women appear for roughly the same amount of time and are given roughly the same number of lines. Where a movie has a male *and* a female co-lead, men were back to receiving way more screen time and lines than the women they were supposedly starring alongside.

Well, fuck me sideways, we wouldn't want people to see women acting like they deserved equal rights and equal attention. They might think it was a movie *for girls*.

Can this gender gap on-screen be considered partly the fault of the gender gap off-screen? PROBABLY! Women are also underrepresented behind the camera. *The Celluloid Ceiling*, a 2017 report published by the US-based Center for the Study of Women in Television & Film, showed that women comprised only 18 percent of directors, writers, producers, executive producers, editors and cinematographers who had worked on that season's top 250 films—the exact same percentage of women who had been working behind the scenes back in 1998.

It can be frustrating to put forward arguments like this, because there's a not insignificant number of people who bend over backwards to make it the fault of anyone but the people fiercely protecting their territory. It isn't that men choose to work with men (whether consciously or unconsciously)—it's that women don't *try* hard enough. It's not that studios (overwhelmingly run by men) insist on having men direct their blockbuster movies because of unconscious bias—it's that women aren't *good* enough. No one defers to a male perspective as writers—they just think women are *boring*.

Or . . . maybe it's that opportunities for women are stifled by the people around them who have more power than they do? Maybe it's that women's hands are tied when it comes to performing in roles that are inherently detrimental to their own identities, because they have to deal with producers, directors and industry players who sexually harass and bully them? The fallout from #MeToo and its revelations, first of Harvey Weinstein's abuse and then the abuse perpetrated by numerous other powerful men in Hollywood, can't be viewed separately from the space in which women in La La Land have been allowed to move in for decades, especially not when there's evidence that opportunites were so often conditional on compliance. Mira Sorvino, Annabella Sciorra, Rose McGowan—these are just a handful of women whose work prospects dried up the moment they either refused or called out Weinstein himself.

In 2008, Jennifer Kessler (founder of *The Hathor Legacy*, a website focused on women in print and film) wrote about her experience with screenwriting professors at UCLA who, she says, taught her *not* to write scripts and stories that passed the Bechdel test. The path to success, she was told, was to write scripts with white, straight, male leads. These would function as the platter on which she could offer up more diverse characters—as long as she never allowed their stories to overshadow those whom the audience 'really paid their money to see'.

And yet, she continues, 'There was still something wrong with my writing, something unanticipated by my professors. My scripts had multiple women with names. Talking to each other. About something other than a man. That, they explained nervously, was not okay.' They were reluctant to tell her why.

She finally persuaded an industry professional to tell her what her professors would not. (Warning: his answer may cause your blood to turn into rivers of lava. I would take a seat.) He said, 'The audience doesn't want to listen to a bunch of women talking about whatever it is women talk about.'

As Kessler put it:

> According to Hollywood, if two women came on screen and started talking, the target male audience's brain would glaze over and assume the women were talking about nail polish or shoes or something that didn't pertain to the story. Only if they heard the name of a man in the story would they tune back in. By having women talk to each other about something other than men, I was "losing the audience".*

Call me crazy, but I don't think women should be punished because men are egocentric dickheads.

From a gender perspective, the most conclusive evidence we have for the success of movies concerned with stories *about women* are

* 'Shut up feminist, men are the ones who watch movies so it's basic sense to give them what they want!' Wrong again! The Motion Picture Association of America's Theatrical Market Statistics report for 2016 revealed that 52 percent of movie-goers were women. Additionally, Asian Americans/Other Ethnicities represented the highest per capita purchasers of movie tickets, with an upswing as well in the number of African Americans going to the movies.

the box office figures. In 2015, an average of US$90 million was grossed by that year's top 100 non-animated films. And according to the Geena Davis Institute, 'Films with female leads made considerably more on average than films with male leads . . . [grossing] 15.8 percent more on average than films led by men.' Films with male and female co-leads were the big winners, earning approximately US$108 million each, an average of 23.5 percent more than films with separate male or female leads.

But sure, women are just sooooooooooo fucking boring and pointless.

Again, it's not just on screen that women are being short-changed. Negative assumptions are still made about the ability of women to handle big projects. Despite breaking the opening weekend box office record for female filmmakers, Catherine Hardwicke's opportunities didn't explode after directing *Twilight.* In 2011 (three years after *Twilight*'s release) she revealed she couldn't even get an interview to be considered as the director for *The Fighter* (ultimately helmed by David O. Russell) because the studio insisted that the director had to be a man. As Hardwicke noted wryly at the time, 'It's about action, it's about boxing, so a man has to direct it . . . But they'll let a man direct *Sex and the City* or any girly movie you've ever heard of.'

These things matter. They matter for the world's population of girls and women. They also matter for the world's population of boys and men, all of whom are being conditioned to view themselves as far more important than they are. That isn't to say that boys and men *aren't* important, or their stories aren't also meaningful. Of course they are! But pop culture and entertainment should broadly try to reflect the world in which we live (if a more polished and generically more attractive version of it), and it is causing untold harm to us all to have such an imbalance of power represented as normal. If we raise girls to be grateful for what they're given, any attempts to ask for more will be met with abuse and punishment. If we raise boys to believe they are the rightful rulers of narrative and adventure, any attempts to redress the balance will be treated as an assault on their liberties and all too many will choose to respond in exactly the ways they've been taught how—by fighting back in an attempt to defeat 'the enemy'.

In *You Play the Girl: On Playboy Bunnies, Princesses, Trainwrecks & Other Man-Made Women*, the film critic Carina Chocano explores how the idea of girlhood is shaped by stories so often constructed by men. Chocano writes about her first foray into film criticism, when her work required her to spend hour after hour watching films in the dark, consuming 'toxic doses of superhero movies, wedding-themed romantic comedies, cryptofascist paeans to war, and bromances about unattractive, immature young men and the gorgeous women desperate to marry them'. She observes that hardly any of these movies had what could adequately be described as a female protagonist. Instead, women were cast in the role of 'the girl':

> 'The girl' was the adult version of 'the princess'. As a kid, I'd believed the princess was the protagonist, because she'd seemed the most central to the story. The word *protagonist* comes from the Greek for 'the leading actor in a contest or cause,' and a protagonist is a person who wants something and does something to get it. 'The girl' doesn't act, though—she behaves. She has no cause, but a plight. She doesn't want anything, she is wanted. She isn't a winner, she's won. She doesn't self-actualize but aids the hero in self-actualization.

Most people don't watch movies and TV and consciously consider the myriad ways in which the voices and stories of men outnumber women's (or see the way in which stories about white people silence the narratives of people of colour.) They think that what they're seeing is an even and equal portrayal, which means they believe that women participating at less than our equal share is *balanced*. The flip side of this is that when women take up more space in both the visual and audible landscapes, we are thought to be dominating. Consider this. The Geena Davis Institute found that women comprise around 17 percent of any crowd scene. But Davis told NPR, 'If there's 17 percent women, [men surveyed] think it's fifty-fifty. And if there's 33 percent women, the men perceive that as there being more women in the room than men.'

Women can participate, but we can't dominate. We must be kept at a distance, told what to say and when to say it, and are expected to smile for being invited along at all.

And if we don't? Oh, my friends. The *rage*.

It's like nothing you've ever seen before.

■

In 2014, the director Paul Feig announced that all systems were go for a reboot of *Ghostbusters*. Feig would be directing and co-writing the script with Katie Dippold, whose writing credits include *Parks and Recreation* and *The Heat*. In contrast to the original films of the 1980s, this new *Ghostbusters* team would be made up exclusively of women.

You know where this is going.

Some people reacted with abundant enthusiasm, me included. Who wouldn't want to see a new team of ghostbusters taking care of New York? And why shouldn't they be women? When

Feig later announced a cast that included Kristen Wiig, Melissa McCarthy, Leslie Jones and Kate McKinnon as the ghostbusters, I felt a rush of excitement. Four hilarious women, giving a fresh spin on a movie I had watched numerous times when I was a kid—a movie I still quoted religiously with my brother and sister. I couldn't wait.

To say that others were less than supportive would be an understatement. As if having to watch four women at once wasn't bad enough, Jones was also black, and it is a truth maniversally acknowledged that anything other than wall-to-wall white dudes is 'unrealistic' and 'pandering to the Social Justice Warriors'. Wait, let me just get my tinfoil hat.

While Feig's Twitter announcement of the cast gained plenty of positive comments, aggrieved man-babies came out in force to let it be known just how much this movie was gonna suck haaaaaaaard. One wrote: 'awful just awful. It's like you're trying to make the worst movie possible while spitting in the faces of ghostbusters fans.' Another observed pithily: 'I didn't realise there was a quota of vagina for every film to fill.' (Oh no, women are taking over Hollywood!) Someone replied with a simple and straightforward 'FLOP!!!!!!!!!!', while another warned: 'Stop you don't know what your [sic] doing stop production NOW! YOU KNOW YOU'VE MADE A MISTAKE! FANS DONT [sic] WANT TO SEE AN ALL FEMALE TEAM!'

Hmmm. As a fan of the originals, I guess I must have missed the official poll on that one.

But my favourite response came from @patrickmoffatt1, who wrote: 'I now know how Star Wars fans felt after Phantom Menace. You have SHAT on Mr. Ramis' grave, and I hope this kills your career.'

Feelings, be in them.

The consensus from the Angry Man Squad seemed to be that Feig (along with the fat, ugly, unfunny and unfuckable bitches he'd chosen to be in his disgrace of a movie) was engaged in a systematic attack on the memories of men who had grown up believing that 'ghostbuster' was actually a real job.

How very dare he.

The toxic backlash got worse, reaching a crescendo with the release of the movie's first trailer on YouTube. The announcement of a movie starring four women that more than thirty years ago starred four men had been bad enough, but having to watch evidence that they were actually going through with it (imagine having your concerns as a fan just *ignored* like that!) was experienced as such an aggressive assault on the very essence of masculinity that men around the world not only down-voted the trailer on YouTube more than one million times (making it YouTube's tenth most disliked video at one point, although at the time of writing it had dropped back to the twenty-second spot), they also started numerous petitions to try to stop Sony Pictures from giving it a theatrical release.

The 2016 release of *Ghostbusters* continued to trigger many raging rivers of tears from millions of whiny childhood defenders all around the world, because watching women perform on-screen in a way that gives zero respect to the integrity of cis-het male erections is just one of the many oppressions men are being forced to endure under the new Matriarchal Order. Ghosts taking over a city is fine (and so too is a space opera where there are more characters with bodies made up of either fur or mechanical parts than actual women), but wanting a movie to pass the Bechdel test is apparently asking too much of an audience's already stretched suspension of disbelief. Even now, men still flock to the comments section of the YouTube trailer to revel in the number of dislikes the video has attracted and share their sophisticated jokes about feminism ('Q: What do you call a feminist with half a brain? A: Gifted!')

Similar (and similarly exhausting) backlashes occurred after the 2015 release of *Star Wars: The Force Awakens* and then its 2017 follow-up *The Last Jedi*. Set approximately thirty years after the defeat of the Empire in *Return of the Jedi*, this new *Star Wars* universe appeared to have had an upgrade. Instead of there being only one woman and one person of colour in the entire galaxy, there were multiple examples of both. Princess Leia was now General Organa, and the new band of plucky Rebels aiming to take down the next Big Bad was more radically diverse than anything the original trilogy had featured in its entirety. White dudes loved it, and for once the comments section became a really positive place to hang out.

Just kidding! They hated it!

It was almost as if they didn't know what to be more aggrieved about—the fact that one of the two new heroes, Rey, was a woman or that the other, Finn, was a black man. Both, according to many of the naysayers, were 'unrealistic', which is a fair enough point to make about a fictional world that includes an entire species of warrior teddy bears. Rey (a young orphan plucked from her home planet of Jakku and drawn into the Rebel fight) was dismissed as a 'Mary Sue', a term used in pop culture to denote a female character who is too good at too many things and therefore functions as a kind of wish fulfilment for the girl or woman writing her. This sledge was aimed at her because Rey shows an early affinity with the Force and proves to be skilled with a lightsaber, and good lord we have never ever seen that before, no sir. #fakenews

As the heroes, Rey and Finn disrupt the parameters set out by the dominant white male gaze. Women and black men aren't supposed to be the heroes. They can be heroic, but the ultimate hero is still supposed to be a white guy. Or, as Jennifer Kessler was taught, 'the people the audience paid to see'. The addition of Rose Tico in *The Last Jedi* (played by Vietnamese American actress Kelly Marie Tran) inspired yet more horrendous backlash and absurd accusations that Disney was forcing a 'feminazi SJW [social justice warrior] agenda' down the throats of the franchise's most loyal fans. Tran was subjected to vile racist abuse, with one person even changing her character's entry in Wookieepedia to read: 'Ching Chong Wing Tong is a dumbass fucking character Disney made and is a stupid, autistic and retarded love interest for Finn. She better die in the coma because she is a dumbass bitch.'

And they say women are sensitive.

Do these kinds of stories cut too close to the bone for men who've never been expected (let alone forced) to fight for representation? White men in particular are raised with an abundance of heroes who look exactly like them(ish) and whose adventures are tailored as perfect aspirational fantasies. For some of them, the thought of sharing that space with the people to whom they've traditionally been encouraged to see themselves as superior is akin to some kind of assault. It's ironic really, because the irrational nature of their response puts them closer into the story than they think. As Kayti Burt wrote on Den of Geek, '*The Last Jedi* is filled with male characters on both sides of the dark/light divide who cause and endure suffering because of their inability to deal with their emotions in healthy ways.'

An inability to 'deal with emotions in healthy ways' is what toxic masculinity is all about. And, in most cases, what this really stems from is fear. They're afraid of the world changing, because then they might have to actually work a bit harder to be seen as important within it. So they shit on women and people of colour and anyone else fighting for political equality alongside them and screech about 'SJWs' and feminism being 'cancer' and think this is enough to mask the stench of fear that rolls off them in waves. But as any true fan of *Star Wars* can tell you, fear is the path to the dark side. Fear leads to anger. Anger leads to hate. Hate leads to suffering.

I find myself wondering how it is that men who align themselves so strongly with hero narratives can be so unaware of what side of the story they sit on. The men lashing out at women online, the ones who use misogyny and racism and abuse to fiercely protect what they see as their territory, consider themselves to be the good guys. But it's like they don't realise that racism, misogyny, homophobia, transphobia, ableism and all the other bigoted views they uphold and gleefully enforce are, you know, *what the baddies do*. They spent their youths daydreaming about being Jedi Masters, and they haven't yet realised that they've grown up to be Stormtroopers, mindlessly doing the bidding of whichever evil leader they're acting in service to. The funniest thing is that, in the real world, they would dismiss all their heroes as cucks and white knights. *Ha ha Skywalker, you fucking soyboy!*

Like the texture of the iconic hair rolls sprayed to within an inch of their life on the head of Princess Leia, the irony is extremely crisp.

■

I love stories. As a girl, I grew up watching movies that predominantly featured male characters. Men being heroes, men being villains, men being funny, men being serious. Men—so many men—navigating the world with purpose and adventure, while women flitted in and out of the scenes around them until they were needed again. At the time, I didn't know how much I was missing out on and it didn't occur to me to ask for anything more.

But it's only been in the past few years that I've realised just how different the experience of watching movies must have been for me and my brother, even as we sprawled next to each other while watching the same ones over and over. It was never a stretch for him to imagine himself as Luke Skywalker or Peter Venkman. He could be Marty McFly or Doc. There were five Goonies for him to choose from, not just the two tagalong girls. I asked him recently what *Star Wars* meant to him when we were kids. He told me he couldn't remember watching it for the first time, but he recalled the very strong feeling of awe he had about the world it depicted. He was drawn to the idea of being a Jedi Master, the battle between good and evil and the operatic tones of the whole story. More than anything, he felt incredibly moved by Yoda's explanation of the Force—that balance between light and dark.

I liked listening to him speak about it, and I was glad he'd experienced something that offered such wonder to him. I wouldn't want to take that away from him. But his is just one of many similar experiences that are provided to boys in a world that insists on always making them the heroes of the tale. I am a thirty-seven-year-old woman, but I didn't get that full slam of feeling until I sat in a darkened cinema in 2015 and watched women, people of colour and political ideas I can relate to finally become part of a universe I have always found magic in but that hadn't, up until that point, ever found me.

We have to demand better. Maybe it starts by changing the pronouns in the books we read to our kids, but then it grows into having conversations that encourage critical engagement and reflection. Why don't more people talk to their children about the stories that are shaping their lives? Become conscious consumers, and teach your children to do the same. Seek out content that doesn't reinforce regressive stereotypes about gender or present the world as a sea of white men with a few supporting characters added 'for balance'. We are not helpless, even if stories have always made us believe otherwise.

I don't want my son growing up in a world that tells him he deserves a greater, more important role than the women he knows just by virtue of his being a boy. I don't want him to think it's normal to always speak twice as much as women, or to take up twice as much space, or assume his opinion carries more weight. I don't want him to punish women when they refuse to fit into the boxes in which he's told they belong. And I especially don't want him to become so unconsciously self-entitled that he lashes out when women—or, indeed, any marginalised group—push back against this.

Surely we can all tell a better story than that.

NOT ALL MEN

Shhhhhhh.

Do you hear that sound? I'm not talking about the clock ticking in the background or the passing cars in the distance. I don't mean your heartbeat, or the soft brush of your thumb against the page.

I'm talking about that persistent buzz in the background, the one that seems to be getting louder and more intrusive. You first noticed it in the middle of the introduction, and you put it down to the tinnitus that sometimes flares up when you're tired or anxious. But no, it's definitely still there. A buzz that turned into a whine which has now morphed into a full-on cacophony.

It's the protest cry reverberating around the world, the one with the power to tune into any conversation that even obliquely references patriarchy, harassment, social hierarchies of gender or the institutionalised protection of abusers. Listen. Can you hear it now?

Noooooooottttttt aaaaaaallllllllllll meeeennnnnnnnnnnn.

headdesk

■

Friend, you have purchased a book about toxic masculinity and how it's weaponised in particular ways to harm both women and men. Naturally, you must be made to pay for your conceit. How dare you just *assume* that there's a problem with men! Don't you realise that *not all men* are rapists, wife beaters or [extremely Dolores Umbridge voice] *sexists*?

Also, *women rape men too.*

There's something sinister about the lengths to which some men will go to make sure they are never held accountable (as individuals and as a class) for the indignities and rampant abuse women are subjected to on a daily basis. It's just gobsmacking that when so many of these guys hear stories from women who've been brutalised, humiliated and/or violated in horrifying ways, their first response is to demand that the speaker acknowledge first and foremost that most men are great.

Unfortunately, the petulant retort of #notallmen has become part and parcel of any attempt to have public conversations about masculinity and the damage caused by patriarchy. There are even internet memes mocking the trend, like the still shot from 1975's *Jaws* which shows the killer shark launching itself onto Captain Quint's boat only to intone, 'Not *all* men.' Or Matt Lubchansky's comic strip about an everyday dude who, after seeing the Man Signal beamed into the sky ('Someone must be doing reverse sexism!'), transforms into Not-All-Man, 'Defender of the defended! Lone protector of the protected! Voice of the voiceful!' Donning a fedora and brown leather waistcoat cape, he races to a nearby diner, where he interrupts a woman as she's confiding to a friend, 'I'm just sick of how men—'

'May I play devil's advocate?' he says.

The potential for #notallmen to be lampooned in meme format has been eagerly taken up by literally thousands of people, if not millions. But while the ridicule certainly tastes sweet, it doesn't make up for the insidious thinking behind the phenomenon's existence in the first place. 'Not all men!' isn't just a mating call for the lazy and aggrieved, it's also a diversionary tactic used to shift attention away from the substantial issues of discrimination and oppression that impact women's lives and channel it instead into men's *feelings*. Worse, it demands that women temper our complaints, that we frame our discussions of the violence we've experienced at men's hands in a way that doesn't implicate any of the men we know or work with or sit next to on the bus or even just casually pass by in any one of the infinite numbers of corridors on the internet. Sure, you may have been raped or beaten or grown up with a violent father or been groped by a colleague—but the important thing to remember here is that *not all men* are like that, and unless you acknowledge this then aren't you kind of just as bad as those men out there who hate women enough to kill them?

Short of falling into a vat of mercury and developing superpowers that turn my brain into a calculator, there is no universe in which I could even hope to count the number of men who've insisted I give them a hall pass when it comes to caring about this stuff. Day in, day out, reports of women being terrorised by family violence, sexual assault or just good old-fashioned gender inequality abound, and still the cries of 'not all men' roll in. It happens with such alarming regularity that I could set my watch by them.

Oh, look, here's an article about how unpaid domestic labour is predominantly performed by women.

Yeah, but here's some anecdotal evidence about my house and how I help my wife out heaps!

What's that, you say? Three-quarters of victims of family violence in the state of Victoria are women and girls, with a quarter of all male youth offenders under the age of nineteen being boys who bash their mums?

This is just more misandering against men! Why don't you acknowledge that 99.9 percent of us are amazing and wouldn't dream of hurting our mums?!

Really? One-fifth of all Australian girls over the age of fifteen will be sexually assaulted at least once in their lifetime, and the vast majority of their assailants will go unpunished.

Stop saying all men are rapists, you she-wolf!

Sigh. It must be 3 pm on a Tuesday.

■

If you plan to introduce the ideas and case studies discussed in this book into your broader community (and I very much hope you will), you'll have to be prepared for the various guises of Not-All-Man when he turns up. In my experience, there are a few basic types you'll find demanding disclaimers in things like comments sections, interpersonal discussions or forum audiences. They use different methods and approaches, but the central message remains the same: *Stop making me feel bad, you bitch.*

1. The 'Well, I'm not like that' man

We've all met a guy like this and felt the spray of his anger because we haven't bent over backwards in our critiques of patriarchy to make sure he knows it's not about him.

Oh hey, here's proof that 90 percent of all sexual violence is perpetrated by men and that this is reflective of a system that considers women's bodies the property of patriarchy and can therefore be exploited as vessels for male rage, entitlement and aggression. This is what feminism is fighting, and this is the reality that we need allies to be conscious of.

Well, I'm not like that and nor are 99 percent of the men I know. Why didn't you introduce this information with the careful acknowledgment that most of us are great?

Yep, you're sounding pretty great there, Not-All-Man. You triumph against evil again.

You don't need to worry too much about how to spot 'Well, I'm not like that' man. The most reliable thing about this kind of guy is that he'll tell anyone who'll listen just how very much *not* like That Guy he is. You can find a smorgasboard of Not-Like-That guy all over the internet and media landscape. He hosts talkback radio shows on networks that only hire other men who look exactly like him, all of whom are paid whopping great salaries while they talk occasionally about how career advancement 'should be about merit'. He's working in local government and federal parliament, voting to defund women's shelters and 'stop the boats' while proclaiming Australia the greatest country on earth. He camps out in the comments section of online news sources, regulating the flow of information whenever it veers too dangerously close to anything that could be seen as 'pro-woman'. He makes sure women are held accountable online for the brazen misandry they show when they link to articles about domestic homicide, sexual assault, men's violence against women and even (or perhaps especially) that mythical wage gap. Like thigh rub in summer time, he'll find you. Babes, if you need to tell women all the time just how 'not like that' you are, then you're probably more like that than you actually think.

2. The 'Male Champion of Change' Self-Saucing Pudding

You may already be familiar with the cookie monsters who loiter in the cloisters of feminist communities. These men have all the lingo about intersectionality down pat, and are always the first to call out other people whose activist vocabularies are a little less sophisticated. They may be *mostly* motivated by a genuine passion for social justice and equality, but there's no doubting that the gratitude with which they're showered for their feminist statements is a nice little bonus.

Feminist men are generally received quite differently from feminist women, and this includes them being expected to do significantly less work to earn significantly more praise. Think of the response any time a man does something vaguely feminist, especially when he's in the public eye. Astonishment! Wonder! Ticker tape parades! The keys to the city, engraved with both his name and the honorific 'Best Feminist Ever'!

People who are conditioned to expect adoration for doing what basically amounts to the right thing tend to get a little bit shirty when their minimal efforts are treated as exactly that. Sometimes, they feel the need to remind you of their allyship and point of difference from the Bad Men you speak of, the men who don't deserve to hear a thousand grillion women talk about how amazing they are and how they just *get it* and how the world needs more men like them or (because sometimes words just aren't enough to adequately portray our damp gusset gratitude) be digitally serenaded with just a string of heart-eye emojis.

In circumstances like these, you might be pressed upon to acknowledge publicly that while, *yes*, this article about a group of schoolboys filming themselves raping one of their school peers is absolutely an example of disgusting, animal-like behaviour, it's not really fair to present such behaviour as being typically male. *I don't do that!* the self-proclaimed left-wing supporter of women might insist. *I've never raped anyone! If you want allies, you need to be nicer.*

I mean . . . good? But, like, do you want a medal for it, bro?

Oh, wait—you do. That's exactly what you want. A shiny 'Not All Men' medal to go alongside your 'Best Feminist Ever' giant golden key. I'll have it sent directly to you as soon as I can summon up the energy to give a damn.

3. The 'None of My Friends Are Like That' Conspiracy Theorist

Reader, meet Matt Damon.

In a 2017 interview with ABC News in the US to discuss the widespread allegations of abuse that had emerged in Hollywood as a result of the #MeToo movement, Damon whined that not enough credit was being given to the men who *don't* abuse women.

Yes, really.

'We're in this watershed moment,' he said, 'and it's great, but I think one thing that's not being talked about is there are a whole shitload of guys—the preponderance of men I've worked with—who don't do this kind of thing and whose lives aren't going to be affected.'

Let me translate that more directly into Not-All-Man speak for you.

'All these women are claiming to have been touched or abused or harassed or whatever, but why are none of them making a big deal about the fact that *I* wasn't the one doing it to them? It isn't fair that the rest of us men should have to feel guilty when we didn't do anything to hurt them. I mean, okay, we didn't do anything to *stop it*, but shit's complicated, you know? Plus, my friends are great too.'

I'd ask you to forgive my sarcasm, but I feel like if I don't wear it as a suit of armour against these kinds of views then I might literally burst into flames and take down an entire city with me.

Damon is a Good Guy, so it pains him to know that people might be associating him with Bad Guys. Sure, he's worked with a whole bunch of them. Harvey Weinstein launched his career, and Damon even admitted that he knew of at least one allegation against the mogul way back when he was filming *The Talented Mr. Ripley* in the late nineties. That allegation just happened to be made during the course of filming by his co-star, Gwyneth Paltrow (who was also dating his best friend, Ben Affleck, another man accused of improper conduct towards women). Let's not forget that Matt 'the preponderance of men I've worked with' Damon has also closed ranks around Ben Affleck's brother Casey, who was accused by two different women of multiple incidents of sexual harassment well prior to the Weinstein revelations yet still went on to win an Academy Award for Best Actor in 2017.

This casual collusion with men alleged to have abused women makes it all the more infuriating to hear Damon argue there is 'a difference between patting someone on the butt and rape or child molestation. Both of those behaviours need to be confronted and eradicated without question, but they shouldn't be conflated'.

Well, gee, thanks Matt Damon for explaining sexual assault to all us silly little women! What would we do without a sensible, rational man to interpret our experiences for us?

In response, the actress Minnie Driver (whom Damon famously dumped on-air during an interview with Oprah by claiming, to Driver's great surprise, that he was currently single—yes, folks, he's just *that* classy) tweeted, 'Gosh it's so interesting (profoundly unsurprising) how men with all these opinions about women's differentiation between sexual misconduct, assault and rape reveal themselves to be utterly tone deaf and as a result, systemically part of the problem.' Alyssa Milano, who has worked in show business since she was a child, responded pointedly, 'There are different stages of cancer. Some are more treatable than others. But it's still cancer.'

The belief that abusers comprise only a tiny percentage of the population is a popular one. One of the most common refrains sung in the Not All Men chorus is the one about how there are a lot of Bad Men out there, but 99 percent ain't one of them. I hear this about as often as I hear I'm an unfuckable man-hating shrew with a rusty shipping container for a vagina that also doubles as a Hellmouth, which is roughly four thousand times a day. I mean, I added a bit of colour there because the men who comment on my angry, shunned snatch are not imaginative enough to have come up with that absolute banger of an insult. But you get the picture.

In the world of Not All Men, anecdotal evidence that barely extends beyond the four or five blokes you occasionally get drunk with is apparently enough to disprove years of comprehensive research, analytical data and crime statistics that place men as the primary perpetrators of violence, be it physical or sexual in nature. This is the natural evolution of the '99 percent of men aren't' argument. It begins as a convenient statistic to whip out of the same collective butthole from which other, similarly unfounded statistics are pulled and then doubles down on it by pretending to offer some kind of proof.

Listen, it's not outside the realm of possibility that an individual's circle of friends is absent of any men guilty of assault, rape or just garden-variety misogyny. We all want to believe that we direct our love and attention to good people. But the thing is, you can't know. You just can't. Maybe your friends have never sexually assaulted someone, but if they had, do you think they'd tell you? Is it the kind of thing you expect them to do in front of you? (I mean, maybe. Let's not forget that some men don't just boast about sexual assault, they actually engage in it regularly as a bonding exercise and a bit of weekend revelry.) When you say your friend has never acted like a misogynist, are you thinking of the *real* kind of misogynist who stones women for committing adultery or murders his wife or abducts women in alleyways or keeps women as sex slaves in his cellar? Or do you mean that other kind of misogyny, the 'fake' misogyny that feminists keep going on about, the one that's actually just light-hearted *jokes* about stoning women or murdering them or kidnapping and raping them?

The other reason why this '99 percent' response is just unmitigated bullshit is that it disrespects the expertise and skills of the people doing the work to heal male aggression and prevent violence. It isn't a surprise to us that you think your friends are faultless when it comes to the treatment of women (or at least faultless enough that they should get a pass). What surprises us is that men think their responsibility to challenge what is clearly a widespread problem only extends so far as vaguely trusting the people they choose to spend their time with.

A friend and I once had an argument with her then boyfriend about his view that women should take responsibility for protecting themselves against assault. He cited the usual nonsense about it being 'common sense' to dress appropriately so as not to 'provoke' anyone. To make 'good decisions' about who they chose to spend time with, particularly when they were alone.

'So you're saying women should feel wary around you?' I asked.

He immediately grew angry.

'No!' he exclaimed. 'What an offensive thing to say!' He was deeply insulted by my suggestion that women should feel anything other than safe in his presence.

'But you just said women needed to modify their dress and behaviour around men to minimise their risk of being assaulted,' I reminded him.

'Yes, but I'm not a threat to them,' he retorted.

'They don't know that,' my friend pointed out.

We explained that if he insisted it was up to women to prevent rape, he had better be prepared to find himself included in the cohort of people they should consider dangerous. And not just him, but all the men he knew and respected.

Oh no, he protested, he and his friends weren't the kind of men he was talking about. None of his friends had ever hurt anyone at all, let alone *raped* a woman!

'How would you know?' I asked, which seemed to throw him for a moment. 'Most women are raped or sexually assaulted by someone they know, so it stands to reason the people assaulting them are also known to others.'

'But I don't know anyone who's been raped,' he replied.

'Yes, you do,' I said. 'They just haven't told you about it.' (And it's not hard to see why, I thought to myself.)

Only moments before, this man had stood there and listed all the things women ought to do to stop men from attacking them. That he did it in such an authoritative manner, as though he was imparting frightfully clever new information, wasn't the most astonishing thing about the whole sorry interaction. No, the most astonishing thing was the unwavering confidence with which he declared that he knew no women who were survivors of rape or sexual assault. The thought that this might be something they chose not to share ('Thanks for meeting me for lunch; I thought we could share a pizza and talk casually about one of the worst moments of my life!') had clearly never occurred to him.

Later, when my friend and I were alone, we rehashed the conversation, appalled.

'I can't believe he said that thing about not knowing any victims!' I screamed.

'I know,' she replied. 'I mean, *I've* been sexually assaulted.'

Needless to say, they are no longer together.

4. The 'Women Do It Too' Equal Opportunity Officer

This is an interesting one, because it doesn't actually deny the problem of abuse and violence. Instead, it tries to create an equal and opposite problem of women perpetrating the same kind of abuse and violence against men, and in the same numbers. I'm going to look more critically at how this argument harms boys too in a moment, but it's important to address briefly the reality of 'equal and opposite abuse' (particularly in terms of family and intimate partner violence, which is where this argument is so often used).

It's true that men can be victimised by family and intimate partner violence. But it's also true that the majority of victimisation occurs either at the hands of other men or as part of a reciprocally violent relationship (i.e. women responding to violence perpetrated against them), a fact that is curiously omitted when men's rights organisations advocate on behalf of male victims.

Australia's One in Three campaign is a good example of how stats and figures are manipulated to create propaganda that actively works to discredit the reality of family violence while undermining the efforts of service providers and healthcare workers. Because of the murky way One in Three reports its (dubious) findings, some of the organisation's followers repeatedly claim that one in three *men* (as opposed to one-third of the affected demographic) are victims or survivors of domestic violence. Additionally, it is blithely assumed that it is women who are responsible for this violence—because if men are the ones killing women at a rate of at least one per week in this country, then it *must* be women who are lashing out when the victim is a man.

In fact, men face a far greater risk of violence from other men, most often in public spaces or entertainment venues and to occasionally devastating conclusions. The growing awareness of one-punch attacks (formerly known as 'king hits' and then rechristened 'coward punches' in an attempt to associate them with weakness—a linguistic rebranding as yet not applied to men's violence against women) seems to indicate that society is prepared to get serious on the issue of male violence, yet concern for its impact seems curiously absent whenever family violence is on the table. Who cares about sons, brothers, husbands and friends murdered or maimed on the street or left with comprehensive brain injuries when there are some points to be scored against the drastically underfunded women's health sector?

But, then, this is what these kinds of not-all-menners are ultimately more interested in—point scoring and deflection. All this swagger and bravado masks an incredible fear of change. Masculinity has not been kind to them, nor has it been ultimately liberating beyond a sort of superficial privilege granted in order to keep patriarchy flourishing. Still, it's a superficial privilege they understand and one that's designed to make it easy to ignore the less enriching aspects of pledging devotion to such a detrimental system. If these men acknowledge the reality of male violence and its impact not just on women and girls but also on men and boys, they'll have to accept responsibility for doing the hard work to change it—hard work that will involve confronting some of the lies they've been told about what it means to be a man.

This leads to another example of how the 'women do it too' brigade work against their own interests so as to justify their refusal to change. Think of the response to child sexual exploitation and abuse. As incredible as it seems that discussing, say, a news article detailing the systematic sexual abuse of a child at the hands of their father or a man known to them could prompt someone to respond with nothing more than a link to a story of a female predator, I can assure you this is a common response. Apparently the most important thing to remember in circumstances like this is not that devastating harm can be (and indeed is) inflicted against children on a regular basis—it's that this devastating harm is not always a man's fault. Because when we're talking about one very specific case that involves a man abusing a child, it must be countered by the acknowledgment that he could have easily been a woman. This is child abuse, for crying out loud—won't someone think of men's feelings about it?

Again, of course women are capable of committing monstrous acts of violence. And yes, the women who do so should be roundly condemned by their communities and treated exactly the same way men are (which, let's face it, more often than not means a light slap on the wrist and almost all of their immediate friends rallying around them while calling their victim a liar). But there's a certain element of convenience to these arguments, and it becomes all the more obvious when you look at how abuse meted out by women is measured differently based on the context of the abuse itself. It's interesting, for example, that the spectre of the female sex predator is often thrown around as a rejoinder to reports of men preying on children. In my experience there are only certain circumstances in which the predatory behaviour of women is considered repulsive. The choices people make in differentiating between the abuse inflicted by men and women go to the heart of patriarchy and the sexual harm it causes. It's feminists rather than men's rights activists who are far more likely to speak out against adult women abusing teenage boys, and they do so against a cultural backdrop where this particular kind of predation is treated in a nudge-nudge-wink-wink fashion. *I wish I'd had a teacher like that when I was at school! What man wouldn't want to be initiated into sex by an older woman?!*

The assumed universality implied in the phrase 'what man wouldn't?' is harmful in and of itself. Men are not a homogenous group of people, and their experience of (and desire for) sexual contact is not operated by a remote satellite circling the earth. Linking masculine strength and identity to how vigorously you rut your way around town not only places fundamental restrictions on male expression, it can also lead to boys and men participating in behaviour they would otherwise avoid or speak out against, because to do otherwise is to wilfully emasculate oneself. The belief that teenage boys must always be willing players in sexually coercive situations (such as an adult teacher grooming their student, or a babysitter building trust in order to abuse) is an insidious one, and it's a key part of why it's so difficult for boys and men to speak out against assault.

Think about the stereotypes of masculinity, and burgeoning adolescent masculinity especially. One of the most fiercely defended foundations of the 'boys will be boys' trope is the idea that male sexuality is a majestic beast that can't be contained. Teenage boys in particular are treated like a herd of wild rhinos, their dangerous tusks constantly poised to spear any hapless antelope that crosses their path as they charge around the plains of adolescence.

Well, listen, I'm not saying it's not *bad*, but girls should know what to expect with that kind of thing. I mean . . . boys will be boys, after all.

According to this definition, being A Boy means having sexual impulses that are stronger than your moral ones. It means being so base in your desires that criminality will always win out over doing the right thing. It means viewing the incapacitation or vulnerability of the girls and women around you not as a responsibility, but as an opportunity.

This is a terrifying prospect. But if you can't bring yourself to care about the fact that supporting these ideals causes quantifiable and direct harm to girls, at least consider the potential harm to boys. It becomes infinitely more difficult for a boy to speak out against the behaviour of an older, wiser, more sexually liberated

'Mrs Robinson' when masculinity is framed in such a way that boys feel compelled to receive sex willingly or else hand in their Man Card.

Yes, women abuse boys too. And we should want to protect boys from abuse by women as much as we do from abuse by men. But if men respond to reports of such abuse by whistling in admiration and regretting the lack of similar opportunities in their own youth, then we are doing a pretty bloody terrible job of offering boys a way out.

It's scandalous that the best argument offered against the demonstrable rates of male violence and its impact on women and children so often amounts to this form of childish finger-pointing. But it's also incredibly sad. Instead of working towards change that will benefit all people, *including men*, we are forced to squabble in the gutter about who's meaner and who has it worse.

What a wasted opportunity.

5. The 'You Lose Credibility with Your Misandry' Man

If the men's rights movement is skilled at anything, it's the ability to figure out new and wackier ways to fight back against equality and the angry witches trying to sweep it in with their broomsticks. Manufacturing false claims of 'misandry' (which isn't even remotely a source of threat to men given that women as a class lack the political, social and financial power to truly weaponise any hatred of men we may harbour) is just a clever way to play superiority politics. It's often accompanied by claims of support, but it's a support that always turns out to be conditional. You might hear it phrased in the following ways:

I believe in equality, but you do yourself no favours by alienating men.

I consider myself an ally, but I refuse to support your nasty man-hating invective.

It's people like you who give feminism a bad name.

I'm not saying these issues aren't real, but you would win more men over to your cause if you were nicer to them.

A few months into the #MeToo movement, after I'd woken on a Saturday to read yet another piece about the 'alleged' repulsive, sexually abusive behaviour of a high-powered male celebrity (in this case, it was Dustin Hoffman), I fired off a couple of tweets in an attempt to express some of the frustration bubbling away inside me.

'Dozens of women can expose the abuse of one man and other men will still insist that they must be lying or that we just can't know,' I wrote. 'When that one man admits to it (like Louis C.K.), those same men are like, well he apologised, what more do you want? #silencebreakers.'

Still fuming, I followed up with: 'And women still have to appease male egos around their belief in their inherent goodness for us to get them to even listen at all.'

For good measure, I then tweeted the succinct catchcry of the angry feminist: #cancelmen

Whoops!

Someone with as much experience as I have in the field of crushingly fragile male egos should have known that by doing this I broke accepted protocol. You're not supposed to punctuate the rage you feel about men's violence with sarcastic references to ridding the world of the male scourge. Your cynical attempts at joking make men feel *marginalised.* And isn't that kind of the opposite of equality?

It didn't take long for one man to reply, 'I swear every time I start to see where Clem is coming from and even nod in agreement she dives right back into this shock value BS.'

It's incredible that this male hypersensitivity continues to surprise me, but it does. For millennia women have been forced to live with the risk (and reality) of rape, assault, forced reproduction, imprisonment and even murder by men, yet we're still expected to pepper every single thing we complain about with disclaimers. Even in agitating for our own liberation and freedom, we're still forced to soothe male egos and make sure none of them walk away feeling bad, let alone feeling even remotely responsible for being part of the change that is so desperately needed in the world. If we fail to soothe, we're subjected to a barrage of male anger and a litany of arguments explaining how it's really our fault that most men are do-nothing fuckfaces when it comes to addressing gender inequality. They were *totally* planning on calling out their friend's next rape joke, but then we did a misandry and now they just don't fancy it.

Men: if you need women to be nice to you for you to accept the reality of our oppression, you are doing allyship wrong. No trophy for you!

■

If you're a man reading this, you may be feeling defensive. It's okay, I get it. It can be hard to hear that you're not as great as you think you are. It doesn't make you a terrible person to feel defensive and uncomfortable. It makes you a terrible person if you refuse to interrogate that discomfort and instead use it as a way of dismissing what it is you're being told.

It takes a radical shift in thinking to understand that those people concerned with the problem of gender inequality, gendered violence and oppression are under no obligation to prioritise your ego. If you've never engaged with ideas like this before (or if you've only ever skimmed over the surface of them), it's probably going to come as a big shock to you to hear that none of us care about how this makes you feel. But that doesn't mean you can't work on your feelings and your reaction and try to be an *actually* decent person as opposed to one who thinks men should be routinely praised for making it through a whole day without raping someone.

One of the things you need to fundamentally understand is that women already know all your arguments about why #notallmen are guilty of [insert any one of the multitude of things men are definitely guilty of doing to women]. The function of this kind of defence isn't to tell us anything new, although you'd be surprised by how many guys seem to think they're blowing our minds. In the great pantheon of crimes against women, of course Not All Men are guilty. There are nice guys out there, and by that I mean men who are actually nice and not just nice until the moment a woman questions their view of the world. But there are also guys who do nothing to constructively or substantially challenge the misogynist foundations of patriarchy that allow for this kind of behaviour to exist. They line up with their hands out for cookies and praise when it suits them, but they do nothing when it really counts. They don't speak out against their friends when they abuse women. They don't challenge the actions of their colleagues or their workplace superiors over sexist comments. They vote for men who work hard to introduce legislation that hurts women.

They don't call out their brothers' misogyny. They side with their sons and say *boys will be boys*. They do nothing to demonstrate true allyship to women, but they're sure as shit ready to wear that white ribbon for one day of the year if they think it'll get them a public round of applause.

If I'm being gracious, I might say that this kind of casual arrogance is understandable. After all, the problems of toxic masculinity are cultural, not biological. Men have been assisted throughout countless generations to believe that their basic efforts and their acts of benevolent sexism are good enough, and it probably comes as a bit of a shock to suddenly (and without ceremony) be told that this isn't the case. But if you men want to be better—if you truly want to live up to the promise that so many of you keep loudly telling women you have—your efforts to address gender inequality and patriarchal oppression have to extend much farther beyond saying a few choice words here and there and being nice to your girlfriend. Women have run out of time and energy to hold your hand through the hard parts of the class.

But one of the saddest parts of all of this is that many of us still will. It is a mark of either immense compassion or immense foolishness that women continue to throw ourselves into the act of loving men despite amassing a lifetime of experiences that tell us how dangerous this decision can be. I am increasingly disagreeing with the view that not all men are part of the problem, and it's because I truly think most of them don't understand that the problem is theirs to solve. I have a male partner whom I love, and I'm the mother of a son for whom I would die a million times over, but the gap between where we live in the world is treacherous and deep. Still, I and billions of women like me try to create safe passage between those two spaces every day. We are building the bridge, while they mostly just watch.

Under his eye, indeed.

In the end, this is perhaps #notallmen's greatest insult. Women don't need to be told to look for the goodness in men, because we try our damnedest to find it every day. We work hard to nurture it, even as we're told to be grateful for it. For our own survival, women must believe that not all men are the enemy.

Yet we are not shown the same respect in return. We search for the humanity in men only to have them turn away from the reality of our pain. It can be pouring out of us in waves, but they'll only consent to look at it if we promise not to hold them accountable for it or make them change anything about their lives in order to ease the suffering of ours. Brutality is not always about physical strength. As Twitter user @thetrudz once powerfully observed, 'Not all men are actual rapists. Some are rape apologists. Some tell rape jokes. Some are victim blamers. Some are silent.'

No, Not All Men are a threat to women.

But we know that any man could be.

And that right there is the difference.

—5—

WE KNOW WHAT BOYS ARE LIKE

When I was twenty-one years old, I took a year off from university and moved to Japan to teach English. I was sent to Okinawa, a small island south of the Japanese mainland. Okinawa accounts for around 1 percent of Japan's landmass, but it hosts 25 percent of the country's US military bases. Basically, there are lots of men in uniform (which was good for me, but that's a story for another time).

My first night there, I found myself chatting to a marine outside a ramen shop. We started talking about the supposed differences between men and women, and how he thought the latter had a responsibility to act 'respectably' if they didn't want to be regarded as sluts. 'Women have to be careful,' he explained to me. 'They shouldn't have sex with a lot of guys because it will make their vaginas loose.' He went on to say that it was important for men to sleep with lots of women because then they'd know how to be good lovers. Convenient.

I think we can all agree that someone who thinks a vagina gets looser every time a woman has sex has no business being allowed near women let alone into their beds. The vagina is a muscle, not a piece of sugar taffy. A few dicks can't upsize it from a studio apartment into a sprawling compound. If that were true, we could just keep all our loose change and keys in there, and we wouldn't be so put out by the fact that none of our clothes are designed with pockets.

Unfortunately, a lack of basic understanding about how bodies work is part and parcel of the double standards that infect so much of society's understanding of sex. In 2015, Victoria's Fairhills High School ran a Christian sex education program teaching its year seven students that girls who have multiple sex partners 'risk becoming like overused sticky tape'. The students were given a booklet titled *Science & Facts*, which included such well-known scientific facts as 'girls are needier than boys' and 'sluts are gross'. (Okay, so it didn't cite that second one in so many words, but I read between the lines.)

The whole 'used vaginas are like old sticky tape' analogy is not a new thing. It sits right up there with Old Okinawan Mate's conviction that vaginas are stretched just a little bit further out of shape whenever they come into contact with a random schlong. Some years ago, students at an American high school made a short film for their health class which showed what happened to a piece of duct tape when it was stuck to different objects like the water cooler or a bin. Duct tape works by using an adhesive backing to stick itself to things, and it stands to reason that it becomes less effective with use. As the tape was transferred from item to item, it not only became less sticky, it also became dirtier and more laden with residue. The not so subtle suggestion was that sex diminishes the sanctity of girls' bodies and turns them into garbage receptacles nobody wants to touch.

A similar experiment is often used to depict the 'ugliness' of a sexually active woman and the supposed lack of respect her behaviour evokes in others. In 2014, an article in *Slate* revealed that over 60 percent of schools in the Mississippi high school district were encouraging teachers to use 'purity preservation exercises'. One such activity asks students to pass around a piece of chocolate to show how grubby and dirty it becomes the more people touch it. The chocolate is supposed to represent a girl's body, and the unwillingness that class members have to eat it at the end of the activity is supposed to show how unattractive she becomes the more people she permits to fondle her. Other examples of this kind of not-at-all-scientific lesson compare sexually active girls' bodies to chewed pieces of gum or dirty toothbrushes, and emphasise the disdain with which others will regard them if they allow themselves to become 'used goods'.

It seems absurd that we're still wrestling with institutional slut-shaming in this day and age, but I guess it's not so surprising when you consider the fact that double standards about male and female sexuality are still uncritically presented as fact. The idea that 'purity' is at all related to the number of sexual partners a woman has is disgusting, as is the notion that her sexual decisions are the business of anybody else in the first place. Women's bodies do not become dirtier and less valuable with the increase of sexual activity, and it isn't our responsibility to shield ourselves from sex in order to 'earn' respect. These kinds of attitudes don't protect women; they endanger us. And they endanger us because they send the message that sexually active women are less deserving of bodily autonomy, and therefore less capable of being sexually assaulted or violated. This is absolutely not the kind of message we should be sending to anyone, let alone children navigating adolescence and sexual desire.

But what I'm really interested in is how these retrograde beliefs about girls' supposed 'purity' send a completely converse message about the sanctity of boys' bodies and sexuality. It was the mother of a boy who first spoke out against the chocolate lesson, telling the *Los Angeles Times* that she believed it was designed 'to show that a girl is no longer clean or valuable after she's had sex—that she's been used'. After all, who wants to touch a girl who's gone and left herself smeared all over the hands of other men? Women . . . are . . . dirty.

Oh, but also remember that you can do whatever you like to dirty women who've let their sticky vaginas get tacky and unclean; they don't respect themselves, so why should you be forced to respect them?

Slut-shaming women is a practice as old as time itself, and it hasn't shown any signs of abating. In 2014, ACCESS Ministries were accused of distributing 'Biblezines' to Australian year six students that asked readers to consider 'how far you can go before you are no longer pure'. Taking that dirty chocolate analogy even further (because why not?), the zines suggested, 'Let's put it this way: How much dog poop stirred into your cookie batter does it take to ruin the whole batter?'

Let's put it this way, girls. If you have sex, you may as well be asking a boy to take a giant shit right inside you and then whenever you touch someone after that you'll just be leaving your dirty, shit-stained hands all over them because you're a dirty girl covered in shit.

Just as troubling were the pamphlet's implied teachings about sexual assault. Girls were advised never to go braless or to wear low-slung jeans and tube tops, because they may be responsible for 'putting sexual thoughts about [their bodies] into guys' heads.'

Aside from the fact that there are few circumstances in which someone in a position of authority should be speaking to girls of any age about their nipples, the preoccupation with pubescent girls' bodies and what they choose to do with them signifies an unhealthy obsession that ought to be questioned regularly and thoroughly. But again, what must also be critically examined is how this particular obsession with turning girls into sexual gatekeepers creates a universal excuse for those 'insatiable' boys who can't help but constantly try to push past that border patrol.

Consider the phenomenon of 'purity balls' (which could perhaps more accurately be referred to as 'creepy incest parades'). Your typical purity ball is basically a weird sort of daddy–daughter dance in which girls on the cusp of puberty dress up in white gowns and 'pledge' their virginity to Papa to look after until it can be passed along to their future husband as a 'gift'. Although mostly popular in America's Bible Belt, the balls are still held in forty-eight out of the fifty states.

It's worth noting that no such equivalent exists for boys. Despite the founder of the purity ball movement arguing that it's really more about 'being a whole person', there's no doubt that the focus is on girls alone. (In fact, one of the few examples I could find of boys participating in something like this was focused less on pledging purity and more on learning how to respectfully treat the women in their lives—which is certainly a noble cause, but problematic in the context of how sex education is interpreted differently based on conservative moral standards.) The practice is deeply patriarchal and intensely disturbing. Participants are given mock wedding rings to wear on the fourth finger of their left hands while their daddies vow 'before God' to act as their protectors and authority until they can be passed along to another man to do the same thing.

There's something more than vaguely disturbing in an activity that literally asks young girls to charge the protection of their vaginas to their fathers. In a *Nightline* report on the ceremonies, the head pastor of the Living Stones Church, Ron Johnson, is seen offering a ring to his twelve-year-old daughter while saying, 'This is just a reminder that keeping yourself pure is important. So you keep this on your finger and from this point you are married to the Lord and your father is your boyfriend.'

Purity balls and chocolate Jesus analogies might be situated at the more extreme end of the spectrum here, but it all spawns from the same essential belief: that girls and boys experience sexuality differently, and that one group must protect themselves from the insatiable and wholly natural desires of the other (particularly in Australia, where men are basically thought to be powered by beer and boobs). Worse, that if girls fail to adequately guard themselves from the hot-blooded desire of boys (or when they inevitably realise as young adults that their thoughts on sex have evolved substantially from when they were twelve), then the shame and filth that evidently follows is theirs alone to bear.

She should have known better. Boys can't control themselves when they get worked up. They get blue balls. It hurts them. They just want it so bad. That's why girls can't wear leggings or short shorts to school—because boys will get distracted and chew their own arms off in class.

Why are people so concerned with protecting young girls from sexual interaction, if not because it's assumed that their sexuality is somehow different to that of boys? Girls are granted fewer rights of exploration and self-expression, and taught that their essential worth and value is tied up in how firmly in place they keep their knickers.

Boys, on the other hand, are shamed for precisely the opposite reasons. For not being sexual enough. For not wanting it all the time. For desiring intimacy and connection instead of an emotionless fuckfest. For needing to be in love in order to sleep with someone. For wanting to wait.

There's a beautiful episode of *Freaks and Geeks* (Paul Feig's hilarious, heartfelt coming-of-age television series about teenagers growing up in 1980s Detroit) that explores this very dynamic. For most of the series, Sam Weir (a late blooming fourteen-year-old) has pined after his classmate, Cindy. When they finally start 'dating', he realises that the reality is a bit more grown up and a lot less fun than he daydreamed about. Cindy wants to go to make-out parties, something Sam's not ready for or particularly interested in yet. After Cindy gets mad at him for wearing a turtleneck jumper to cover up the hickey she's given him, he tells her he wants to go back to being just friends.

'No, Sam, you can't break up with me,' Cindy says. 'You're supposed to be nice. That's the only reason why I'm going out with you in the first place!'

'Hey, I am nice!' he replies. 'I'm just not having any fun. Are you?'

I love this scene because it reveals so much about the truth of adolescent sexuality. Cindy wants to experiment with sex and intimacy, and she selects someone she thinks will make that a safe bet for her (both physically and emotionally). But Sam wants to wait until all of him is ready for it—his body *and* heart.

It reminds me of another show, the television adaptation of *Puberty Blues* that ran on Channel Ten between 2012 and 2014. In that, viewers are shown a very different vision of teen sex, one in which the young girls growing up in the beachside suburbs of 1970s New South Wales are used as little more than holes for boys to plunge both their dicks and their disdain into. Having experienced this degrading, dehumanising treatment firsthand, Sue (also fourteen) confides in her mother that she's had sex and 'hated it'. Her free-spirited mum responds by giving her a copy of *The Joy of Sex*, and Sue proceeds to work her way through it with one of her schoolfriends, Woody. The arc that follows is a rare televisual example of truly affirmative and enthusiastic consent, with both Sue and Woody treating the activity almost as a fact-finding mission in which they both get to be Chief Scientists. After Sue has her first (unexpected) orgasm, she walks home alone along the seafront in the early morning light. The camera trains itself on her face, watching as it slowly morphs from an expression of deep thought into one of pure, unbridled joy.

Why isn't the sexual awakening of boys like Sam considered as precious as that of girls? Why isn't the freedom of girls like Sue considered as worthy of defence as that of boys?

One thing is clear: these contradictions are weaponised in a way that causes harm to everyone. Changing the narrative around sex isn't just about liberating girls from harmful stereotypes—it's also about protecting boys from those same damaging ideas. The world is made up of Sams and Sues, and they have a lot to teach us if we just let them.

■

The question of what we learn from representations of sex goes well beyond basic pop culture. I knew I couldn't write this book without looking at the impact that easily accessible pornography has on young men and women, but I'd be lying if I said I wasn't nervous about wading into it. The conversation itself is fraught, with advocates on both sides of the argument too often unwilling to give an inch towards middle ground. Allow me to generalise for a moment.

Anti-porn feminists (who are frequently also unsupportive of the autonomous rights of sex workers to choose their own form of employment, and porn performance *is* a form of sex work) will say there's no place for orchestrated voyeurism in the fight for liberation from patriarchy. In their view, porn is not just universally harmful but often a catalogued depiction of rape (or at least a how-to). The stance is that there can be no liberation from patriarchy as long as women's bodies are exploited to provide sexual fulfilment for men, and the sheer mass of pornography is evidence of how far we are from achieving this goal.

On the other side, you'll find people who argue that porn itself isn't the problem. They believe there's nothing wrong with depicting all manner of sexual proclivities on film, because fantasy isn't the same as reality and porn is meant to be entertainment, not education. According to this argument, violent porn isn't necessarily drawn from misogyny but rather from the fact that some people—and yes, that includes women—enjoy BDSM and humiliation, and they shouldn't be kink-shamed for this. Rather, what's needed is better understanding of the fact that pornography is a text like any other and it requires literacy.

I've watched my share of porn through the years, and I sympathise with elements of both points of view (except for the anti-sex work stuff). It does disturb me that a good proportion (if not the majority) of freely accessible porn has aspects of misogyny (and in some cases is just a full-on celebration of it), and that it's being watched by millions of viewers who either aren't used to or aren't interested in critically engaging with the impact of this. We live in a misogynistic, capitalist patriarchy; I'm hardly surprised that one of our biggest global industries routinely reflects the hatred of women that permeates all other areas of society. So does Hollywood, for that matter.

At the same time, I don't think that voyeurism and pornography is in and of itself harmful. Watching pornography doesn't make you a misogynist, nor does it necessarily disconnect you from a healthy sexuality. Using visual and erotic aids as a means to get off is hardly an invention of modern technology, and dismissing it as such is an oversimplification. As the academic Bianca Fileborn noted in a 2016 article for *The Conversation* titled 'Gonzo: We need to talk about young men and porn':

> Pornography is neither an uncomplicated positive force, nor an oppressively negative one. It can be a tool for sexual gratification, or used to explore nascent sexual desires, or a source of amusement, or of reassurance that one's burgeoning sexuality is 'normal'.

This last one is particularly key. Well-made porn—which is to say, porn that's founded on principles of consent, mutual pleasure and respect—can help people to understand their own desires and kinks, while reassuring them that there's nothing 'wrong' with them. It can be used in sexual relationships to start dialogues that might not otherwise have been explored. It can be a space for people to receive positive, sexual validation denied to them in mainstream society—a place where different kinds of bodies are celebrated and respectfully depicted as sexual. For young queer and gender-diverse people especially, it can provide an essential outlet for safely exploring their own sexuality and identities without the risk of being harmed either by people around them or by narratives that reinforce exclusion.

The problem as I understand it lies at the point where capitalism, patriarchy and misogyny intersect. The global porn industry pulls in roughly US$4.9 billion per year. One-third of all internet downloads are pornographic in nature. Supply meets demand, and considering that misogyny pervades most of capitalism's global structures, why wouldn't it also exist in a content provision business that just happens to sell sexual fantasies? And that's an essential fact to remember—that what's being sold here is *fantasy*, not reality.

Let's be real. You can find anything online if you look hard enough for it. (I once fell into an internet hole reading about 'starseeds', and that was a real trip. Go on and Google it, it's safe for work I promise.) More concerning to me than the prospect of people searching for visual sex aids online is: a) the age at which they first start looking for it; b) the ease with which it's possible to find truly heinous and brutal expressions of sexual violence against women *for free* and absent of any depiction of consent or prior negotiation; and c) whether or not individuals have been given the literacy tools to fully understand what it is they're looking at, and whether they understand it's not 'real'. I'm not saying that, for example, pornography featuring BDSM should be banned. BDSM is a valid form of sexual delight for many people, and operates as a culture with its own specific set of rules. But consensually navigated BDSM isn't the same thing as sex that involves non-consensual violence. Does a thirteen-year-old boy watching either scenario play out in a free eight-minute video online really have the cognitive skills yet to understand the difference? For that matter, should we always assume that a thirty-five-year-old does?

Sexual violence wasn't invented alongside modern pornography, although the latter can certainly amplify attitudes that help the former to be perpetrated. The abundance of amateur pornography (which isn't guaranteed to have been made safely, or with performers who've been paid properly—or at all—and given control of their consent) provides a template for behaviours that can become toxic depending on how and what they're used for. The steady rise in men filming sex without the consent of their partner is a good example of this, as is the even more horrifying practice of groups of men filming sexual assaults and then sharing them online as a form of toxic bonding. In fact, it isn't unusual for young men to use porn and degradation as a bonding activity. In his 2008 book *Guyland*, Michael Kimmel writes that, 'guys [like this] tend to like the extreme stuff, the double penetrations and humiliating scenes. They watch it together with guys and they make fun of the women in the scene.'

But the heightening of sexist attitudes and unhealthy expressions of masculinity among peers isn't the only risk posed by excessive porn consumption. Studies have shown a heightened risk of erectile dysfunction in men who consume large amounts of porn, with the idea being that it can decrease the ability to maintain sexual stimulation with a partner. With respect to intimacy, a 2017 meta-analysis of more than fifty studies (comprising more than 50,000 respondents) conducted by researchers from Indiana University and the University of Hawaii found that viewing porn resulted in a lower sense of relationship satisfaction, with one suggestion for this being that mainstream porn leads to men having unrealistic expectations of sex.

But still, I'd argue that the problem here is less to do with the concept of porn as erotic voyeurism and more to do with how gender inequality, capitalism and society's rampant misogyny informs its creation. Like I said, supply and demand is the governing force of all economic industries and pornography is no different. To change the way porn is consumed and understood, we can't just get rid of it. Nor should we have to sacrifice entirely a tool that can be used so positively for sexual pleasure. Instead, we should focus on changing the culture that creates both an economic and social market for unethical, sexist pornography to abound in. This has always proven to be a much trickier proposition.

That said, there *are* ways we can do this. Contrary to popular belief, boys in fact have a far richer relationship with sexuality than traditional gender stereotypes would have us believe. They need to be invited to have a conversation about the complexities of sex and expression. One of the obvious ways to do this is by talking with them about porn sex versus real sex, and incorporating discussions of consent into this. It isn't just imperative that we do so to promote positive emotional health in kids; it's also vital from a physical health perspective.

For example, research conducted in 2014 by the London School of Hygiene & Tropical Medicine among adolescents from three different British locations found there's an inadequate transmission of accurate sex education in a porn-viewing culture. One of the consequences of this can be seen in the 'expectations, experiences and circumstances of anal sex among [heterosexual] young people'. Many of the girls responding to the study said they felt expected to 'do anal'. Conversely, while some young men said they avoided anal sex out of concern for their partner's comfort, others admitted to pushing for it despite believing it would probably hurt her. In fact, researchers found that girls' pleasure was 'often absent in narratives of anal heterosex' and that this was seemingly accepted as normal. Of more immediate concern though was the lack of adequate health education available on how to have healthy and safe anal sex in the first place. The consequences of ignoring it cannot be downplayed. In 2018, the Australian journalist Patrick Wood reported on the impact pornography was having on adolescent sexuality, with one of the most distressing stories told being that of a sixteen-year-old girl who will now spend the rest of her life wearing a colostomy bag after 'attempting' anal sex with a *group* of boys. While we absolutely must focus on improving consent dialogues (in adolescents particularly), the knowledge that some of them are engaging in potentially risky sexual behaviour without proper precautions or preparation means we also have to significantly improve the practicalities of sex education so that girls stop turning up to the doctor complaining of rectal bleeding and tears so severe they become permanently injured.

But alongside encouraging literacy in the viewing of porn, we also need to prioritise literacy in the *having* of sex. There's a subtle difference between consenting to an act freely and consenting to it because you feel it's expected of you. In having dialogues about sex and intimacy with young people, we should be encouraging them to think about what desire actually is. Do they want to do something because they have a genuine curiosity or erotic thrill over it, or does their impulse stem more from the sense that this is what's expected of them? Remember, professional porn performers are paid and have contracts, directors and catering on-set. It's one thing to watch porn for entertainment and sexual release, but part of that aforementioned need for literacy involves its consumers understanding that what they're seeing isn't a field guide; nor does it have to be instrumental in directing their tastes. If we're going to talk about the problems of porn, let's not discount the fact that it sits in this weird cultural space where libertarianism meets abject prudishness. Attempts to address sex education realistically with young people frequently results in the Helen Lovejoys of the world freaking out. But issues of pleasure and consent should be considered central rather than peripheral to comprehensive sex education, and porn is realistically going to form a huge part of that discussion. If young men can happily watch a woman being ploughed by three dicks at once, they should also have the fortitude to talk openly about the importance of lube and how to make sure it feels good for her.

Gone are the days when parents and educators could focus exclusively on the matters of biology and reproduction, leaving children to figure out everything else in the back seats of cars and in other people's bedrooms. We live in an internet era and, like it or not, most kids today have their first sexual experience by way of searching for or stumbling across porn online. For boys, the average age at which this occurs is eleven, which means we need to start teaching kids about sexual health and consent much earlier than that.

And really, having an open dialogue about porn is an excellent way to talk to adolescents about consent. I know these conversations can be difficult to have. It's hard to imagine children who only yesterday seemed to be toddling around the playground suddenly diving into adult experiences you think they may not be ready for. The advent and growth of sexting alone is a terrifying prospect for parents suddenly confronted by their child's burgeoning sexual exploration, and it's understandable—if unwise—that some people want to ignore it for as long as possible. But healthy sexual choices are best made by people who've been encouraged to talk about sexuality in all its complexities. Yet as we keep seeing time and time again, this dialogue still appears to be largely absent in Australia's education institutions.

There are ways to talk to your kids about porn that are helpful and respectful of their burgeoning sexuality—but the conversation also needs to go far beyond just the physical. Talk to them about sexism and misogyny, and how each of these things inform the gender inequality that exists across all industries, not just pornography. Research some of the people within the porn creation community who are actively challenging sexism in their industry and championing really important, positive things, like women's sexual pleasure and consent. Encourage the young people in your life to be critical of all the media they consume, not just the sexy kind. Ask them to consider the potential power imbalances in play. Do they even really like the porn they're watching? Tell them about this amazing thing called feminist pornography.* Use this as an opportunity to talk to them about the economics of production, too. If they're using pornography to get off, they should make ethical choices about how they consume it, starting with paying for it and knowing where that money goes, and having assurance that the performers involved are all being appropriately compensated and respected. If it's easier for fathers or a trusted male figure to have this conversation with boys alone, then do that.

Talk to them about consent.

Talk to them about consent.

Did I mention you need to talk to them about consent?

Foster the kind of relationship with your children that lets them know they can speak to you about anything, and that they will find love and safety in your arms.

Because it's true that children mimic what they see in media. It's true that the rise of young men filming women without their consent (or filming actual sexual assaults) and then sharing it around is underpinned by a learned misogyny that finds a bigger platform through the media, including mainstream pornography. Slut-shaming and victim-blaming have always been used as weapons against women, and the internet in general makes it easier for this to happen on a widespread level. These things wouldn't disappear if you got rid of porn, because the root cause of men's violence against women isn't sex—it's misogyny.

---

* Sex worker, sex educator and porn producer Gala Vanting has an excellent feminist porn resource list on her website galavanting.info. But don't just stop there. Search 'feminist porn' on Google and discover how amazing and positive porn can actually be!

The fundamental truth is that we live in a world where gender inequality is still a reality, and myths about male and female sexuality are still fiercely held with all the intensity of someone trying to stop a slippery butt plug from falling out of their well-oiled hole.

But if the reality of women being harmed by this shit isn't enough to make you sit up and take notice, then maybe you'll start to care when we look at how it hurts men too.

■

In 2015, the small American town of Dietrich, Idaho, was rocked by revelations of sexual abuse emanating from the high school's football team. The *Washington Post* described Dietrich as 'a community on edge' after charges were filed against three players who were alleged to have sexually assaulted a fellow student.

While it's not uncommon for residents to rally around young men with 'promising futures', there's one key difference between this case and most of the ones we hear about—in Dietrich, the victim was a male teammate. He was also an intellectually disabled young black man in an overwhelmingly white town, which can't be discounted when considering the weight of community defence typically offered to young men who've put themselves in situations like this. Had he been white and neurotypical, would supporters have been so quick to back the perpetrators? It's hard to know for sure, but I think we can safely say that the situation would have been a bit less clear cut for them.

It seems that the assault was at least partly planned, as the young man testified that it began with an invitation for a hug. While he was being held, another player pushed a coat hanger into his anus. The only man named in the trial, John R.K. Howard, then kicked the hanger, pushing it further into the young man's rectum. As the victim told the court later, 'Pain that I have never felt took over my body. I screamed, but afterwards, I kept it to myself.'

It's hard to imagine a situation in which anyone could find this kind of behaviour defensible, but it's incredible how flexible people can be when it comes to forgiving their heroes. Local resident Hubert Shaw told the *Washington Post*: 'They're 15-, 16-, 17-year-old boys who are doing what boys do . . . I would guarantee that those boys had no criminal intent to do anything or any harm to anyone. Boys are boys and sometimes they get carried away.'

The case isn't too dissimilar from one that occurred at a party in Brisbane in early 2015. A young man drank too much and passed out in a bedroom. Four of his 'friends' coordinated an attack that involved two holding him down, another sexually violating him with a glass bottle and the fourth filming it. Afterwards, the footage was shared on social media. After a week-long trial, Bailey Hayes-Gordon, Nicholas Jackson and Jacob Watson—all of whom had pleaded not guilty—were convicted of rape and sentenced to two years in prison, to be suspended after six months. The fourth man, Frazer Eaton, had pleaded guilty from the outset and was given a sentence of eighteen months, to be wholly suspended.

When I read about this case, I remember thinking how brave that eighteen-year-old lad was for coming forward and pressing charges—not because what happened to him was significantly worse than the rapes that women are subjected to, but because the framing of his assault as some kind of hilarious 'prank' must have made it that much more difficult to speak out.

'Don't dog the boys' is still the ridiculous catchcry used by young men when they circle the wagons in defence of each other, and a man speaking out must have been perceived as some kind of deep betrayal of this form of toxic brotherhood. After the trio who pleaded not guilty were sentenced, friends and family members didn't just openly weep in the courtroom, they also took to social media to lament the supposed miscarriage of justice that had happened that day. It was a joke! Their lives were being ruined over a joke!

There is a delight in humiliation that rests at the centre of this swaggering machismo, and it must be asked what it is about seeing another human humiliated that is considered a) entertaining and b) a cheap night out. In her book *Night Games*, Anna Krien explores the notion of the 'prank' that underpins so much of the exploitation of others undertaken by groups of men: the secret filming of women engaged in sex acts, the sudden appearance of a second or third or fourth man during intercourse (even to the point of attempting to substitute one for another without her realising), the degradation of unconscious people's bodies while others watch and laugh (even if, as the judge in this case decided, there was 'no sexual gratification').

It speaks to the absolute repression of male emotional maturity that some circles of men require the use of women (and sometimes other men) as inanimate objects in order to connect with each other and/or use this degradation as a means of elevating their own status. At one point, Krien recounts the story of a woman who agreed to consensual group sex (very, very different to the pack sex so often defended in these scenarios as a mutual activity) with a small group of footballers. But I guess her consent was a problem in the end; being unable to dehumanise her sexually and therefore fulfil the purpose of the standard sexual 'prank', one of the footballers decided to do the next best thing. He defecated into her shoe, and waited for her reaction when she went to put it on.

And to think, when I want to laugh I just watch old episodes of *Blackadder* and *Gavin & Stacey*. Is it true what the online trolls say to me? Have I been doing humour wrong all these years?

Sarcasm aside, I often wonder what it is that draws these men to each other. Is it as simple as falling into line behind a ringleader? Maybe. Patriarchal order that favours you can be a helluva drug, and conforming to the rigid codes of masculinity in your own peer groups must seem easier than challenging it. No one likes to be ostracised as the party pooper. (Except feminists; we live for that shit.) But I suspect what's probably going on is that a lot of young men want to say no to this kind of activity but don't really know how. I don't think that makes their complicity forgivable, but it does give us a point from which we might start to try and disrupt it.

Of course, we first have to disrupt the impulse shown by broader society to make excuses for them. Consider this example. Around the same time as the sexual assault in Dietrich, yet another group of young men had their community rally around and protect them from the consequences of their actions. A young football player in Florida was arrested after footage was uncovered showing him and up to twenty-five other boys engaged in sexual activity (some just as spectators) with a fifteen-year-old girl in a school bathroom. Afterwards, Lee County schools superintendent Greg Adkins corresponded with parents, urging them to 'move forward from this incident without further harsh judgment of those involved . . . They are adolescents who have made a serious mistake. They must now be afforded the opportunity to learn from their mistakes.'

The media and public were predictably quick to condemn the girl. When incidents like this occur, people are often scathing about the 'sluts' and 'hoes' who need to 'respect themselves more', because if we can't shame teenage girls for being sexually exploited then what *can* we do? It's political correctness gone mad!

It's telling how much leniency is granted to boys allowed to 'learn from their mistakes' while girls continue to be subjected to scrutiny and shame for similar engagement. But there's an unusual element in this situation that not only compounds this girl's exploitation but makes the shaming of her especially repugnant. At thirteen, she was trafficked into sex slavery and spent the next two years being raped for the sexual gratification of large groups of adult men. As her advocate argued at the time, she was a victim who had been conditioned into sexuality at the threat of extreme punishment. For her to be now labelled as 'promiscuous' by a community more intent on sheltering its boys was simply inflicting further abuse on her.

But the sexuality of boys is both revered and given free rein to experiment without risk, even as a regressive patriarchal mindset also denies it healthy and positive avenues for exploration. Shortly after the incident in the school bathroom, a twenty-four-year-old female teacher was arrested elsewhere in America and charged with grooming and raping her thirteen-year-old male student. The teacher, now pregnant, briefly tried to flee authorities but was soon captured. And although there is commentary from the public calling this what it is—rape and paedophilia—there's also a significant amount of back-slapping and praise being foisted on the thirteen-year-old, whose ability to 'nail and impregnate the teacher' is apparently the stuff of envy.

These stories all share the commonality of reducing male sexuality to something base. Why is a thirteen-year-old boy not entitled to the same protection from predatory adult behaviour as a thirteen-year-old girl, just because the society he lives in views his sexuality as something dominant and invulnerable? To what extent do those attitudes inform the behaviour of a pack of boys who gather in a bathroom to watch as sequences more suited to a porn film are re-created with a fifteen-year-old rape victim? Isn't it at least *possible* that some of those boys stood there and watched only because they feared not doing so would expose them as somehow less manly in front of their peers? Isn't it *possible* that teenage boys aren't always ready to fuck or to watch someone be fucked? Isn't it *possible* that some of them just want to stay kids for a bit longer?

If all that might possibly be true, how does this kind of uncritical acceptance of What Men Want help to feed an unhealthy pattern of behaviour that might lead a trio of young men to brutally rape a teammate or friend 'as a joke'?

It's perplexing how fiercely some people will defend what they see as the natural impulses of male sexuality, while also demonising feminists for what they argue is some kind of criminal stereotyping. How many times have you either heard or perhaps even expressed the sentiment yourself that it's feminists who 'paint all men as rapists', while ignoring the tacitly accepted belief that this kind of inappropriate and even illegal sexual behaviour in young men is either unavoidable or just what happens when a prank goes too far? Stop making men feel bad, you *misandrissssssssst*!

But what could be more misandrist than conditioning young boys to view their sexuality as a weapon that empowers them but is also outside their control? Every time society defends or perpetuates this absurd stereotype, it reinforces to boys that the vibrancy of their masculine identities is dependent on how forcefully they not only express their sexuality but perform it for other men to admire. This is what encourages them to view girls and women as conquests instead of human beings, while denying them the right to prioritise intimacy over physicality, if they choose, or indeed to reject sexuality altogether when it suits them.

We are doing damage to our young boys, and this in turn compounds the damage we already do to our young girls. We should all be disgusted to live in a world where an assault on either of them can be met with high fives or praise. We should absolutely demand more of boys. But we should also demand more *for* them.

I don't want my son to join in while his friends viciously attack someone who trusts them. I don't want him to think that 'humour' relies on someone being humiliated. I don't want him to be afraid of showing too much of his softness out of fear others will use it against him. I don't want him to stand in a bathroom one day, watching a young girl be fucked and filmed by his school friends, and not know how to *speak up* about it to say no. But worse still is the thought that he could be the one filming it. That he could be the one organising it.

I don't want that world for him.

I will *not* have that world for him.

■

In his book *How Not To Be a Boy*, the comedian Robert Webb jokes that it's not so much that masculinity is in crisis as that masculinity *is* a crisis. He immediately denounces this conclusion as too simplistic, but I'm tempted to agree with the original premise. Boys might be conditioned to believe that their sexuality is a fire-breathing dragon whose life force must never be tamed, but let's be honest—that's bullshit. It seems to me more likely that boys are *fucking terrified* all the time. Terrified that they won't measure up to what they're told men have to be, terrified that they're not doing sex properly, terrified that they're doing it with the wrong people, terrified that they'll never get the girl, terrified of what it means that they don't *want* to get the girl, terrified that someone might discover that they have *feelings*, terrified terrified terrified.

Women may have few advantages over men in this crazy little sideshow we call life, but one thing we definitely don't have to do is shove all our icky human emotions into a metaphorical box and send it on a one-way trip to the centre of the sun.

And it isn't just about what men mean to themselves. It's also about what they're allowed to mean to each other. You may have heard the homophobic rejoinder of 'no homo' to anything that even vaguely implies an expression of affection or admiration between men determined to maintain their reputations of strict heterosexuality. In this context the phrase is intended to be humorous rather than threatening, a way for otherwise straight men to share their feelings with each other, but maintain what ethnographer C.J. Pascoe referred to as 'compulsive heterosexuality' in her 2007 book, *Dude, You're a Fag: Masculinity and Sexuality in High School.*

Pascoe coined the phrase to describe the ways in which masculine power is codified within a community of teenage school peers. While it almost certainly begins in the nightmarish halls of secondary education, it's a concept that can also be easily recognised alongside our society's boring, ongoing, mainstream paranoia about men and homosexuality. Pascoe conducted field research for eighteen months at a racially diverse high school in California, interviewing more than fifty students about how gender, sexuality and the concept of masculinity played out for both the male and female students. In the male students' interactions with each other, she found that homophobia was rife as a bullying tactic between both enemies and friends. The 'compulsive heterosexuality' she writes about thus becomes the institutionalised antidote to the emasculation always waiting to undermine boys and their place in the broader social hierarchy.

And they accuse women of hysteria.

My son isn't quite two years old, but he's perfected the art of the gentle hug. I watch him when he meets his little friends. At first he seems astonished to be suddenly surrounded by people who are the same size as him. But then you can tell he just wants to love on them like crazy. He'll approach them slowly, carefully wrap his arms around them and then bury his head in their shoulder. The kids aren't always into it, at which point we have to gently navigate some early lessons about bodily autonomy and respect. But there's no two ways about it—he just bloody loves hugging people.

I find myself wondering sometimes at what age this might stop. Will he succumb to the pressures of compulsive heterosexuality and the repressed masculinity that comes with that? And what does this mean for his ability to relate to men later on? Perhaps this is where we need to start: not just teaching men how to navigate healthy intimate relationships with women, but encouraging them to embrace healthy intimate relationships with each other. It breaks my heart to know that men—and young men especially—are conditioned against embracing the pleasures of a physically expressed platonic love for each other for fear that the authenticity of their manhood may be challenged.

My family was always affectionate when I was growing up, and my father and brother still hug and kiss and say 'I love you' today. But it's sad and surprising to realise how many men don't express gentle intimacy with their sons, particularly as those boys enter adolescence. That touch isn't necessarily replicated in their friendships with other men because of the pressures that compulsive heterosexuality presents, which means their emotional isolation from each other often starts at a very young age. More worrying are the dynamics that replace this physical affection. High school boys aren't the only ones who enforce compulsive heterosexuality, and they're clearly not the only ones prone to gross, obnoxious 'pranks' and the gleeful indulgence of truly toxic misogyny. If the men who frequent my Facebook page are anything to go by, a lot of this harmful shit is being passed down from father to son and nurtured as an obscene replacement for true intimacy.

Failing to teach and encourage men to express healthy intimacy not just with women but with other men is causing significant damage. For those of us raising boys, it's vital that we try to counter not just Pascoe's sense of compulsive heterosexuality but the homophobia that keeps men from truly connecting with one another. How else do you explain a bonding activity that involves four young men shoving a glass bottle up their unconscious mate's arse and filming it, because who could resist recording the high-brow comedy?

We all have a role to play in dismantling the twin towers of homophobia and misogyny. You might not think any of this is a problem in your house, but in fact you just can't know. Questioning toxic masculinity and the harm it does to boys and men is an ongoing activity (which is fun for the whole family!). It's not just about double standards and it's not just about porn. It's also about the ways men are socialised to communicate and *commune* with each other.

We can be a part of disrupting that, but we have to start by taking it seriously. Make it a practice to have in-depth conversations about *all* this stuff—about touch, intimacy, healthy expressions of emotion, consent, porn, relationships, feelings and how sexism impacts negatively on all these things. We are doing young men no favours when we allow masculinity to be dictated to them by the status quo.

Because here's some news for you. The status quo might revere men as a class, but it destroys them as individuals. And it teaches them to destroy others in return.

—6—

MASS DEBATE

UNFUCKABLE, it screamed, the fluorescent yellow letters filling half the cheap projection screen mounted in the bowels of a suburban function centre in Adelaide. The damning word was superimposed over the top of an extremely unflattering photograph of me, taken when I was roughly nineteen years old and here, almost two decades later, reproduced for the amusement of a 1500-strong crowd of men's rights activists, online shitlords, teenage boys and the handful of women who can always be found laughing uproariously at events like these because they're 'not like other girls'.

The shabby crowd was there to see Milo Yiannopoulos, a man who has come to symbolise in many ways the toxic nature of online discourse. Hailed as a hero by his followers and derided as a bigoted fool by his critics, Yiannopoulos represents the chasm that exists between actual dialogue and something far more chaotic and lawless. He has built a career on saying things that are not only deliberately 'shocking' (for example, he 'jokes' that lesbians aren't real) but also purposefully cruel and offensive (like his repeated claim that transgenderism is a mental disorder). Although he positions himself as a thinker and influencer, he really acts as little more than a microphone for the repulsive views of his fans, most of whom appear to be young white men who fancy themselves somehow oppressed by the successes of the feminist movement.

Adam Morgan, the editor-in-chief of the *Chicago Review of Books*, once described him as 'a clickbait grifter who has made a name for himself spewing hate speech'. It's an apt summary, but it's not the whole story. Yes, he spews hatred in exchange for fame and money, but he also has the relative advantage of being able to do that from a place of extreme nihilism. He appeals to his target demographic not just because they're angry and entitled, but because they want to be excused from having to prosecute their arguments. This is what makes him and what he represents so dangerous. It isn't his bigotry, although that mustn't be downplayed. It's the way he revels in laziness and in turn gives permission to his followers to revel in their own. It's in how he uses words like 'snowflake' and 'triggered' to deride the opposition while sending the message to his fans that it's actually *them* who deserve special consideration. It's in how his own intersection of identity (he is a gay man married to a black man and he claims without real evidence to have Jewish heritage, though he grew up a practising Catholic) is used as the ultimate identity politics card by people who otherwise spit on the invocation of identity as any kind of defence. He can't be homophobic! *He's gay!* He can't be racist! *He's married to a black man!* He can't be a Nazi apologist! *He's Jewish!*

Anyone who challenges or disagrees with him can be dismissed as one or more of the following: libtard, leftard, white knight, cuck, snowflake, feminazi, fake news. Yiannopoulos didn't invent these terms, but he uses them with such bombast and swagger that he emboldens his followers to do the same. *Cuck!* they yell at the men who dare to challenge their sexist views. *Feminazi!* they screech at the woman whose Facebook page they've found so they can try to mock her into silence. So successful has Yiannopoulos been at mobilising childish young boys and men (and some girls and women) to behave this way that he's basically ceased to be a real person and has instead become a cheap cardboard cut-out sent out as part of the sad promotional kit of a low-budget movie. If his fans could buy an action figure, they probably would.

My photo appeared in Yiannopoulos's set on the opening night of a five-city Australian tour for this self-described 'internet supervillain'. I'm sure the main reason he singled me out for scorn was because I'm a relatively well-known feminist in the places he was visiting and, seeing as his audience undoubtedly loathes all us scary man-haters, he knew it would play well. It's a bit like a bad comedian changing the locations and landmarks of all their stories because they think it will resonate more with the punters. But the other reason Yiannopoulos singled me out that night (and the ones following) was because I had refused his demands for a 'debate' in the lead up to his tour, correctly describing him online as someone who has been captured on video cavorting with neo-Nazis and white supremacists while also being revealed only a few months earlier to have made comments that appeared to support sexual relationships between adult men and adolescent boys. I questioned why numerous (male) journalists had reached out to me on his behalf, wanting to set up this absurd meeting. Why were they acting as publicists for a man with hateful views on some of the world's most marginalised people, and why were they downplaying these views as merely 'controversial'? Why were the same newspapers that dredged up nonsense to write defamatory and, in some cases, wholly made-up articles about me and my 'shocking' behaviour describing this Islamophobic misogynist and Nazi supporter as a 'provocateur'? Why were prominent talking heads and one-time prime ministerial candidates hosting this garbage fire on his nationwide tour, practically licking his butthole all around the country in their rush to welcome him to our shores?

Free speech, apparently: the most important of all the speeches. When women refuse to let men force their free speech on us, what we're doing is *silencing* them. It's because we're *afraid*. It's because we know we'll be *destroyed*. So instead, we just get to be punished for denying them.

Debate me, bitch! *Or get ready to take your medicine.*

■

If you haven't heard of Milo Yiannopoulos until now, congratulations—you've so far managed to avoid being infected by any of the steaming pile of pig shit that is his entire personality and existence on this earth. Please accept my sincerest apologies, because I'm about to ruin that for you right now.

Yiannopoulos has been sliming around the media landscape for at least a decade. For a time, he worked as the tech editor at the right-wing jizz factory known as *Breitbart News*. There, he wrote articles with such delightful headlines as TRANNIES ARE GAY (in which he argues against transgender people being able to access public bathrooms that accord with their gender), THE LEFT'S BLOODY WAR ON WOMEN: SENDING CHICKS INTO COMBAT BETRAYS MEN, WOMEN AND CIVILIZATION (which sounds fairly hysterical to me, but okay) and NO, JC PENNEY, FAT PEOPLE SHOULD ABSOLUTELY HATE THEMSELVES (in which he confirms, not for the first time, that he's a massive cunt). He popularised the phrase 'feminism is cancer', a deeply average joke that is rivalled in tragic weeniness only by the numerous man-babies who throw it around as if it's the height of sophisticated comedy. We get it, guys—women scare you.

Make no mistake, although Yiannopoulos exploits the bigoted views of his fan base to further his fame and weirdly superficial popularity, there's only one thing the two-time university dropout actually believes in—himself. He courts the slavish devotion of his fan base not by creating anything of substance to earn their political allegiance, but by exploiting their own hate and insecurity, and feeding it back to them in colourful sound bites that give them unprecedented freedom to say whatever they like and have it affirmed. Yiannopoulos's fans (mostly young men under twenty-three and David Leyonhjelm) praise his intelligence and bravery, but what they really mean is: *This man makes me feel intelligent and brave.* Who doesn't want to be given licence to not only say what they like, but to have every thought that swirls around in their brain validated? You might hear fans say of Yiannopoulos that 'he really makes you think', but what they actually mean is, 'he gives me permission not to have to think too deeply at all'. Or, as Vox writer Aja Romano put it in 2016, '[Yiannopoulos] has essentially played commander to a veritable army of mostly male extremists hailing from Reddit, 4chan, and Twitter.'

If it didn't have such dangerous implications for people's safety, it would be easy to dismiss his existence as little more than a juvenile fandom. But over the years, Yiannopoulos has targeted women, Muslims, people of colour, trans and gender-diverse communities, gay people and fat people among countless others, directing toxic pile-ons their way in a desperate attempt to mask the deep insecurity he so clearly feels about his own place in the world by threatening the stability others have found in theirs.

He began his rise to what I guess you could call international prominence and/or infamy proper when he became one of only a few people in the short history of Twitter to be permanently banned from the platform after inciting a racist mob to attack the actress Leslie Jones, who had recently starred in the 2016 reboot of *Ghostbusters* (which, as we saw in chapter three, made a whole bunch of whiny man-babies lose their shit). Much like the way he piggybacked on the fetid stench of the GamerGate movement (after initially mocking it, he quickly switched his allegiance once he realised that morals can be exchanged for treasure in the land of fragile masculinity), the man who would later laugh off accusations of racism because of his marriage to a black man stoked the bigotry and supreme sensitivity of his followers by claiming *Ghostbusters* was doing so poorly that Jones had been deployed to 'play the victim' on Twitter; that she was 'barely literate'; and, as he wrote on more than one occasion, that she was a 'black dude'. Because disparaging a woman's appearance is how you show people you're not only smart but also really funny.

What stoked Yiannopoulos's braying mockery? It was Jones having the audacity to share some of the abuse she'd received after appearing in a movie millions of men loudly pledged they would never watch. This abuse included tweets likening her to a gorilla, images of men's naked bodies, and an image of her face onto which someone had ejaculated.

This is classic Yiannopoulos: he'll accuse a woman of colour of 'playing the victim' when she shares the dismay and deep hurt she feels after being subjected to cruel and vicious racism, misogynoir and straight-up whiny baby-boy tantrums simply because she worked on a movie by which they felt personally victimised, but he'll cry foul when he's forced to suffer consequences for it. When Yiannopoulos had the blue tick on his Twitter account officially removed at the start of 2016 (which basically just means he became 'unverified' in the user system of the Twitterverse), both he and his army of mouth-breathing twonks threw a huge tantrum about it. One outraged soul tried to start a petition (and listen, I have to say that for a group of people so deeply committed to online anarchy and libertarianism, they are *very* fond of gathering signatures to protest all the pointless shit that makes them mad), demanding then president Barack Obama 'issue a statement demanding the restoration of Milo Yiannopoulos's Twitter verification badge'. This petition was retweeted by Yiannopoulos, alongside a flurry of tweets making light of the death of David Bowie. When his account was suspended a few months prior to the bullying of Jones and then cancelled in response to it, the hashtag #FreeMilo trended worldwide.

So it ever was and so it ever shall be—misogynists, racists and homophobes want to be empowered to say whatever they like without vilification or accusation, both of which will result in them crying about being bullied or hard done by. After the permanent suspension of his account, Yiannopoulos told CNBC, 'There's certainly no suggestion whatsoever that I was involved in any kind of racist or sexist harassment of Leslie Jones.' Incorrect. 'What I did was dislike her movie, and write a very critical review that she didn't like.' Also incorrect. 'After that, I teased her a little on Twitter.' Incorrect. 'If a journalist can't tease a Hollywood blockbuster actress, I don't know what this platform is about.'

He reiterated this faux astonishment on *Breitbart*, the ultra-conservative site for which he was then working as the tech editor. 'Honestly, this is why I say feminism is cancer. She used to be funny but being involved in a social dumpster fire like *Ghostbusters* has reduced her to the status of just another frothing loon on Twitter.'

On *ABC News Nightline*, he tried to joke, 'Trolling is very important. I like to think of myself as a virtuous troll, you know? I'm doing God's work.'

I'm loathe to spend this much time discussing an adult man who behaves like an overgrown child, but the fact is that he legitimises hatred and ignorance to an increasing number of young men who are unable or unwilling to critically examine the snake oil he's selling them. This is what it looks like when decidedly non-oppressed people are empowered to 'fight back' against a system they falsely believe is in the process of disempowering and emasculating them—they become internet 'edgelords' who consider it a personal success to force people into a meltdown while claiming they had nothing to do with it, that it's actually the inherent weakness of their victim that's to blame. *Everyone* gets bullied online, and they should grow up and get over it. If they can't handle the heat, they should get out of the kitchen (but also get back into it and make me a damn sandwich).

You might be wondering why, if all this is happening primarily in the online space, the women affected don't just get off the internet. Why not just ignore men like Yiannopoulos and all those he encourages to behave like petulant, bullying children?

It's a common question, one that's asked by journalists, members of the public and the police officers who are called on to take down reports of online harassment and abuse filed on occasion by the women subjected to it. I mean, no one's *forcing* you to turn your computer on. If you choose to wade into these scenarios, aren't you sort of partly to blame?

Yeah, nah. The internet has been accessible to the general public for more than twenty years and has been considered an essential tool for communication, business and employment for at least the last ten. To suggest that the people most likely to be victimised by online misogynists and bullies should just 'remove themselves' isn't only unfair and unreasonable, it's also cavalierly dismissive of the realities of the world today.

The fact is, Milo Yiannopoulos is not so much a disease as he is a symptom. A pus-ridden boil of a symptom, yes, but a symptom all the same. As much as he might fancy himself indispensable to the shitlord movement, in reality almost anyone could perform the role he's created for himself were they to share a similar level of narcissism, moral bankruptcy and love of making mischief. It isn't the demon they are drawn to—it's the chaos the demon unleashes.

In the fantasy role-playing game Dungeons & Dragons, player characters, non-player characters and creatures are all categorised according to a cross-reference of ethical and moral perspectives that's referred to as 'alignment'. The alignment is decided by players choosing what their character's position would be on 'law versus chaos' (ethical) and whether they act for good or evil (moral). There are nine possible alignments: lawful good, neutral good, chaotic good, lawful neutral, true neutral, chaotic neutral, lawful evil, neutral evil and chaotic evil.

The alignment chart itself has become a popular internet meme, with everything from *Star Wars* to *Harry Potter* and even US legislators being categorised according to where they fit in the grid. For example, Han Solo is considered to be 'chaotic neutral'; his ethical framework embodies chaos (he rejects authority, shuns the law and has no respect for convention) and his moral framework is guided by neither good nor evil, but preservation of the self. Harry Potter is neutral good (as is Luke Skywalker) because he holds no unwavering respect for the rules but he acts in the service of good. Hermione Granger, on the other hand, is lawful good, because she is both morally and ethically drawn to goodness that accords with the observation of protocol. Dolores Umbridge is lawful evil because she operates maliciously within the authoritarian framework of the wizarding world to inflict sadistic harm on others, including children. She's more terrifying than Voldemort, in my opinion.

Yiannopoulos is what I would characterise as chaotic evil. In the D&D universe, this is known as the Destroyer, an entity that thrives on blood lust, greed and self-interest. Holland Farkas at *Geek & Sundry* said of the Destroyer, 'If you find yourself identifying with chaotic evil, not to judge or anything, but . . . I'm scared. But hey, some men just want to watch the world burn.' Well, Yiannopoulos did name his twitter account @Nero after all. How's that for hubris?

The Joker is considered to be chaotic evil on the alignment charts, which might appeal to Yiannopoulos's hyper-inflated sense of self. But, then, so is Joffrey Baratheon, the petulant, sadistic pissbaby who ruled Westeros until he was poisoned at his own wedding. Chaotic evil might sound appealing to people who lack the maturity to aspire to anything better, but it's not all it's cracked up to be. The *easydamus.com* website (where you can take an extremely comprehensive test to tell you what your character type is) describes the typical chaotic evil character as doing 'whatever his greed, hatred and lust for destruction drive him to do. He is hot-tempered, vicious, arbitrarily violent, and unpredictable. If he is simply out for whatever he can get, he is ruthless and brutal. If he is committed to the spread of evil and chaos, he is even worse.'

This sounds a lot like Yiannopoulos, but don't worry too much. Chaotic evil is undone by the ultimate ineffectiveness of its character types: 'Thankfully, his plans are haphazard, and any groups he joins or forms are poorly organised.

'Typically, chaotic evil people can be made to work together only by force, and their leader lasts only as long as he can thwart attempts to topple or assassinate him.'

Sure, it's a bit of silliness to place a human with demonstrably awful politics and terrifying sway over uncritical minds in a chart for a fantasy role-playing game, but truth can be found in the strangest places. (By the way, I took the test and I'm a 'neutral good'. So I am basically a Jedi *or* a wizard. Probably both, to be honest.)

It's easy to dismiss the behaviour of Yiannopoulos and his acolytes as just sheer, unbridled entitlement, but it's important to recognise the elements of chaotic evil in there. The desire to watch the world burn is not a good one, but it's definitely becoming attractive to more and more young men who feel themselves forced to watch as the world they thought they had been promised steadily slips away—a world where men have dominion over women, where white people have dominion over people of colour, heterosexuals over queer people, and so on and so forth. History has celebrated and elevated men and masculinity for as long as we've had a collective cultural memory, but this celebration has been of a superficial veneer that doesn't actually dig beneath the surface. If it turns out they don't have the power they have grown up believing their masculinity entitles them to, what *do* they have?

They have an internet connection and a giant chip on their shoulder. It's a recipe for disaster, and it's blowing up in all of our faces.

■

Contrary to claims that it's their ideological opponents who suffer from being 'snowflakes', these men are defined not by iron-clad fortitude but by extreme fragility, and this is what bonds them together beneath the leadership of men like Yiannopoulos (and Jordan Peterson, and Rush Limbaugh, and Bill O'Reilly, and Alex Jones). It's obvious from their reaction to simple politics. Conservative (some might even say fascist) governments are being installed worldwide, but there's also a healthy resistance to them. The people who have historically been forced to remain silent on pain of punishment or death are rising up and fighting back in new ways that are increasingly hard to ignore. The Black Lives Matter movement, the recognition and embrace of trans and gender-diverse identities, the people fighting for rights and dignity for the disabled, women oppressed by domineering and abusive men—these voices will no longer be quelled.

And it fucking *terrifies* some people. White supremacists may have always existed, but they're mobilising again to reclaim a more visible place in mainstream society. Ironically, the newly invigorated white supremacist movement itself embodies everything its practitioners claim to reject in the 'freedom-hating, liberal elites'. Despite being quite emphatically racist, they lash out at being described as such. Despite being enthusiastically misogynistic, they will not stand for being called sexist. Despite insisting that others toughen up and take brutal language on the chin, they become vitriolic and defensive at being called names, decrying what they see as the penchant for 'ad hominem' in the 'weak, predictable Looney Left'. We are at a point in history (again) when Nazis are not only proudly congregating in public spaces, but having their horrendous bile defended as 'freedom of speech'. For almost a century, the United States of America has cultivated a grand reputation of hunting Nazis in literature, movies, television shows, comics and basically any form of pop culture you can think of, so it shows a remarkable level of cognitive dissonance to *still* hold on to the image of oneself as a hero fighting on the side of good while defending the rights of white nationalists to light up tiki torches and march towards the town square.

Where does Yiannopoulos fit into this, and what does it have to do with the central concern that boys are being bred in a culture of toxic masculinity, entitlement and dangerous rage?

As I said earlier, Yiannopoulos isn't so much an ideas man as he is a conduit for a particular kind of white male entitlement and hostility. Once upon a time, men were allowed to be men and this meant men were allowed to be in charge. White men in particular were given authority over certain groups of people, which I'm sure made the simultaneous inequalities they may also have experienced a little easier to stomach. The vast majority of Yiannopoulos's fans are so young that this cultural memory is little more than idealised nostalgia, but my goodness does the nostalgia taste ideal.

When Yiannopoulos sneers that 'feminism is cancer', what he's really offering to men is an easy and flippant rejoinder to anything that remotely threatens the stability of their position in society. Feminism is cancer, because boys should be allowed to be boys without fear of censure or discipline from the horrendous schoolmarms trying to spoil their fun. Why should they have to engage with the concept of rape culture and its documented harm on women in particular, but also men? Why should they be required to investigate the social advantage that being men gives them in the workplace, the public sphere, the private sphere . . . basically, the entire fucking world? Why should they have to *apologise* for being men, as if there's something shameful about this? Feminism is the thing trying to make them do this! Feminism makes them feel bad, annoyed, angry—*it's a cancer destroying the very fabric of their world.*

The sense they're being asked to personally apologise is interesting, because it not only assumes a generic and universal state of masculinity that is somehow being subjected to widespread cultural shaming right now (which is not true, even if certain aspects of male entitlement are being scrutinised and critiqued) but also that this supposed universal state of manhood is so beneficial to boys that the removal of it will cause untold damage.

Let's be clear about what is and isn't harmful to boys. Having faith in oneself is an important part of self-esteem. Having faith that one is never wrong and indeed that one's masculine status gives them licence to test that theory every day leads to harm being done to others and a failure of the self to progress beyond a crude ego. There's a pretty big fucking difference, and it's doing no one any good to let it continue unchecked.

Of course, this devotion to the unparalleled excellence of the self is not shared by all boys, but it's held in some way by the ones who eagerly embrace the teachings of a man like Yiannopoulos. It may spawn from unbridled arrogance (think here of the private school boys whose parents pay top dollar for their school fees so that their teachers are never allowed to discipline them or even say that they're wrong; the same boys who participate in online communities that exploit and criminally abuse their female peers because it's 'funny', who are backed up sometimes by parents claiming the girls 'asked for it', and who view it as a good way to solidify the relationships they share with their figurative brothers). Or perhaps it stems from the opposite—a false bravado born out of a crushing sense of inadequacy and a desire to right this clear wrong (feminism has gone too far, men are the oppressed ones now, this is why men are killing themselves etc.) Whatever its motivation, the end result is the same: a collective sense of invincibility that has a recognisable thread of cherished masculinity woven through it.

But what these boys and men also share is a desire for blood. Not literally, of course, but blood in the sense of destruction. It's obvious in their language and online dynamics that they want to watch someone they consider an enemy be torn to pieces and 'destroyed', as they put it, not only for their amusement but also because they think that witnessing this annihilation is somehow owed to them. This is why one of the most common challenges demanded by the average internet edgelord is that you (and anyone else whose political position threatens them) agree to 'debate' either them or whichever infamous troll they happen to be fapping over that week.

Over the last year or so, I've had to field numerous demands from men—most of them adolescent boys, from the looks of their profiles—that I 'debate Milo' in particular. My refusal is regarded as proof that I know he'll 'destroy' me (there's that word again). Sometimes the two ideas are joined together, I guess in the spirit of playing an open hand.

'Debate Milo,' they shriek, 'because I want to watch him destroy you!'

Sounds fun!

It's easy to dismiss Yiannopoulos as a sort of poor man's Puck, but he represents a much broader problem with how some young men are being socialised to act in online spaces. The British journalist Laurie Penny once wrote of Yiannopoulos: 'I have seen the death of political discourse reflected in his designer sunglasses.' It is perhaps one of the most accurate things ever to have been written about the man who calls Donald Trump 'Daddy', and in doing so encourages in his followers a feverish loyalty and devotion to the self-proclaimed 'pussy grabber'. It's a level of engagement that appeals especially to the boys being bred to have complete and unwavering faith in their own supremacy, providing them with an easy means of discounting anything that remotely challenges them and one that conveniently requires no experience, knowledge or intellectual rigour to uphold. (Mitchell Ivers, the editor working on Yiannopoulos's book before Simon & Schuster cancelled the contract, even suggested in his copy-edits: 'Careful that the egotistical boasting that your young audience finds humorous doesn't make you seem juvenile to other readers.')

Who needs facts and conversational convention when you can just scream 'fake news' at anything you don't like and claim the speaker is angry, ugly, afraid and mentally unwell? How liberating for the young men drawn to this level of discourse, and empowered further by the mirthful hollers of the braying crowd?

Like me, Penny has also been frequently instructed by the internet's enthusiastic bloodletters to go head to head with Yiannopoulos, but has responded with characteristic insight and vulnerability. 'I have never understood this game,' she wrote in 2016. 'That's why I've always refused to debate Milo in public. Not because I'm frightened I'll lose, but because I *know* I'll lose, because I care and he doesn't—and that means he's already won. Help and forgive me, but I actually believe human beings can be better than this.'

Human beings can indeed be better than this, but that doesn't mean they will be. And this is what one comes to understand about engaging in this kind of battle online, where the rules and conventions of formal debate were long ago lost and any vestige of them has been disdainfully thrown away: the only way to 'win' is to understand that winning at any cost is all that matters. Qualifications, knowledge and expertise are irrelevant—if you can shout the loudest, you can box in the ring. Because it isn't just Yiannopoulos who feels entitled to a public showdown with the people with whom he disagrees—it's everyone, from the administrator of the local men's rights chapter's Facebook page to the anonymous teenage shitlord whose primary experience of the world comes from hanging around on 4chan or Reddit (if he's feeling sophisticated that day).

Your opponent may have no better argument than to dismiss an entire political movement as 'cancer', to mock its practitioners as fat, feral and sexless, or to recite obnoxious and easily disproven statements such as 'the wage gap doesn't exist' and 'rape culture isn't real', but the use of sound bites and sneers as a means of dialogue will sadly be more than satisfactory to an audience of his supportive peers and fellow ideologues. This is what makes dealing with this kind of repetitive arrogance so infuriating—not that the request for a debate is unreasonable, but that it is repeatedly made in bad faith. Why would anyone feel inclined to offer themselves up to a room of angry, spoilt and entitled men to be verbally torn apart—and not by eviscerating intelligence but by the crudest and most basic of insults?

Call me crazy (and so many people have), but I consider finding ten different ways to tell someone they have a floppy, diseased vagina to be slightly more than a difference in opinion. And yet when women choose not to engage with this kind of repulsive and wholly unproductive dialogue it isn't because we recognise that it's beneath us. No, it's because we're hypocrites who can't defend our ideas. We're snowflakes who crumble under the weight of gentle critique. We're scared of facts and logic, babies who need to be agreed with otherwise we'll be #triggered. Also, we're fat and ugly and that's why we hate men.

There's a question in here with which all of society should be concerning itself, and it goes beyond the more philosophical query of what happened to actual debate. It's the question of how the language of misogyny most hateful became incorporated into the standard vocabularies of boys and men all over the world—boys and men who would, like today's modern white nationalists, become visibly irate at the suggestion they held anything other than exemplary views towards the group of people they routinely denigrate and dehumanise.

Let me share some examples of the reasoned 'critique' I received after a men's rights website wrote a blog post comparing me to Hitler and very kindly directed their enthusiastic readership to my page.

'You're obviously mentally retarded, being a "feminist" and all.'

'I swear, all this chick needs is a good solid rogering in her arse, by like 5. No. 6 dudes from across the world (no discrimination here) and she'd be happy again.'

'If your [sic] feeling hurt because someone calls you and [sic] ugly fat discusting [sic] snowflake fucking layde [sic] boy then get over it.'

'There is not one "woman" on this page that men would want to have sex with.'

'Hitler does not deserve to have feminist [sic] called feminazis. Poor Adolf. He could have prevented this.'

'I think women deserve equal rights, and lefts!'

'You're just craving some cock and don't know how to say it.'

'You shit-thick thundercunt.'

'Shut up retard.'

'Go sit on a butcher knife swine.'

'A real man keeps his woman batered [sic].'

'Good job you slimey [sic] fat cunt, I really do hope you are the next one raped.'

What can you say to that? To engage is to willingly open oneself up to a discussion devoid of facts or any real arguments, and in which points are awarded by the audience based on how many 'sick burns' can be made about owning cats (remembering, of course, that these insults are only allowed if they go one way—if you were to respond in kind, you'd be guilty of 'ad hominem' and 'typical feminazi behaviour, resorting to insults instead of facts'). To ignore them is to admit defeat and acknowledge your inferior abilities and intellectual vacuity.

The impossibility of it reminds me of the arguments I used to have with my brother and sister when we were small enough to be forgiven for being intolerable little shits. Anyone with a sibling will be familiar with the game Wave Your Finger Around Your Brother Or Sister's Face Until They Scream For Parental Intervention,

At Which Point You Gleefully Repeat Over And Over, 'I'm Not Touching You! I'm Not Touching You!'

The internet's Angry Young Men, stuck as they are in a state of arrested development, operate in much the same way. It isn't their fault if you *choose* to get personally offended or upset by their behaviour. They're not even touching you! If you can't handle a bit of gentle antagonism when they're not even touching you, then you're the one with the problem.

Being expected to tolerate such mindless, brain-numbing verbal diarrhoea with good grace is a burden frequently placed on women, and this is what Yiannopoulos represents to the men who eagerly herald him as their messiah (and yes, he does have female fans who are no doubt attracted to his racism, his transphobia and his hatred of the left but who also have enough internalised misogyny to think that if they can just be the best Official Woman ever, these men will somehow treat them as an exception): his deliberately offensive bombast provides cover for those who think they should be absolved from ever having to face up to the consequences of their actions. They scream for a debate while at the same time lashing out at any of the women who dare to fight back against them. They don't want women to stand up for themselves or to be given the opportunity to defend their ideas and arguments in an adult environment. They want us to sit there like good little girls, absorbing their hatred and anger and reassuring them of their supreme importance to this world. This is what a debate looks like in their minds. It's a thousand men forcing a woman to silently endure their animosity, insecurity and unbridled rage while they collectively jerk off before ejaculating all over her face.

■

It's all too easy for people to think this behaviour is confined to the worst and most immature of teenage boys, but the reality is frighteningly different. It's becoming more commonplace online and more normalised in the mainstream media we create and consume. Yiannopoulos slowly clawed his way from being an obnoxious troll at the fringes of the far right (the new wave of which is known as the 'alt-right', a term that seems obscenely sanitised to me) and onto airwaves beamed directly into people's homes across America and the world beyond. He regurgitates basic, outrageous bigotry as a way of exploiting the short attention span of modern-day consumers so he can cultivate the appearance of being an expert, and it's effective in both recycling and reinforcing views that would otherwise be subjected to intellectual testing. But a readership that forms its opinions on the basis of headlines rather than news content responds very well to ostentatious sound bites, which makes someone like Yiannopoulos a sinister choice for establishment industries to propel into the mainstream.

Which brings us back to that function centre in Adelaide. After losing a series of employment and speaker opportunities following his guest slot on a podcast in which he appeared to condone sexual relationships between adult men and adolescent boys, Yiannopoulos needed somewhere to regroup (and refuel his ego). Where else for him to head but the welcoming bosom of his vast Australian fan base? We are a country girt by rednecks, racists and misogynists, after all. More pertinently, we slobber over any North American or British import, no matter what their philosophy or actual talent. The American media had spurned Yiannopoulos when he revealed that condoning even paedophilia was a depth to which he was willing to sink, but the Australian media wasted no time in rolling out the red carpet for him. His five-city tour was sponsored by *Penthouse Australia* magazine (I was *shocked* to discover they hated women—shocked, I tell you!) and promoted by 'celebrity agent' Max Markson. It also featured hosts Andrew Bolt (a newspaper columnist, radio and television presenter, and convicted racist—so maybe not that much of a surprise, really), Mark Latham (an unhinged collection of used aeroplane vomit bags that have been sculpted into the approximate shape of a human male, and also a former prime ministerial candidate) and Ross Cameron (a knob). David Leyonhjelm, the Libertarian senator and universally recognised Awful Human, also invited Yiannopoulos to speak at Parliament House in Canberra, with members of Pauline Hanson's One Nation (of Dickheads) racing to occupy the front row.

God, we're a country of embarrassing eejits.

My own personal feelings about Yiannopoulos aside, I find it deeply concerning that a man who espouses such relentlessly hateful views has found such a substantial audience here. As Laurie Penny so eloquently wrote, he represents the death of political discourse. How can we possibly hope to have productive conversations around gender inequality when the rules of engagement are so decidedly nasty and lawless?

As far as fighting goes, it's seductive. Who hasn't experienced a spike in adrenaline when they've gone head to head with someone in the comments section of an *ABC News* post? Even when the tide of public opinion (full of shit and debris as it is) turns against you, it's still impossible not to keep checking on those notifications.

Cuck!

Feminazi!

Snowflake!

Fat bitch!

Man hater!

Cunt!

Gone are the days when you would be required to convince an audience of your argument by using conventional methods that involve an actual critical understanding of your topic. Now it's just humiliating the other person and talking over the top of them while everyone present laughs uproariously (see also: the behaviour of Donald Trump during the 2016 US presidential debates and, indeed, his entire presidency). Ironically, the same people who bay for blood at the thought of this kind of event are always first in line to complain if they think a man somewhere might be being unfairly picked on. It's true that I give as good as I get, and I've definitely thrown my fair share of insults. But funnily enough, this tactic coming from me is never defended as 'free speech' or a 'debate'. Instead, it's always loudly framed as an assault while the goalposts are quietly shifted once again in the background. Women (for it is mostly women) are expected to stand there and absorb the staggering amount of hatred that men can collectively direct towards us as some kind of payment for even having audible opinions, and fighting back often just opens us up to more abuse.

I have never cared that Milo Yiannopoulos and his band of merry misogynists think I'm unfuckable. It's not the first time I've been called that and it certainly won't be the last now that men all over the world have a convenient meme they can just tweet at me whenever their penises get a bit twitchy. I couldn't be happier that they don't want to subject me to the three minutes of bad to average sex they invariably offer to the other, unluckier women (or men) in their lives.

What angers me, though, is that this use of images and slogans to dehumanise and discredit women is a form of abuse that's becoming far more common. I have the power to fight back against it, but countless others don't. And in addition to the general abuse we have to field online, we have to deal with a new form of stalking that follows us into the digital space despite all our efforts to put up boundaries. I was very clear that I didn't want to have anything to do with Yiannopoulos when he visited Australia. With the exception of a handful of tweets explaining why, I didn't write or say anything about him publicly because I refused to give him the attention he so desperately craves (and please note the irony that women are often told to 'just ignore it', as if this will somehow make 'it' magically disappear). Yet I was still effectively harassed by mainstream media outlets determined to make a story out of our political opposition. I was still bombarded by comments and messages on my public social media accounts from his followers demanding I debaaaaaaaaate Miiiiiiiilo. And in the end, when I *still* refused to play the game according to his rules and give him what he wanted (which was basically the opportunity to call me a fat cat lover with daddy issues on national television, despite the fact I fucking hate cats), he decided to just insert me into his pathetic sideshow act anyway.

This whole game is so insidious and dastardly, and anyone with any kind of moral conscience at all automatically begins playing it on the back foot. The onus is always on the person being targeted to defend themselves for being so 'weak' that they can't just deal with it and move on. To show vulnerability is to lose.

How fucking sad is that?

In the end, this is one of the things that should concern us most. Boys raised in our patriarchal world need no help with killing off the parts of themselves that are vulnerable and earnest. Raised with the tropes of stoic masculinity and boorishness, men can find an easy home in a community of Milos. Yes, from this place of privilege they are capable of causing untold harm to anyone who threatens their inflated sense of self. But the compassionate side of me also feels sad for them. It must be very lonely to live in a world where 'cuck', 'white knight', 'mangina' and 'soy boy' are seen as legitimate ways to emasculate each other—to *destroy* each other and to do it gleefully and with no regrets.

Make no mistake, we absolutely need to challenge the vicious abuse girls and women are bombarded with every day. It hampers our ability to live free and autonomous lives, particularly in the unavoidable landscape carved out by modern technology. It has a severe impact on our mental health, and contributes to the widespread gaslighting that's part and parcel of growing up female in a patriarchal world. We do not have to show compassion to our abusers if we don't want to, nor are we obliged to hold their hands through the inevitable change in power structures that's coming. It's not an overstatement to characterise the toxic teachings of men like Yiannopoulos as being central to the radicalisation of today's young white men, and marginalised people (which includes women, but certainly isn't limited to us) do not have to negotiate with terrorists to secure their right to live peacefully.

But society—particularly that which thinks these problems are peripheral or nothing to do with them or just another case of 'boys being boys'—might also think about the impact this perpetration of abuse does for the young men being indoctrinated into its ideology. As bell hooks warned, 'If an individual is not successful in emotionally crippling himself, he can count on patriarchal men to enact rituals of power that will assault his self-esteem.' So it is that young men are not only destroying the tenacity that exists in the women they're being taught to mistrust and fear; they're also obliterating the vulnerability that exists in themselves. And as the grenades go off one by one, no one's spared from the violent, bloody fall-out.

—7—

THE MANOSPHERE

A few months after the release of my first book, I was invited by the University of Melbourne to deliver a lunchtime lecture on the subject of rape culture. When I arrived at the library, I was surprised to learn that the organisers had arranged for a security guard to be present. Apparently they had received a complaint from a men's rights activist who was upset that a man-hating feminazi terrorist (I'm paraphrasing) had been considered an appropriate speaker. He was concerned for his safety, he told them. He had reason to believe that I might try to hurt him, because of my known vendetta against straight white men. (His fears were not ill-founded. It's a well-known fact that I am amassing a collection of straight white men in the crawl space beneath my house, and when I have properly trained them they will be released back into society with a terrifying new skill set that includes knowing when their bedsheets need washing and being able to appreciate a gentle joke at their expense.)

My contacts at the university reassured the worried fellow that he would be perfectly safe. However, if he was concerned, then they recommended he consider staying far, far away from the venue where I would be speaking.

It probably goes without saying that the security guard was for my benefit.

Having just had a baby and hence being in a slightly more vulnerable state of mind than I would normally be, I was grateful for the organisers' consideration. Unfortunately, I can't say I was surprised that they deemed it necessary. It's not uncommon for me to turn up to events and hear straight away about the various people who took issue with me being there and the things they've done or said to make their anger about it known. Men who don't even live in the same state (and frequently not even in the same country) flock to Facebook event pages to leave abusive comments to organisers, links to defamatory blog posts about me and images of satirical tweets I've written that are presented as evidence of my violent hatred of the world's male population. Despite their fury over what they see as feminist and SJW attempts to 'censor' the voices of MRAs (men's rights activists), they sure do pull out all the stops when it comes to trying to fuck with your shit.

Before it was cancelled, I was due to speak at the 2018 Global Atheist Convention in Melbourne. The post announcing me as a speaker was inundated by thousands of angry men, all eager to share their incandescent rage that I might have anything to do with a movement that rejects the concept of deities. There's a stark irony in the fact that so many men who count themselves as atheists are also furious about women who refuse to bow down and worship them. I was told that a number of rape threats had

had to be deleted from the post's comments section, because of course the best way for men to disprove a feminist's central world view that 'world is fukt' is to gather together and threaten her with sexual violence.

The threats made against feminists are not always explicitly violent in nature. Sometimes, they amount to a concerted effort to destroy your financial opportunities. In 2017, I published a Facebook post announcing I had just signed a contract to write this book. That post was shared by Avid Reader, a bookstore in Brisbane with a wonderful reputation for supporting writers, artists and the tenets of basic human decency. Almost immediately, Avid Reader's Facebook page was bombed by one-star ratings accompanied by reviews blasting them for being 'anti-men'. The source of the backlash was quickly traced to an online group named *Anti-Feminism Australia*, a noxious community of MRAs whose leader seems to be particularly fixated with me. In addition to trolling businesses that support my work, the group has circulated a petition calling for my book contract to be cancelled, trawled through my Instagram archives to find photographs to publish under the headline WHO IS THE FATHER OF CLEMENTINE FORD'S BABY? and suggested I should be investigated by authorities for abusing my son. After Avid Reader shared my post, *AFA* posted a link to the store's business page with the caption: 'Avid Reader Bookshop and Cafe in Brisbane are promoting Clementine Ford's man hating book. Be sure to leave them a one star review for promoting the hatred of men.'

AFA have had success with this approach before. A Dymocks bookstore on the North Coast of New South Wales closed down their Facebook page after being flooded with one-star reviews by *AFA* members also complaining about their 'promotion' of me. Afterwards, *AFA* wrote a celebratory post declaring: 'A big thank you to everyone who helped expose Dymocks Charlestown bookstore for promoting Clementine Ford's book. As a result of many 1 star reviews and comments they have removed their page! That's what we call a success!'

The post went on to outline their motivation more clearly: 'We need to keep exposing and shaming any business or organization that promotes Clementine Ford or gives a platform [sic] to preach her hateful ideology. If she is rejected by enough businesses she will have no where [sic] to go and will eventually fade away. Remember this misandrist makes a living out of hating men.'

Well, now. I would hardly call it a *living*. A stipend, perhaps. A bit of pocket money at the most. But not a living. If only it paid that well!

AFA's attempts to troll Avid Reader backfired spectacularly. Not only did the bookstore's social media manager respond by thoroughly ridiculing them, prominent members of Australia's literary scene (some of whom were actually Avid Reader staff alum) rallied others to leave their own glowing five-star reviews. By the end of the day, Avid Reader's page likes had increased by a few thousand and their rating hovered at roughly 4.8. As an added bonus, Dymocks Charlestown reinstated their Facebook business page and very quickly re-established a four-star rating too.

It's childish behaviour from men who feel angry because they aren't taken seriously, but tantrums such as this in response to my work are so common that it seems almost normal now. I once missed a phone call from the (now former) editor of the *Sydney Morning Herald*. The voicemail he left sounded so grave and serious that I was convinced I was about to lose my job. I phoned him back in a panic, preparing myself for annihilation when he said there was something he needed to discuss with me.

'We've received some quite concerning correspondence in relation to you,' he began.

'Oh really?' I replied, scanning my memory to see if I'd done anything illegal recently—like how you drive past a police car and suddenly freak out that you might have stolen the vehicle you're in and somehow forgotten it.

'Yes,' he replied. 'It's a photocopied picture of you with some pretty nasty things written on it. Look, I don't really feel comfortable reading them out loud to you, but I wanted you to know that we're taking this very seriously and we've forwarded it on to police.'

Adrenaline suddenly flooded through my body and I burst out laughing.

'Is that all?!' I exclaimed. 'For a minute I was worried something really bad had happened!'

It's an odd feeling to find yourself explaining to one of your most senior employers that a handwritten letter calling you a whore is actually on the tamer end of the scale when it comes to your daily fan mail. It's an expression of aggressive misogyny, sure, but it's also nice to see that there are some people who still know how to use a pen. The vast majority of the abuse I receive is meted out in the same default fonts favoured by social media platforms and email accounts, and it gets a bit samey. You want to see the flourishes of someone's personal calligraphy as they call for you to be throat-raped or fucked by a donkey, and I naturally offer humble admiration to anyone who continues to persevere with the Australian postal service.

I think some people are surprised by how easily I deal with the torrent of abuse sent my way but, honestly, it's because it's difficult to imagine a more pathetic group of people than the men who, for various reasons, have decided to spend their lives telling women on Twitter that a good hard cocking would cure them of their bitterness. And they could get one, too, if they weren't so fucking fat.

Imagine the world's most unappealing assortment of chocolates, with flavours like 'urinal cake', 'unwashed dick' and 'silent fart in an elevator' all crammed into a plastic tray that's covered in the slick grease of an unwashed barnet. Men's rights activists, internet shitlords, teenage boys who spend too much time on conspiracy websites, Mark Latham—they might each have their own specific grievances and concerns, but if you threw them in a cauldron (you probably have a few floating around) and boiled them all down together you'd find that their flavours were fairly indistinguishable.

At least, this is the impression gleaned after spending even the barest amount of time surveying the internet's 'manosphere'. Drawing together users from 4chan, 8chan, Reddit, YouTube, Twitter, Facebook, independently run blogs and the sewerage pipes that connect the lot of them, the vast toilet system that makes up this manosphere can be accurately summarised by three words: angry, paranoid and entitled.

In his book *Alt-America: The Rise of the Radical Right in the Age of Trump*, David Neiwert refers to MRA websites in particular as being 'like wildlife refuges for misogynist ideas'. As he notes, 'They call feminists "a social cancer," and assert, "Feminism is a hate movement designed to disenfranchise and dehumanize men."' To illustrate his point, Neiwert references a blog written by an MRA with the moniker Alcuin. Alcuin argues, 'Just as the Nazis had to create a Jewish conspiracy as a way to justify mass slaughter, so feminists have to create patriarchy as a way to justify mass slaughter of innocent unborn, and the destruction of men and masculinity. Rape is now a political crime, not a crime of sex or violence.'

Alcuin appears to have made his blog private now, but I managed to track down a post in which he rails against the characterisation of MRAs as 'angry' and 'hate-filled'. MRAs are kind creatures, he argues, but the 'feminist-run media' has painted them in a bad light. Instead, he says, 'A lot of articles and comments simply offer observations based on experience. A guy finds out that western women prefer alphas, sleep around easily, turn their love into hatred at a moment's notice, use shaming language, are sweet only when they want something, fuck their boyfriend's best friend, walk out on their family or, more common, kick the husband out. Why shouldn't he warn others about this behaviour? It's a public service, actually.'

It's misogyny, actually.

Despite their solid standing in the world's legion of Angry Men, MRAs are a slightly more worrisome breed of creep because they use some of the genuine issues men face as a sort of Trojan Horse via which they can sneak a far more insidious agenda into the public discourse. MRAs are capable of recognising the harm that patriarchy does to men—the increased risk of suicide, the shunting of their emotional selves, the substantial impact that violence has on men's lives—but instead of working with feminists to dismantle this system of structural oppression, they've identified women as its source. The curious logic of the average MRA holds that feminism and the fight for women's liberation is not only unnecessary (because women *obviously* have more power and privilege than men because we can have sex whenever we want—*yes, really, this is an argument that some of them earnestly expound*), but that every harm identified by feminism can be countered by an equal and opposite harm being enacted by women against men. Misogyny and misandry are treated by MRAs as interchangeable, with the latter being widely viewed as 'just as bad, if not worse'. According to Newton's Third Law of Motion, for every action there is an equal and opposite reaction. So it is that MRAs view the battleground of sexism. Every time a bell rings, a she-witch somewhere commits a radical misandry against an unsuspecting man.

Yes, Ben Folds said it best when he observed that, 'Y'all don't know what it's like / Being male, middle class and white.'

Central to the MRA argument is their insistence that women experience some kind of disproportionate 'female privilege' that actually provides them with more advantages than men. In the MRA handbook, female privilege includes the following: being able to speak to men without being considered predatory; being able to have sex 'whenever you want'; being able to decide whether or not to continue with a pregnancy (as opposed to 'having a child forced on you so that a scheming bitch can rob you blind for the next eighteen years'); being able to have sex with a man and then later change your mind while accusing him of rape; having the right to leave a marriage because the courts will *automatically* favour you in a custody dispute, despite this not having been the case for over twenty years; not having to pay for dinner or drinks. Female privilege is also receiving, as the Pulitzer prize-winning journalist George F. Will put it in the *Washington Post*, the 'coveted status' of being a rape survivor on a college campus and all the advantages that come with that ('Colleges become the victims of progressivism', 6 June 2014).

With the exception of that last charge, which is so despicably offensive that it's almost impossible to believe it came out of an actual person's brain, all these examples of 'female privilege' seem less indicative of a rising gynarchy poised to crush whimpering men with a gigantic, comfortably shod foot than they are things some men either want or don't want women to be able to do (say no to sex; pursue sex; have an abortion; have a baby; report sexual assault; get a divorce). It is not 'female privilege' for a woman to have the final say over whether or not she grows a foetus inside her for nine months before birthing it and then raising it. Having done all those things (the third is an ongoing project), I can assure you it's not a fucking frolic in the park. While we're at it, can we all agree that it's a curious bit of cognitive dissonance to argue against paying to support children you don't want in one breath while ranting about how the legal system helps women steal them from you in the other? And by the way, the belief that women can just walk out of their house and fall on a dick of their choosing is patently false. For example, I have never fallen onto Oscar Isaacs' dick and it's not like I haven't tried.

The argument that the fight for gender equality has swung 'too far' to the other side is simply ludicrous. One woman is still killed by her partner or ex-partner every week in Australia. The World Health Organization estimates that 30 percent of women worldwide who have been in a sexual relationship have experienced some form of violence within that partnership. The two issues most integral to women's equality—reproductive autonomy and financial independence—are still not considered legally sacrosanct for the overwhelming majority of women in the world today.

And we've got men (and some women) not just complaining that feminism is subjugating men, but claiming that it's gripped them in a vice so tight they need to stage their own *movement*?

I'll let you in on a little secret. The feminist mafia in Australia *is* trying to erode men's rights, and we've had some success over the years. Like the right for a man to rape his wife. Destroyed that. Or the right of men alone to determine who rises to political leadership. We nailed that one too. Or how about the right of husbands to consider their wives as their physical property, and for a husband to have the right to commit his wife to a mental asylum (as many did) as a means of securing a divorce, leaving him free to marry another (often, younger) woman? Yep, got rid of that. So referring to 'female privilege' (particularly in a world where, in some places, it's still considered a privilege when girl babies are even allowed to live) as some kind of nefarious threat to the psychic wellbeing of men isn't just offensive, it's also dangerous. It provides a focal point of blame for the frustrations of men who feel they've somehow been denied all that was promised to them, and it can have terrifying and often violent ramifications for the women in their lives.

■

You'll notice that a good deal of the angst and fury of Angry Internet Men is wrapped up in sex: specifically, women who will not have it with them. More criminal than their rejection, though, is the fact that these women are *obviously* having sex with everyone else, because they are trashy sluts who have had a parade of cocks in them, so who do they think they are to be so fucking *discerning*?

It's a stance eagerly embraced by *Return of Kings*, established in 2012 as 'a blog for heterosexual, masculine men' with the aim to 'usher the return of the masculine man in a world where masculinity is being increasingly punished and shamed in favour of creating an androgynous and politically correct society that allows women to assert superiority and control over men'. Articles published on *RoK* boast such titles as: 'Women should not be allowed to vote', 'Young girls are better than older women', 'The Intellectual inferiority of women' and '27 attractive girls who became ugly freaks because of feminism'.

As the founder and face of *Return of Kings*, Daryush 'Roosh' Valizadeh has become something of a hero to the insecure, occasionally deranged men who make up his fan base. He claims to have coined the term 'neomasculinity', a wackadoo ideology that basically states women are only valuable if they're young and fertile, and that men prove their value by fucking them. Roosh started his career as a pick-up artist (or PUA), teaching men how to hook up with women by asserting their 'alpha' status and borderline raping them.

That may sound like a hyperbolic accusation, but you need only look to his own work to see how close it is to the truth. For a long time, Roosh's primary source of income came from his *Bang!* series, a collection of travel guides aimed at men who wanted to screw their way around Europe and South America. I say 'screw', but they've been widely condemned not just for encouraging rape but for recounting Roosh's own numerous experiences as a rapist.

In *Bang Iceland*, Roosh writes:

> While walking to my place, I realised how drunk she was. In America, having sex with her would have been rape, since she couldn't legally give her consent. It didn't help matters that I was relatively sober, but I can't say I cared or even hesitated. I won't rationalize my actions, but having sex is what I do.

As David Futrelle, author of the anti-MRA website, *We Hunted the Mammoth*, wrote in 2015, 'Sex with women too drunk to consent is considered rape in Iceland as well as in the US.'

In *Bang Ukraine*, Roosh brags about the time he turns an initially consensual sexual encounter into rape. *(Warning: the following excerpt contains a graphic description of sexual assault.)*

> I was fucking her from behind, getting to the end in the way I normally did, when all of a sudden she said, 'Wait stop, I want to go back on top.' I refused and we argued ... She tried to squirm away while I was laying down my strokes so I had to use some muscle to prevent her from escaping. I was able to finish, but my orgasm was weak. Afterwards I told her she was selfish and that she couldn't call an audible so late in the game.

So, to recap, his sexual partner told him to stop and he not only refused, he also 'had to use some muscle' to hold her down and 'prevent her from escaping'. And after he finished raping her, he called her selfish.

Neomasculinity, hey?

Roosh is not an outlier in the MRA world, even though he publicly distances himself from the movement. The belief that men have been stripped of their natural roles as 'leaders' (and the rewards that come with it, which always, *always* include access to nubile young women's bodies) is fundamental to the MRA philosophy, as is the conviction that they must work towards restoring this balance. That's why they embrace philosophies like that of the Red Pill movement (MRA dork code for 'taking the Red Pill' à la *The Matrix*, and 'seeing' the true reality of the femofascist dictatorship under which we labour), pick-up artistry and 'returning' to those glorious days of yore in which they were 'kings'. It's why they're drawn to the work of Milo Yiannopoulos, Alex Jones from *InfoWars* and even (perhaps especially) Donald 'The President' Trump, all of whom give them licence to say what they want to whomever they want and ignore any and all consequences. Feminism is cancer! Women are whores who think everyone should pay for their birth control! Grab 'em by the pussy—they'll let you do it!

Those who are drawn to this kind of rhetoric ignore the fact that patriarchy has generally never favoured men of their calibre. It may soothe them somewhat to fantasise about (or even act on) taking what they want from women through violence or force, but their real gripe should be laid at the feet of patriarchy itself. Unfortunately, this would require actual work and introspection. It would require challenging *other men*. Far easier (and less intimidating) to pretend that uppity women are the problem.

The lack of wholesome, positive communities for men in a society that so often denies raw sensitivity to them can't be underestimated. Opportunities for bonding are limited, and too many of the ones available require the degradation of somebody else. Men who frequent MRA websites (or PUA ones, or basic shitlord communities whose only goal is to out-edge each other) derive an enormous amount of satisfaction from trolling the people they believe are somehow denying them power. They argue that women manufacture rape claims, and so express their anger over this by coordinating with each other to threaten to rape them. They are pathologically afraid of women encroaching on the spaces and communities they feel belong to them. Women who transgress these rigidly enforced boundaries can be doxxed (internet slang for documents being deliberately leaked), their home addresses, phone numbers and private details published online to make the world just that much more terrifying for them.

When game developer Zoe Quinn's *Depression Quest* received positive reviews in 2013, she began to receive hate mail almost immediately. But the harassment escalated when Eron Gjoni, Quinn's bitter ex-boyfriend, published an online rant alleging she had slept with a journalist in exchange for a positive review. As it turns out, the journalist in question had never written the review—but Quinn may have slept with him, and in a community that pulses with image-based exploitation (more commonly known as 'revenge porn'), slut-shaming and aggressively entitled masculine dominance, that appears to be the more unforgivable crime.

The unwarranted backlash spawned #Gamergate, a thinly constructed Twitter 'movement' that pretended to be about 'ethics in gaming journalism' but, as prominent feminist games and media critic Anita Sarkeesian observed, very quickly revealed itself to be a 'sexist temper tantrum' more concerned with silencing critics of misogyny in gaming culture and keeping women out completely. Sarkeesian had already inspired the wrath of gamers all over the world when she used a Kickstarter campaign to create her *Tropes vs. Women in Video Games* YouTube series, and gamergaters wasted no time in ramping up the abuse. Video game developer Brianna Wu was likewise targeted after she posted a series of tweets about gamergaters, quipping that they were 'fighting an apocalyptic future where women are 8 percent of programmers and not 3 percent'. Quinn, Sarkeesian and Wu were all doxxed by furious gamergaters, each receiving dozens of death threats and/or rape threats. In September 2014, an anonymous message was posted to 4chan, that community of juvenile 'edgelords' feverishly committed to their campaign of abuse and silencing.

'Next time [Quinn] shows up at a conference we . . . give her a crippling injury that's never going to fully heal . . . a good solid injury to the knees. I'd say a brain damage, but we don't want to make it so she ends up too retarded to fear us.'

A month later, a Twitter user named 'Death To Brianna' (@chatterwhiteman) tweeted at Wu, 'I've got a K-Bar and I'm coming to your house so I can shove it up your ugly feminist cunt.' It was part of a series of tweets that included threats like, 'Your mutilated corpse will be on the front page of Jezebel tomorrow and there isn't jack shit you can do about it,' and, 'If you have any kids, they're going to die too. I don't give a shit. They'll grow up to be feminists anyway.'

But remember, it's about ethics in gaming journalism.

Roosh may have been peripheral to this, but the festering community of rage-wankers he comes from shares a lot of similarities with #Gamergate. Chief among them is the unbridled hatred of women who not only refuse to know their place but seem oblivious to or disregard the place to which men are *entitled* as a birthright. Shortly after @chatterwhiteman publicly threatened to rape and murder Wu, Roosh published a post on *Return of Kings* pledging support to the #Gamergate movement and its efforts to destroy what he saw as a common enemy (people with a moral conscience, I guess). He wrote:

> Gamergate is an exciting development for our sphere because an external group is going up against our enemy. While gamergate is not our movement, I have chosen to aid them as much as possible. I won't take any credit for their victories,

> but I sure will enjoy the satisfaction of having my enemy defeated.

The idea that women (and the men who support them, and collectively fight for a better, more equitable world) are perceived as The Enemy is fundamental to understanding the mindset of the men who move through the manosphere, whether as out and proud MRAs, Red Pillers, 4channers, territorial gamers or lonely pick-up artists. They have been successfully conditioned by the patriarchal lie that says 'real men' are defined by their ability to dominate others and, in turn, command their respect. For some of them, their inability to embody these so-called 'masculine' values is felt as a source of deep shame. Others will exhibit naturally bullying traits, comfortable with the abuse of others and confident in their rule as Supreme Alpha Male.

The risk of the manosphere is in the way toxic behaviour and rage become weaponised against the people perceived to be standing between men and their 'biologically gifted power'. Roosh dehumanises women to an audience of thousands, encouraging the belief that we exist only as vessels for men to plunge their dicks into and only then if we happen to be young and fertile enough to 'deserve' them. To developmentally arrested men desperate to assert themselves as strong and virile, it's a pretty intoxicating message. Gamergaters nerd out over the integrity of the gaming space while secretly enjoying the fact their pretensions to some kind of larger moral goal allow them to get away with (and get off on) treating real-life women the way they treat the background character sex workers in *Grand Theft Auto*.

The vast majority of these men will swear blind that they don't hate women at all; that your accusations of misogyny or entitlement are ad hominem attacks; that they love women (the good, *nice* ones); and that death/rape threats posted on the internet are always just a joke. Is it their fault if women can't take a joke?

Easy things to say but if you really want to see toxic masculinity in action, you only have to look at how these same men excuse and sometimes even make martyrs of the men who actually do commit these acts of violence in real life.

After all, it's obvious, isn't it? If women would just be nicer to men, then men wouldn't be forced to hurt us.

■

> It's not fair. You girls have never been attracted to me. I don't know why you girls have never been attracted to me, but I will punish you all for it. It's an injustice, a crime, because I don't know what you don't see in me. I'm the perfect guy, and yet you throw yourselves at all these obnoxious men, instead of me, the supreme gentleman. I will punish you all for it.

These words were spoken as part of a video titled *Retribution*, filmed and uploaded onto YouTube on the night of 23 May 2014. The creator of the video was a twenty-two-year-old man named Elliot Rodger. *Retribution* was just one of many videos in which Rodger raged against what he saw as the 'injustice' of his virginity and lack of sexual prowess with women, but it was the one that outlined most clearly his violent plan for revenge.

> On the day of retribution, I will enter the hottest sorority house of UCSB, and I will slaughter every single spoiled stuck-up blonde slut I see inside there. All those girls that I've desired so much, they would have all rejected me and looked

> down upon me as an inferior man if I ever made a sexual advance towards them. While they throw themselves at these obnoxious brutes, I'll take great pleasure in slaughtering all of you. You will finally see that I am in truth the superior one. The true Alpha Male.

Shortly after posting 'Retribution', Rodger embarked on a massacre that saw him take six lives and seriously injure thirteen others. After fatally stabbing his three male housemates, he drove his black BMW through the Californian college community of Isla Vista and began shooting random members of the public. A stand-off with local law enforcement ended with Rodger shooting himself in the head.

Investigations after the massacre found that Rodger followed several men's rights channels on YouTube and was an active member in one online MRA community. In addition to *Retribution*, he also uploaded a 137-page manifesto titled *My Twisted World: The Story of Elliot Rodger.* The manifesto is an exhaustive recount of Rodger's life, each grievance and outrage described in meticulous detail. As numerous others have said, the clinical language is reminiscent of that used in Bret Easton Ellis's *American Psycho*, a novel about a similarly privileged young psychopath with a homicidal hatred of women. The fictional Patrick Bateman may not have had Rodger's sexual ineptitude, but he was likewise obsessed with measuring his worth as a man against the achievements and possessions of other men in his social sphere. And like Bateman, Rodger had a very clear idea of what he thought it meant to be a successful 'alpha' male. This dangerous belief system was fostered and indulged by the MRA and hyper-masculine communities he immersed himself in online. Despite growing up with money, Rodger was obsessed with winning the lottery. 'I mused that once I became wealthy, I would finally be worthy enough to all the beautiful girls.'

Being considered 'worthy' by 'beautiful girls' is a repetitive motif in Rodger's manifesto. At one point he writes, 'It's all girls' fault for not having any sexual attraction towards me.' Shortly after, speaking about his friend Dale, he laments bitterly, 'Women were never cruel to *him*. They gave him sex and love his whole life.' Chillingly, he observes towards the end of his tirade that: 'Women's rejection of me is a declaration of war, and if it's war they want, then war they shall have.'

Rodger's online footprint included frequent visits to the website *PUAHate*, a community of men committed to exposing 'the scams, deception, and misleading marketing techniques used by dating gurus and the seduction community to deceive men and profit from them'.

On paper, pushing back against the creepy and misogynistic fug of pick-up artistry sounds like a community service. In practice, *PUAHate* was a kvetching place for men who had poured thousands of dollars into learning how to bed beautiful women only to wallow in the same swamp of rejection. They'd paid their money and applied the techniques, so where were the women they were promised? Fucking hot guys, apparently. What a bunch of shallow, superficial *cunts*.

At least, this is how the members of *PUAHate* saw it, seemingly unaware of the double standard. As Katie J.M. Baker wrote for *Jezebel* in 2012, 'Isn't it a tad hypocritical for PUAHate posters, who seemingly think they deserve a bevy of beautiful ladies ready to have sex with them on command at all times, to criticize women who date attractive guys?'

PUAHate no longer exists (the site was closed down shortly after the massacre in Isla Vista) but at its heart it represented what's known as the 'incel' community. Short for 'involuntarily celibate', incels are predominantly straight, cis men who feel they are being forced into celibacy against their will because women refuse to have sex with them.

Yes, really.

So gripped by this idea of no-sex-as-oppression are incels that misogyny abounds. In their world view, women are not fully formed humans with rights to autonomy of their bodies *and* desires. Instead, they are cruel banshees who exploit a supposedly unfair hierarchy of attraction and need to purposefully humiliate and exclude the 'average' and 'below average' men who fail to live up to its superficial standards. Although it's not unique to them, there's a curious narcissism to incels that reflects the simultaneous strength of their self-hatred and self-obsession. Instead of just being ignorant of their existence or vaguely turned off by them, women are instead thought to be keenly aware of incel desperation. Denying sex to incels is perceived as more than basic rejection—it's an act of humiliation, deliberately waged and cruelly enjoyed by women who devote a lot of time to thinking about how much better they are than these men. To put it bluntly, incels behave as if they're the biggest piece of worthless shit floating right smack bang in the centre of the universe.

Basically, we're looking at a turducken of toxic masculinity, entitlement, self-obsession and rank misogyny.

Don't be tempted into feeling pity for incels. While some of them may be genuinely clueless chaps unable to figure out a way to overcome loneliness and social awkwardness, most are furious at women for (as Rodger lamented) refusing to 'give' them love and sex. Instead, they go for 'Chads', the jocks and d-bags (of course) who get laid whenever they want despite being arseholes because women are FICKLE BITCHES. (Incidentally, and to literally nobody's surprise, a number of the posts on *Anti-Feminism Australia* are rooted in incel ideology. In February 2018, a post appeared with the title 'Why Aussie men face dating inequality'. The author defends men who get angry or lash out following rejection, writing, 'Can you really blame those men? They probably just got rejected for the 100th time because they weren't in the top 10% of men that women go after. That is, men who are muscular, tall and rich.' Yanno, 'Chads'.)

In an unchecked community, this furious male entitlement to sex (and the subsequent rage felt at being denied it) feeds off itself. It isn't uncommon to discover incel threads of men discussing the ethics of having sex with dead bodies or the imperative a just society has to make rape legal. (In his manifesto, Rodger also wrote, 'Women should not have the right to choose who to mate with. That choice should be made for them by civilized men of intelligence.') In the incel world, shared fantasies of revenge homicide are not the exception; they're the norm. When news of Rodger's massacre hit incel communities, he was widely heralded as a hero. Even today, fan pages exist praising his actions—and no, not all of them are run by morality-free edgelords trying to get some 8chan cred. Some are genuinely agitating to follow in his footsteps.

Others would argue that venting about revenge doesn't necessarily mean a person will act on it. This is undoubtedly true. The vast majority of people who unleash angry tirades online are probably not going to go on a homicidal rampage. But enough of the people who *have* perpetrated massacres began by building an online portfolio of rage, indignation and pointed commentary outlining if not their exact plans, then something that arguably formed the basis of them.

In April 2018, a young man named Alek Minassian commandeered a white van in Toronto and drove it into a group of pedestrians. He was arrested and charged with ten counts of murder, and multiple further counts of attempted murder. Facebook later confirmed that a profile linked to Minassian had published a post shortly before the attack. It read: 'Private (Recruit) Minassian Infantry 00010, wishing to speak to Sgt 4chan please. C23249161. The Incel Rebellion has already begun! We will overthrow all the Chads and Stacys! All hail the Supreme Gentleman Elliot Rodger!'

Not too long after Minassian staged a mass murder in Toronto, a young man named Dimitrios Pagourtzis took a pistol and a shotgun into his Texas high school and opened fire, murdering eight students and two teachers. It later emerged that his first victim, Shana Fisher, had spent the previous four months rejecting Pagourtzis' 'aggressive' advances. Her mother told the *Los Angeles Times* that 'a week later he opens fire on everyone he didn't like, Shana being the first one'.

A month before Rodger slaughtered six people in Isla Vista, a sixteen-year-old Connecticut teen named Christopher Plaskon fatally stabbed his classmate Maren Sanchez, also sixteen. When police officers arrived, he announced, 'I did it. Just arrest me.' It soon emerged that on the morning of the murder, Plaskon had asked Sanchez to be his date for the upcoming junior prom. Sanchez and Plaskon were friends, but she had recently started dating another boy at the school. When she declined his invitation, Plaskon pulled out a knife and plunged it into her chest.

Afterwards, he threw her down the stairwell. Apparently, Sanchez had tried to alert the school's administration to Plaskon's violent tendencies but they had failed to act.

This is the terrible bind in which women find themselves within a toxic cultural mindset that prioritises men's 'need' for sex and affection over women's right to determine what feels unsafe or undesirable for us. When we listen to our instincts and complain about male behaviour, we're accused of seeing things that just aren't there. Stop making men feel bad! They're allowed to ask you out! How will the human race survive if men can't ask you out anymore? Stop doing that wishy-washy girl thing and just say no! What's the worst that could happen?!

As we know, there is a lot of 'worst' that could happen. We know it because we know what misogyny and male entitlement writ large looks like. The denial of its existence is what allows violence against women to flourish, from incessant street harassment to sexual assault to murder. This violence is the shadow under which we live and the threat we fear. It's what allows a young man to believe so fervently that he is 'owed' female attention and adoration. And it's what makes him decide to punish those who deny it to him. This isn't theoretical. It's proven time and time again by the actions of men who choose to enact violence against women they believe have emasculated them.

Shortly after Isla Vista, a Tumblr site appeared called *When Women Refuse*. The project was established as a direct response to the massacre, particularly the subsequent claims that violence of its kind was 'an isolated incident'. *When Women Refuse* documents in blistering, brutal, devastating detail the violent retaliation that is often inflicted on women when they reject men's sexual advances. From image-based exploitation to beatings and, in all too many cases, even murder, the sheer number of men who seem unable to handle being denied access to women of their choosing is staggering.

There's Christopher O'Krowley, who shot and killed his co-worker, Caroline Nosal, because she didn't want to pursue a romantic relationship with him. There's Raelynn Vincent, whose decision to ignore a man catcalling her from a car one night resulted in the stranger stopping his vehicle to pursue her and punch her in the face hard enough to break her jaw. There's no shortage of irony in the fact that women are also told to 'just ignore street harassment' or even respond positively to it because 'it's a compliment, if anything'. Tell that to Janese Talton-Jackson, who turned down Charles McKinney at a Pittsburgh bar. As she left for home later that night, McKinney followed her and fatally shot her in the chest. And what about Yan Chi 'Anthony' Cheung, an Australian pharmacist who pled guilty to one count of poisoning to injure or cause distress or pain after his victim and colleague, Pamela Leung, observed CCTV footage of him drugging her water and coffee at least twenty-three times over the course of a year. Leung had previously confronted Cheung over his sexual advances, which included '[brushing] past her breasts, buttocks and hands'. Cheung retaliated by drugging her with medications like Phenergan, doxylamine, Endep, Seroquel and Deptran.

A few months before he killed six people in Isla Vista, Rodger posted on *PUAHate*, 'If we can't solve our problems we must DESTROY our problems. One day incels will realise their true strength and numbers, and will overthrow this oppressive feminist system. Start envisioning a world where WOMEN FEAR YOU.'

Newsflash. Women already fear men, with good reason. It isn't just because some of them, like Rodger, believe their masculinity is anointed by putting their dick in a vagina. It's because beyond the terrifying incel community, there are people whose pity outstrips their rationality when it comes to socially awkward men who are 'shackled' by their virginity or fumbling attempts to connect with women. And here's where we come to the most frightening aspect of incel ideology and misogynist retribution against women viewed as the root of men's problems: it's that altogether too many people are able to recognise the abhorrent nature of Rodger's actions *while also expressing sympathy for what must have driven him to them.*

He did a terrible, horrible, no good, very bad thing—but if women had just *given him a chance* then he wouldn't have been so angry. Rejection is hard! Humiliation is harder! Sexual frustration is the hardest! I'm not saying it's women's fault necessarily when men take all these things out on the world, but maybe if women weren't so picky about who they bone then he wouldn't have had to. You know?

On *Return of Kings*, Roosh condemned the massacre but still found a way to blame it on American women, who, according to him, 'have been encouraged to pursue exciting and fun casual sex in their prime with sexy and hot men as a way of "experimentation".' As ripper as that actually sounds, it's apparently bad because 'until you allow and encourage all men to get sex by some means, these massacres will be more commonplace as America's cultural decline continues'.

Roosh is a particularly awful person, but the view of women as sexual gatekeepers extends well beyond his PUA rape corner of the internet. Men 'need' sex in a way that women don't, and not being able to access it makes them go cuckoo. It's our job, therefore, to release their pressure valves once in a while . . . or on our heads be it.

Not every boy will turn out like Elliot Rodger, Christopher Plaskon, Alek Minassian, Dimitrios Pagourtzis or even Roosh, but these men are also not outliers in an otherwise unproblematic system. They are frightening end points on a spectrum of behaviours that, even at the less homicidal end, still conditions boys and men to feel entitled to women's attention and bodies as a means of establishing their masculine power. The concept of 'alpha masculinity' is almost entirely destructive to both the boys who are raised to measure themselves against it and the girls who are expected to succumb to it. We do a disservice to young men (even the pitiful ones) when we make excuses for them or trivialise their participation in these subcultures. We need to disrupt the messages that are filtered through every aspect of culture: messages that tell young men their masculinity is defined by how well they command the people around them, particularly the women; messages that frame women as rewards for men who compare favourably to other men, that have for generations shown fictional male heroes 'winning' women at the end of their quests.

In his brilliant article 'Your princess is in another castle: Misogyny, entitlement, and nerds', writer and self-proclaimed nerd Arthur Chu reflects on the lessons boys are taught from pop culture about what they 'deserve'. He writes:

> . . . the overall problem is one of a culture where instead of seeing women as, you know, people, protagonists of their own stories just like we are of ours, men are taught that women are things to 'earn,' to 'win.' That if we try hard enough and persist long enough, we'll get the girl in the end. Like life is a video game and women, like money and status, are just part of the reward we get for doing well.

Again, not every spurned man will respond to his own unexamined rage by grabbing a gun or a knife or even just a well-organised online harassment squad and slaying whichever woman has pissed him off that day. But enough of them do for us to know that it's a problem. We don't stop it by isolating them from each other and passing their deeds off as the result of mental illness or depression. We understand it by recognising it as part of a culture of learned entitlement *in which the logical endpoint for falling short is violence and retribution.*

We change it by going back to the beginning, and starting again.

—8—

YOUR HONOUR, I OBJECT

I have ideas about women who spend evenings in bars hustling men for drinks, playing on their sexual desires . . . And the women who drink and make out, doing everything short of sex with men all evening, and then go to his apartment at 2:00 a.m. Sometimes both of these women end up being the 'victims' of rape.

But are these women asking to get raped?

In the most severe and emphatic terms possible the answer is NO, THEY ARE NOT ASKING TO GET RAPED.

They are freaking begging for it.

Damn near demanding it.

And all the outraged PC demands to get huffy and point out how nothing justifies or excuses rape won't change the

> fact that there are a lot of women who get pummeled and pumped because they are stupid (and often arrogant) enough to walk through life with the equivalent of a I'M A STUPID, CONNIVING BITCH—PLEASE RAPE ME neon sign glowing above their empty little narcissistic heads.

So wrote Paul Elam in November 2010, in an online post titled 'Challenging the Etiology of Rape'. Perhaps the world's most famous MRA, in 2008 Elam founded *A Voice for Men*, a for-profit men's rights website with an annual revenue estimated at around US$120,000 as of 2014, and with only one paid employee: Elam. Revenue is sourced mostly from online donations and advertising, but on the Red Pill shop (named for the Red Pill movement), *AVFM*'s CafePress online shop, you can buy t-shirts that say things like 'My Wallet, My Choice' and 'It hurts when you are in love with a heartless bitch'.

(Sidenote: In 2016, an American filmmaker called Cassie Jaye made a documentary about the men's rights movement called *The Red Pill*. The film was heavily financed by MRAs, including Paul Elam and members of the *AVFM* community, and was subsequently criticised for being little more than an advertorial. Of particular concern was Jaye's failure to press Elam on his more violent declarations, including his aforementioned views on rape victims and their apparent culpability. A planned Australian premiere was cancelled by Melbourne's Palace Kino cinema after a petition was circulated characterising the movie as 'misogynistic propaganda'. MRAs, both those who had financially supported the film and those who were simply counting on it to enlist more people to the movement, were up in arms. When they coordinate to sabotage feminist events it's acceptable political activism—but when feminists protest content and behaviours that quantifiably promote harm to women, it's *censorship*. Funny, isn't it? In the ensuing fallout, I was repeatedly accused of having either created the petition myself or of fiercely promoting it, when the truth is I did neither. As I said at the time, I support a general release for *The Red Pill* if only because I think we can all use a little more absurdist comedy in our lives.)

The sentiments expressed in Elam's 2010 post sit nicely alongside some of the articles you can read on *AVFM* a full eight years later, which include 'Feminism and "gender narcissism"', 'The rush to paint men as sexual abusers', 'Pathetic stupidity of cucks described in medieval Latin literature' and—my personal favourite—'Should we execute women who delayed their #MeToo accusations?' In a January 2018 post titled 'How to get your man to punch you in the face', Elam argues that women are the primary cause of intimate partner violence. Our 'relational aggression' is what pushes men to hurt us, and thus men shouldn't be blamed when they do. In fact, Elam writes, '. . . if [relational aggression] one day results in that man punching her in the face, the only criticism I would have is that he should have left before making himself legally vulnerable to even more of her [abuse].'

In his tenure as *AVFM* founder and publisher, Elam has openly stated that if he ever sits on a jury in a rape trial, he would vote to acquit on principle *even in the face of overwhelming evidence that the charges were true*. This is because he believes America is overrun by a swathe of false rape accusations and that the legal system is 'patently untrustworthy when it comes to the offense of rape'. I mean, he's not wrong. The system *is* 'patently untrustworthy when it comes to the offense of rape', primarily because the system itself was built by men to service a patriarchal society that continues to interpret the law based on masculine ideals. Only 3 percent of those accused of rape will ever be convicted, while the survivors of rape face a lifetime economic burden of over US$100,000, not to mention all the victim-blaming that goes along with it ('Lifetime economic burden of rape among US adults', C. Peterson, S. DeGue, C. Florence, C.N. Lokey, *American Journal of Preventive Medicine*, 2017).

But wait, that's not what he means! No—Elam thinks the legal system is untrustworthy because 'in this, the age of misandry, not one aspect of a rape case can be trusted . . . the accuser cannot be trusted.' And of course, as he argued back in 2010, 'stupid, conniving bitches' are just asking for it. Despite the fact that criminal studies consistently show roughly 2 to 8 percent of rape allegations are false (incidentally, the same rate as false reports for other crimes), MRAs doggedly pursue their belief that false reports actually account for around half of all sexual assault accusations. But while Elam and his global acolytes dismiss rigorous, peer-reviewed studies and accurate criminal statistical data on rape as the product of a sinister feminist conspiracy, their own sources are lacking, to say the least.

As Kate Harding writes in her 2015 book, *Asking for It: The Alarming Rise of Rape Culture—and What We Can Do About It*, the primary 'evidence' used by MRAs here is a small and highly questionable study from 1994 in which researcher Eugene J. Kanin investigated 104 sexual assault complaints made to a small Midwestern police station between 1978 and 1987. According to Kanin, 41 percent of these allegations turned out to be false.

Well, now that's a compelling statistic! Sure, it relies on data that's almost four decades old and has to be placed within the context of Midwestern attitudes towards women, sexual agency, second-wave feminism and male entitlement—but *41 percent*! I mean, it's no surprise that bitches lie, but it's just so *handy* to have some evidence that tells us definitively and without any bias whatsoever that they lie *all the fucking time*.

Yeah, nah.

The problem with Kanin's study (and indeed almost all assessments of 'false' allegations in a crime as hotly disputed as rape and sexual assault) is that determining duplicity has occurred is both difficult and extremely flawed. In 2009, David Lisak co-authored a report for the National Center for Prosecution of Violence Against Women looking in part at difficulties inherent in defining a 'false' report. He wrote, 'Kanin's 1994 article on false allegations is a provocative opinion piece, but it is not a scientific study of the issue of false reporting of rape. It certainly should never be used to assert a scientific foundation for the frequency of false allegations.' Lisak (who's widely regarded as an expert in the field) argued that Kanin's study failed to question the police methods used to assess the veracity of sexual assault allegations in that small Midwestern town and that any potential biases 'were then echoed in Kanin's unchallenged reporting of their findings'. Basically, it's scientifically unsound to use as a control group a selection of people who, history and sociology inform us, are unlikely to be impartial when it comes to judging whether or not a woman is telling the truth about her own rape.

Rape allegations can also be declared 'false' if law enforcement officers and/or prosecutors decide not to pursue charges, which might be because they don't believe the claimant (understanding, of course, that social attitudes towards rape, victim-blaming and sexual violence are just as likely to be found within the institutions we rely on to protect us as they are outside them, especially as these institutions continue to be male-dominated) or because it's felt that successful prosecution will prove difficult if not impossible. Sometimes, as was the case with those reports declared 'false' in Kanin's study, rape allegations are withdrawn by the person filing them.

Well, gee willikers, I wonder what it is about the society we live in that would make someone withdraw a complaint of sexual assault? I mean, who doesn't love the idea of being grilled about their behaviour, their clothing, their previous sexual encounters and their complicity in a violent situation, first by law enforcement officers, then by defence lawyers and, last but not least, by members of the public?

You don't have to look very far to see how women are treated when they allege sexual misconduct against them. Branded liars and sluts, they're often terrorised for trying to 'ruin' a decent man's life or accused of going through the entire rigmarole of a rape report and subsequent trial because they irresponsibly fucked someone one night and woke up with a case of the whoopsies. Yeah, opening your entire sexual history up to public comment over a period of months sounds way less complicated and time-consuming than spending the day huddled under a blankie, watching a *Drag Race* marathon and vowing never to drink again.

Isn't it incredibly interesting how society in general has no problem characterising women as vindictive, illogical harlots who will happily 'destroy' a man's entire life rather than take responsibility for their own sexual choices, but that same society cannot equate their knowledge that rape exists with the fact that this means a proportion of men are actually rapists? The idea that millions of women—almost 50 percent!—who purport to be rape survivors are in fact conducting elaborate schemes of revenge or 'attention-seeking' (as Kanin characterised one of the motivations for filing false reports) rather than being, you know, actual rape survivors would be a bizarre enough fantasy in a world that rewarded women for opening up about such things. But the reality is that women who come forward with rape allegations are treated like garbage. Contrary to popular opinion, a truckload of cash doesn't arrive at a woman's doorstop the moment she opens her mouth to screech '*J'accuse!*' at some poor, innocent man. She isn't carried into the courthouse atop a diamond-encrusted throne, deposited into the witness stand and given a relaxing spa treatment for the next three hours. The friends and family members of the accused do not seek her out to thank her for alerting them to his scurrilous ways. The #MeToo and #timesup movements might have put the fear of God into the world's men (particularly those with something to hide), but even their success isn't enough to erase the fact that silence-breakers are still accused of lying, still bombarded with death threats and still risk losing their jobs, social standing and entire relationships. Daisy Coleman, fourteen when she was raped by a classmate in Missouri, but whose family was later driven out of the town; the anonymous young female victim of the Steubenville rape, who had to watch as news anchors lamented the loss of 'promising futures' for her assailants; the female students featured in the documentary *The Hunting Ground* about rape on US college campuses, many of whom ended up leaving school after facing administrative failure to act as well as bullying from their classmates; Saxon Mullins, raped by Luke Lazarus outside his father's nightclub in Sydney and then forced to watch as a parade of well-heeled community members lined up to provide character references for him. These are just a drop in the vast, vast ocean of women who have been punished to varying degrees for daring to besmirch the names of the men who can always count on being protected by their communities.

None of this is to say that women don't ever lie about being raped or are incapable of such duplicity. There are circumstances in which people's lives have indeed been destroyed by false allegations or convictions, and there are people who have served incomprehensibly long prison sentences for sexual crimes they were later discovered not to have committed (but it's worth pointing out this is infinitely more likely to happen to men of colour than to white men). But it is altogether too common for suspicion to be directed at *any* woman who alleges rape, especially when it implicates the kind of man considered valuable by broader society. The phrase 'innocent until proven guilty' is shouted ad infinitum whenever an allegation hits the news (or even just the grapevine), but very few people seem to have a problem with assuming that women are guilty of either lying or being complicit, even when it involves dozens of them speaking out against the same man and demonstrating a pattern of access and abuse played out over decades. See: Bill Cosby, Harvey Weinstein, Donald Trump.

Leaving aside the extreme contortion required to listen to these kinds of repeated testimonies and still find them unconvincing, it's also important to remember that the determination of what makes something automatically false is flawed. Someone falsely imprisoned for a crime they didn't commit isn't evidence that the crime itself didn't occur, only that the justice system might have failed to identify the correct perpetrator. Someone withdrawing their allegation of a crime is not the same as admitting they lied, particularly when moving forward frequently carries such a heavy burden. A rape victim changing their story or proving unreliable with their testimony is not definitive proof that a story has been manufactured; on the contrary, it's consistent with a neurobiological response to trauma that sees the brain more likely to form memories based on sensory rather than visual or linear recollection. A verdict of Not Guilty doesn't mean She Lied, especially when it is notoriously difficult to secure convictions for sex crimes.

And yet, these nuances are all too often discarded in preference for a simple true/false binary that denies not only the complexities of interpreting and reporting sexual assault but also the ease with which the evidence of it can be hidden or obscured. While this reality is dismissed, the trope of the archetypal, vengeful woman painted as fact by large swathes of society (and weaponised by aggrieved MRAs) holds fast. As Harding argues:

> Let's not act as though one woman's false testimony is, by itself, sufficient to create the Kafkaesque hell of a wrongful prosecution—especially when a genuine victim's credible testimony is still often not enough to merit an arrest. The idea that any given vengeful, embarrassed, or simply bored woman can 'cry rape' and automatically send an innocent man to prison is pure fiction.

The term 'fake news' might be relatively recent, but the tendency to dismiss inconvenient facts as a conspiracy has been around since long before Donald Trump pussy-grabbed his way to the presidency. MRAs have been beating the false-accusations drum for decades, pointing to studies like Kanin's and individual high-profile cases (such as a discredited *Rolling Stone* article about rape on campus at the University of Virginia) as definitive proof of the rape industrial complex and the feminist crones who sacrifice men at its altar. Study after study has disproved the claims of high rates of false reports, but the myth persists. Why?

Unlike the feminist movement, which throughout its rich and storied history has sought to liberate all humans from the oppressive structures of patriarchy, the men's rights movement is founded on the basic conviction that women are trying to fuck men's shit up and it isn't fair. In relation to their view of rape particularly, there's a bizarre disconnect. Women need men to protect them, MRAs say, and feminism's disruption of this necessary relationship puts those same women at risk. But when MRAs also deny men's complicity in the violence women experience—indeed, when they argue that women are the ones who are just as likely, *if not more likely*, to be guilty of perpetrating gendered violence—who is it exactly that we need men to protect us from? We're instructed to modify our behaviour, our clothes and our movements in order to 'prevent' rape, yet we're also apparently just as likely to lie about it as we are to be subjected to it. If male-perpetrated violence against women isn't the risk we've been conditioned to believe it is, why are we still warned against going into parks after dark or getting drunk or wearing a short skirt or kissing someone we aren't also prepared to 'see it through' with? And if women are in fact the real danger—if it is us and not men who have the capacity and the desire to inflict pain on others in order to exercise our female privilege—why aren't men expected to minimise and reduce their own engagement with the world in order to not make themselves a target of its violence?

You would think these questions would be of concern to MRAs, but I guess they're too busy conspiring to take down women who do speak out against assault and/or attempting to jam the systems being put in place to try to help them. (See also: when MRAs tried to impersonate women of colour online to get #endfathersday trending, thereby creating the evidence they needed to prove their claims that feminists wanted to . . . end Father's Day).

In 2013, a liberal arts university in LA created an online anonymous reporting system for rape and sexual assault. Victim advocates at Occidental College devised the ground-breaking system as a way for students to 'log' their rapes with the school for the purposes of supplying statistical data and seeking support in a safe environment. To be clear, this was never meant to be an official avenue for students to report their experiences of one, both or either to authorities.

But it didn't take MRAs long to get their hands on a link to the reporting tool, misrepresenting its directive from the outset. On the Men's Rights subreddit (r/mensrights, just in case you want to spend an evening in cyber hell), a poster linked to the reporting tool with the explanation: 'Feminists at Occidental College created an online form to anonymously report rape/sexual assault. You just fill out a form and the person is called into the office on a rape charge. The "victim" never has to prove anything or reveal their identity.'

This wasn't even *remotely* true. Occidental created the tool not just to provide a resource for students who had been raped or assaulted while attending the college, but because a federal Title IX lawsuit had directly accused the administration of under-reporting on-campus sexual assaults to the appropriate authorities. But even if they had wanted to use it as a means of funnelling into the prison system douche-haired young men raping (sorry, 'dating') their way around campus, there's no jurisdiction in the world that will issue a rape charge on the strength of an anonymous tip alone.

Not that this stopped the MRAs spurred on by the Reddit post. In just over thirty-six hours, more than 400 false rape reports were submitted via the online tool, with many of them naming actual students (most of them women). One commenter on r/mensrights wrote: 'The quickest way to shut this one down is to anonymously report random women and let them sweat in the hot seat. This will be over before it begins.' Another wrote: 'Step one: Get a list of every "Feminist" at Occidental College who supported this system. Step two: Anonymously report them for rape.'

MRAs repeatedly bemoan what they see as an abundance of false rape accusations, but at the first opportunity they conspire to flood the system with—wait for it!—false rape accusations. Take a moment to feast on the fucking irony.

As Lindy West wrote on *Jezebel* in her article 'Occidental College Finally Addresses Persistent Rape Problem' in 2013, 'I can barely fathom the putrid mental contortions required to look at a list of rape crisis hotlines, treatment centers, and counseling services and see a threat that must be destroyed.'

But, then, destroying the progress made by women who seek nothing but their own liberation from violence and oppression has always been the primary objective of the men's rights movement. It doesn't matter that a service like the one provided at Occidental would have benefited male victims as well. The very existence of a rape reporting tool is an acknowledgment that rape might actually be a real problem. And unlike Jeff Bridges' iconic turn in *The Big Lebowski*, these dudebros will NOT abide.

■

It isn't just rape convictions for which MRAs hold the legal system to account. The family court is one of the biggest bugbears of the men's rights movement, with an almost psychotic fixation on the 'lying bitches' (because whether she's stupid, conniving, lying or heartless, she's still always a bitch) who evidently collude with judges to abduct children from their fathers. *AVFM* eagerly stokes the flames of this discord, encouraging the false view that family court judges are in the business of ruining men's lives. (Ironically, in addition to denying loving dads the right to see their kids, feminism is also responsible for forcing men to become dads in the first place and extorting them for child support they don't want to pay and probably aren't even responsible for because paternity fraud is also A Big Problem according to the charter of paranoid man-babies. Don't be alarmed if you find it confusing; MRAs make sense to nobody but themselves.)

To his followers, Elam presents himself as a kind of vigorous, take-no-prisoners defender of male dignity. He reserves particular viciousness for the family court system in his article 'The family courts have got to GO and I mean right fucking now' in 2011:

> I am a pacifist. I do not advocate violence. [LOL WHATEVS PAUL!] But I tell you this. The day I see one of these absolutely incredulous excuses for a judge dragged out of his courtroom into the street, beaten mercilessly, doused with gasoline and set afire by a father who just won't take another moment of injustice, I will be the first to put on the pages of this website that what happened was a minor tragedy that pales by far in comparison to the systematic brutality and thuggery inflicted daily on American fathers by those courts and their police henchmen.

The passion of Elam's declaration is more than slightly at odds with his actual knowledge of custody battles and family law. To hear him speak, you'd think he'd had a particularly heinous experience of both—that behind the scenes was a wife who'd conspired to keep him from his children and whose actions, for better or worse, were the spark that set Elam's meninist convictions ablaze. But the truth is a lot more embarrassing for the man who once wrote of disgruntled fathers, 'I am an older man and have witnessed this silent, ignored tragedy for far too long . . . This sort of thing cannot be allowed to continue.' The truth is that Elam willingly abandoned his own kids not once but *twice*.

In 2015, *Buzzfeed* journalists Katie J.M. Baker and Adam Serwer reported that Elam's parental history was less than exemplary. Rather than being a victim of the feminazi family court system, Elam turned his back on his biological children twice—once following his divorce from their mother and then again after his daughter sought a reconciliation as an adult. He speaks bitterly of child support as a kind of crime syndicate racket that fathers are forced into against their will, but as Baker and Serwer revealed in their 2015 article 'How men's rights leader Paul Elam turned being a deadbeat dad into a moneymaking movement', 'he accused his first wife of lying about being raped so he could relinquish his parental rights and avoid paying child support'. Reader, I'm shocked. *Shocked*, I tell you. As his daughter Bonnie (not her real name) told *Buzzfeed*, 'People come to Paul for advice on parenting, even though he has two estranged biological children that he did not raise or take care of.'

There's a racket taking place, for sure. And given Elam's the only financial beneficiary of *AVFM*, it's fair to say he's running the whole damn thing.

But let's be fair. As reprehensible and vindictive as a good proportion of MRAs seem to be, it's also true that some men *are* disenfranchised and disadvantaged by a legal system that has the power to keep their children away from them. The fact that they form the minority of men's experiences with the family courts doesn't mean they don't exist, and in some ways it's understandable that such desperation would attract them to a movement that claims to want to right these wrongs. I have sympathy for these men. I mean, it's hard *not* to sympathise with the thought of a loving parent being kept from their children. Since giving birth to my son, I've conducted more than a few thought experiments about what I would do if he were taken from me or if I were forced to live apart from him. Even contemplating it makes me feel numb and broken inside. It would be like a form of banishment, like being cast into a dark room underground where the air was stale and nothing beautiful could ever grow. As much as some people might not like to believe this, I take no pleasure in the thought of loving, committed fathers being parted from their children. And, yes, of course I acknowledge there are some women who use their kids as a means of exacting revenge.

But—and this is a crucial point—this scenario is not actually representative of the reality of the family court system. The trope of the hard-done-by dad might be compelling, but in reality it's an outlier. In fact, modern family law has never been more disposed towards securing a 'fair deal' for fathers than at this point in time, even in cases where the men have proven themselves a risk to the safety of the child and/or their mother. As the Walkley Award-winning journalist Jess Hill reported so brutally in her piece 'Suffer the children: Trouble in the Family Court' (*The Monthly*, November 2015), changes to family law in Australia in the last three decades have actually made it progressively more difficult for women to obtain sole custody.

In 1995, the Keating government introduced amendments to the *Family Law Act 1975* that shifted the court's focus from awarding custody to a child's primary caregiver and instead emphasised the right of the child to have regular contact with both parents. Not a bad idea, right? But as Hill's piece asserted:

> By 2000, these reforms had in effect 'turned back the clock' on Family Court responses to domestic violence, according to legal practitioners quoted in an extensive study by the Family Court of Australia and the University of Sydney. This study found that the 'safety from family violence' provision had done nothing to dissuade abusive fathers from believing they now had a right to their kids; fathers who would never have even tried to get access before were now being encouraged to fight tooth and nail.

In 2006, the Howard government pushed these amendments even further, introducing changes that included the so-called 'friendly parent' provision which, as Hill reports, 'mandated judges to consider the willingness of each parent to encourage a close relationship between the child and the other parent'. The consequences of this were devastating, resulting in a no-win situation for mothers who were seeking protection orders against abusive ex-partners:

> Parents hoping to raise abuse allegations in the family law courts now faced what former Family Court judge Richard Chisholm termed 'the victim's dilemma': abuse allegations

> could be viewed as vindictive or punitive, and consequently, a judge may order that the child be placed with the perpetrator for longer periods, to protect them from the other parent's 'alienating' behaviour.

Hill's piece is gut-wrenching, particularly in its detailing of the children whose testimonies of abuse experienced at the hands of their fathers has been interpreted by 'single experts' (third-party evaluators appointed by the parents or the court to assess children alleged to be victimised by one parent). One passage highlights how patriarchal notions of women's 'hysteria' can be invoked when judging cases such as these. This is the story of Emily, a mother who filed abuse charges against her son's father (who had also been abusing her for years) in 2006. Hill recounts:

> The single expert assigned to Emily's case wrote that she presented in a 'self-absorbed manner' and had an 'over-valued idea' that Alex had been abused. He noted that the father's two former wives had also separately accused him of sexually abusing their young children, both under five. This was 'hard to dismiss', but he could see nothing in his assessment of the father or his relationship with Alex that confirmed sexual abuse. Alex's 'features of trauma', he believed, were instead caused by a 'toxic relationship' with his mother, who over-loaded Alex 'with anxiety and the demands of the parental conflict'. If Alex continued to live with his mother, the single expert observed, it was unlikely he would have a relationship with his father. In a separate investigation instigated through the Family Court, child protection also concluded there was no risk of Alex being harmed by his father.

In the midst of Emily and Alex's case, the Howard government's amendments to the Act were passed. By fighting so vigorously to protect her son from a man Alex had told school staff he wanted 'dead or in jail' because he was 'a bad man', adding that he didn't like it when 'he kisses me or hugs me or licks me', Emily failed to pass the 'friendly parent' provision. Under the modified Act, the judge was able to view Emily's 'alienating' behaviour as a reason to grant interim custody to Alex's father.

And this is exactly what happened, when Alex was only seven years old. Hill reports:

> Emily can still remember the last thing she said in court. 'I could see I was being painted as this terrible mother. In my last statement to the judge, I said, "If you have to take Alex away from me, please don't give him to his father." My lawyer told me later that was the exact moment I lost my son.'

For the first three months, Emily was denied all contact with Alex. It would be another three years before she was allowed to care for him on weekends. Alex repeatedly tried to report the physical and emotional abuse that his father inflicted on him, but found that no one believed him. When he was twelve, he ran away and went to Emily's house, threatening to kill himself if he was forced to return to live with his father. A single expert was again appointed by the court to assess Alex. His conclusion was that it was all 'stress-related', and recommended that the judge return Alex to his father's home and advised that 'to help them reconnect emotionally, Alex should not contact his mother for a month'. The judge agreed.

Alex continued to reject the court orders, but was stymied at every turn. Eventually, the police applied for an AVO on his behalf. After spending two months in a refuge (because his father refused to allow him to stay with his maternal grandmother), Alex was finally granted a court order that allowed him to live with his mother. It had been five years since he'd been separated from her against his will, forced to live with a man he had consistently claimed had been abusing him and whom the courts acknowledged at the time had been accused by two former wives of sexually abusing their young children. And the Family Court is supposedly working in tandem with the feminazi government superpower to slander men on record and turn their children against them.

But this is what those in the men's rights movement will never admit and perhaps lack the self-awareness to even understand. It isn't women who lie about abuse to keep men from their children; it's men already abusing women who use the loopholes that have been made available to them by the family courts to continue their campaign of violence. For example, a woman in Australia may have an existing family violence order in place that prevents her former partner from contacting her or being within 100 metres of her, but federal law allows for that order to be overridden under the *Family Law Act*. Basically, there's no Australian AVO available that will prevent someone from continuing to harass, bully and abuse their former partner as long as they make sure to ask a question about their kids while they're doing it.

More recently, political parties like One Nation have pledged their support for fathers' rights groups, even those that advocated violence as a means of action. Ahead of the 2017 Queensland state election, the party unveiled a new policy platform that would 'not unnecessarily restrict a father's visitation rights [even though] a court had awarded an emergency protective order'. One Nation candidate Tracey Bell-Henselin argued that women claiming to have been victimised by violent partners should be forced to prove victimisation through their own injuries and medical files or their partner's criminal past. In the financial year 2016–17, a record number of offenders—25,678 to be precise—breached domestic violence protection orders against them. Awesome work, One Nation! But, then, they also chose to align themselves with the Australian Brotherhood of Fathers, a terrorist group whose founder has urged men to suicide at their local MP's office to 'let them witness your final act in person'. Perhaps that's where the ABF's similarly bonkers #21fathers social media campaign gets its fabricated statistic from; the campaign claims that each week twenty-one Australian fathers are killing themselves as a result of vicious women and the family courts keeping them from their kids. I've tried repeatedly to get the mastermind behind #21fathers to reveal the source of this statistic, but his response has only ever been to direct me to his own website. Dude, that's not how data works.

Despite the sheer and obvious lunacy of these groups, the success of the MRA propaganda campaign has proven effective with a public easily swayed by feelings rather than facts. And the lies MRAs tell about their oppression at the hands of family court judges in particular have passed from fringe conspiracy theories into a commonly held belief system. A 2013 VicHealth survey found that 53 percent of respondents believed that mothers fabricate domestic abuse allegations against their partners in order to keep them away from their kids. As Hill illustrated so devastatingly in 'Suffer the children', even women who have existing orders against men are often too afraid to raise those matters in custody disputes because they fear they'll be painted as vindictive and their children will be taken away from them. Even after the Gillard government removed Howard's 'friendly parent' provision in 2012, women still reported feeling pressured both to sign consent orders and to avoid raising allegations of abuse in court because they risked being assessed as hostile. During the course of writing this chapter, I shared 'Suffer the children' on my Facebook page (again) only to read numerous defeated comments from women who reaffirmed that, based on their own current experiences, nothing has changed in the system. Worryingly, news broke in late May of 2018 that Australia's federal government may have even done a backroom deal with One Nation to 'reform' the family courts. Power corrupts etc.

Okay, what about men elsewhere? After all, Elam (the modern grandfather of the men's rights movement) is from America. Isn't it possible that the system's different there?

It's true that a preference for sole maternal custody prevailed in America during the 1980s, but it's been steadily dropping. A comprehensive study conducted in Wisconsin looked at the outcomes of divorce and custody proceedings between 1996 and 2007. Here, the percentage of cases in which mothers received sole custody dropped during this period from 60.4 to 45.7. On the flipside, the percentage of cases in which custody was determined to be shared equally doubled from 15.8 to 30.5. A 2018 survey conducted by the American Academy of Matrimonial Lawyers found there's also been an increase in mothers paying child support and alimony, which kind of challenges the deeply held MRA belief that money between estranged men and women only ever goes one way. Interestingly, the grand sum of child support forced out of Elam, before he agreed to terminate his parental rights, was a measly $1200. Those thieving women, though!

Speaking of child support, in Australia at least the national childcare debt sits at about $1.5 billion. Mothers are more likely to be financially worse off than fathers after a separation. And while heavy penalties exist for non-payers in other countries, no such formal punishment exists in Australia. Dr Andrew Lancaster, a former federal government economist, has even published an online guide titled *How to Avoid Child Support Legally.* Nice guy, hey.

In 2017, Kidspot journalist Alexandra Carlton asked readers to submit screenshots of the child support they were owed. Amounts ranged from a few thousand dollars to at least $65,000. One mother, whose ex-partner currently owed a backlog of $26,000 in child support payments, told Carlton, 'He tells me he will never pay me a cent. Just bought himself a Harley [Davidson motorcycle].' Another said, 'My kids' father pays $35 per month for 2 kids while he travels around Australia on permanent holiday earning cash money. I provide my kids with everything they need. If I thought I could count on their father I would still be with him.'

Stories like these abound, and it's not like this inequality and economic burden gets bad just after a break-up. It's telling how often women report feeling let down emotionally and financially by their partners after they have children, even when they're together. It's hard not to feel cynical about MRAs complaining they aren't being allowed fifty-fifty shared care of their children when, both anecdotally and statistically speaking, there ain't a whole lot of men fighting to do 50 percent of the work before their marriages disintegrate. And although I've found no official data to track this, I'd be really interested to know how many men pushing for fifty-fifty shared custody do so under circumstances where they've re-partnered. It's a bit easier to parent when you can rely on your new girlfriend to do everything your old one did.

But back to the US where, like Australia, the 'friendly parent' provision has also marked a shift in family court decision-making. According to Hanna Rosin, in her article for *Slate* in 2014 called 'Dad's day in court' about America's family court system, 'Mothers who get in the way of a father's involvement can in fact be penalized by the courts.' Contrary to the popular myth peddled by communities like *AVFM* and its ilk, since the 1970s 'the vast majority of states moved toward an assumption of joint custody'. In fact, so beholden to the push for fathers' rights is the American judicial system that women throughout the country have even found themselves fighting custody battles over children produced *as a result of rape.*

Yes, you read that correctly.

If that didn't disgust you enough, here are some further sobering facts about rape and parental rights in the good old US of A:

- Seven states have no legislation whatsoever to prevent rapists from petitioning for custody.
- While forty-three states and the District of Columbia provide at least partial protection to rape survivors from having to fight their rapists over custody rights, in twenty of those states (and D.C.) the request for a termination of parental rights can only be made if a rape conviction has been secured.
- Some states have 'carve out' laws which provide exceptions based on the relationship between the victim and the perpetrator. For example, if a pregnancy occurs as a result of a man raping his wife or de facto partner, she may not be able to

prevent him from petitioning for custody of that child. And given the prevalence with which sexual violence occurs as part of ongoing intimate partner violence, that's a terrifying notion indeed.

- In April 2017, an all-male panel in Maryland shut down a proposed bill that would have allowed the mothers of children conceived by rape to block the parental rights of the men who raped them. It had been Maryland state delegate Kathleen M. Dumais' ninth attempt at passing the bill.

This is abuse.

In fact, the MRA fixation on family court injustices isn't just misguided, it's also a deliberate and repetitive lie that undermines the already tenuous rights of women trying to escape abusive relationships—remembering, of course, that MRAs also cite divorce rates as being one of the many oppressions experienced by the world's subjugated men. (And chew on that for a moment. To women, abuse is when their partners physically, emotionally and sexually violate them, often in situations in which they are held hostage out of fear that they and/or their children will be murdered. To MRAs, abuse is women leaving them.) Worse, the indulgence of the MRA male victim mentality, which is really just outrage at being suddenly unable to demand total obedience from family members they consider their lowly subjects, forces already at-risk women and children into even more dangerous situations.

■

There's a pattern here, not just in how the men's rights movement seeks to classify women but in how formal legislative bodies are actually reflecting that classification. Women lie about rape to punish men. We take our children away to punish men. We lie about being raped by men in order to stop them from seeing their kids, because we're lying liars who hate men. The system hates men, and works with women to punish them even though the system is almost entirely run by men who systematically and wilfully fail to acknowledge and *respect* what it is women go through and need if we are to survive.

Men like Paul Elam, a man who abandoned his own children and refused to pay the meagre funds required of him to help support them, pretend to thousands of similarly frothing misogynists that they have been manipulated, abused and exploited by women. It's no coincidence that the majority of men who are drawn to pages like *A Voice for Men*, *Anti-Feminism Australia*, #21fathers, the *Australian Brotherhood of Fathers*, *Dads Are Kool Dudes* (okay, I made that last one up) are white, cis, straight and pissed off. There's nothing wrong with caring about men's issues (and lord knows, they gotta lotta them), but the men's rights movement itself is less about equality between the sexes than it is about maintaining power and privilege over women. Women (with ugly, angry feminists at the helm) have been identified by MRAs as the source of an imaginary subjugation and emasculation that's been steadily stripping them of power since the suffragettes first chained themselves to railings and demanded the right to vote.

And here we come to the heart of the MRA agenda. It isn't to liberate men from the systems that, among other things, cause them to die earlier, to suffer in silence from debilitating mental health issues, to be denied the opportunities to express their emotional selves. Their agenda is to force women in the process of liberation back into the subservient roles that make all of patriarchy's negative consequences for men easier to bear. Rather than look inwards to see how men can strive for a similar autonomy and independence—one that doesn't, for example, involve women working as unpaid domestic maids for them, raising their children, cleaning their houses, cooking their food and servicing their dicks—they instead lash out, believing themselves to be oppressed.

This is about fear, pure and simple. The men who are drawn to the MRA movement see women's liberation as an assault on their fundamental right to power. They may not be able to compete with other men in that hierarchy, but now they can no longer even assert themselves as superior to the women in their lives. As a result, they resent us, they're afraid of us and they work as hard as they can to punish us for making them feel emasculated and weak. Women have always been forced to absorb the brunt of men's emotional distress and rage—it's just that now we have the internet to disseminate both of those things more widely.

Plus ça change, plus c'est la même chose. The more things change, the more they stay the same.

—9—

THE KING OF THE HILL

When I woke on the morning of 7 October 2018, it was to the expected, rage inducing news that the Republican majority (minus only one woman, plus one male Democrat) had voted together to confirm a man with multiple sexual assault allegations against him to the United States Supreme Court.

I believe survivors, so I understand that what this means is a man with a history of sexual assault (and clear anger management issues) has now been given immense jurisdiction over the lives of Americans and American women in particular. It's no coincidence that his nomination was pushed for and strongly endorsed by another blatantly misogynist man with multiple sexual assault allegations to his name, President Donald Trump.

I am a pretty tough person, but I was surprised by how deeply it hit me to hear coverage of the confirmation. I stood in the kitchen and unexpectedly began to cry, because there is nothing and no one privileged white men won't do and fuck over to affirm their power. Their depth of entitlement should no longer be astonishing, yet it continues to stun in its audacity. Throughout the course of those confirmation hearings, they conducted themselves like the snotty little schoolboys they are. It wasn't so much whether or not they believed Dr Christine Blasey Ford's allegations—it's that they truly didn't care if they happened at all. Brett Kavanaugh was their guy, and they were going to be damned if some uppity professor from the past was going to stand in the way of that.

The person charged with the most disgusting display of behaviour was, unsurprisingly, the President. Throughout the process, he maintained a base level of disdain for Dr Blasey Ford and her supporters, repeatedly and arrogantly affirming that Kavanaugh was a 'good man' and that he had no doubt the 'right' outcome would be achieved. Presidential behaviour would have demanded at least some nod to the possibility that Dr Blasey Ford was bringing forward accurate and relevant information, but Trump is not now and has never been presidential. Only days before Kavanaugh was confirmed, Trump stood before a crowd of thousands (at one of the many rallies that seem to constitute the sole focus of his presidency) and mocked Dr Blasey Ford. Behind him, a row of men could be seen guffawing raucously.

Shortly after this repulsive display, Trump tweeted that SCOTUS protesters were hired by George Soros, and that Ana Maria Archila and Maria Gallagher (the two women in particular who bravely and famously confronted Senator Jeff Flake in an elevator to implore him to consider what his complicity in this vote represents to survivors of sexual violence) were actually paid actors. Trump's enthusiasm for the new internet era of conspiracy theories and 'fake news' is central to the erosion of democracy in America, and witnessing it is simultaneously terrifying and maddening.

But this is how men like Trump and those who model themselves on him operate. Despite insisting that it is women who cannot rein in our emotions and maintain rational perspective, it's the furious guardians of power who froth and spit at anyone they perceive to be a threat, whether actual or just ideological. What message does this send about power and its rightful claimants?

More than anything, it was Dr Blasey Ford's immense dignity that left the most lasting impression. With a measured voice that belied the memories she was being forced to relive, she was professional and controlled, repeatedly offering her apologies that she couldn't be more helpful. As it was, she described how she remembered Kavanaugh and his friend, Mark Judge, pinning her down on a bed in a secluded room and attempting to remove her clothes. 'Indelible in the hippocampus is the laughter,' she testified, 'the uproarious laughter between the two [men] and their having fun at my expense.'

Perhaps Dr Blasey Ford would have liked to have been angrier. Goodness knows the millions of women watching that day (not just from within America but also around the world) felt that deep rumble of fury rip through us all, as scars we've held dormant across our own bodies and memories suddenly tore open once again and began to flood us with pain we thought we'd sealed away long ago.

But anger belongs to men, and so Dr Blasey Ford could not appear before the world and show what the rage of abuse and trauma really looks like. That was a privilege reserved for Brett Kavanaugh, like so many of the privileges he's enjoyed before it. The privilege, say, of being able to attend the kind of expensive, elite all-boys school that looks good on an application to Yale Law, the school your grandfather graduated from. The privilege also of being able to drink beer, lots of beer, enough beer to get drunk and perhaps not even remember everything he did while in that state, but never be held responsible for any lack of 'common sense' that occurred as a result of it. The privilege of growing up male in an era that explicitly represented sexual assault in popular movies as some kind of hilarious jape that red-blooded young men get themselves involved in but never have to face the consequences for.

And yes, the privilege of standing in front of a Senate committee and behaving like a belligerent, petulant child and knowing with absolute certainty that this won't impact his professional reputation in the slightest. Because anger belongs to men.

In 2018, the journalist Rebecca Traister wrote, 'Women are taught that if we express anger, we will not be taken seriously. We will sound "childlike," "emotional," "unhinged," "hysterical." And so, many of us take immense care not to express our anger, lest we undercut the very point we want to make.'

Anger in women is pathologised as something foul and noxious. An angry woman is an unstable one, her rage never able to be understood as something correct and justifiable, only unwieldy and volatile. In the not-too-distant past, angry women were institutionalised by husbands, fathers and brothers—men for whom women's anger was seen as an inconvenience at best and an embarrassment at worst. They were institutionalised for other things, too. Being raped was one of them. Becoming pregnant out of wedlock another. Reading books, also a sin.

Why are you so angry? the angry woman is asked.

It is not a genuine enquiry, but a judgment.

Kavanaugh could spit and sputter his way through that hearing because anger belongs to men. If Dr Blasey Ford had shown a shred of his temperament, she would have been excoriated. Instead, she does exactly as she's supposed to—exactly as she's been trained, as a woman—and she can now suffer the other indignity reserved for us of being called confused.

Anger belongs to men.

And yet, women are the masters at storing it. We can and should start using it again, despite what conditioning has taught us. Elizabeth Warren put it best when she tweeted the following:

'Brett Kavanaugh was allowed to be angry. Dr. Ford wasn't. Women grow up hearing that being angry makes us unattractive. Well, today, I'm angry – and I own it. I plan to use that anger to take back the House, take back the Senate, & put Democrats in charge. Are you with me?'

■

Of course, anger is nice in theory but the punishment for women who embrace it is vast. The treatment of women in public life is frequently disgraceful, even when they're doing everything they can to keep whatever it is in check that we are instructed to. Is it any wonder Dr Blasey Ford's testimony was ultimately judged by a collective made up almost entirely of men? The same collective of men who assign themselves the power to decide what happens to women's bodies and who is entitled to basic human rights like reproductive healthcare? Women can't have any influence over that! How could we possibly be trusted to know what we're talking about? Hell, how could we be trusted at all? The more women in a room, the fewer men *and that doesn't sound like equality to me!*

Even women who are *adjacent* to public life are still considered fair targets for boorish observations by men who really shouldn't be throwing stones. But this is par for the course in a society that turns a blind eye to sexism and fiercely clings to its right to reserve positions of power for men. Men who will be given political portfolios, cabinet positions, Senate seats, prominent media voices, seats on ASX boards and unfettered access to decision-making—but who will almost never be made to fall on their swords when there is a woman around to do it for them.

The depressing fallout from the 2016 US presidential election is proof enough of that. It wasn't misogyny that lost Clinton the election. No, it was that she *stole* the nomination from Bernie Sanders. It wasn't racism that caused Trump's supporters to respond gleefully to his calls to BUILD A WALL. No, it was that Clinton was ugly and 'shrill'.

How frustrating must it have been for the most qualified candidate in US history to lose to a man so incompetent, dangerous and cartoonish that he is living satire. That enough people in the right places preferred an ignorant, racist, misogynist, dangerous imbecile (not to mention an accused rapist) to a woman with decades of political experience is proof of how much further we have to go. Hillary Clinton has endured a lifetime of abuse about her looks (they were even blamed for her husband's infidelities), her 'shrill' personality, her mannishness, her hawkishness, her sensitivity (heaven forbid a person be seen to cry once in a while) and her general 'lack of appeal'. People still seem to be baffled by the idea that a woman could be powerful in her own right rather than have it bestowed on her by the male gaze. I'm not saying she's above critique or that none of it is fair—I'm saying there's a flavour to it that is purely due to her being a woman that isn't found in critiques of men with similar political leanings.

Speaking of Clinton, Monica Lewinsky has fared no better. In the decades since the exposure of her affair with President (Bill) Clinton, she has been hounded, harassed, shamed and mocked. From the very start, she was made a target of ridicule—her big teeth, big gums, big hair and big bottom all fodder for caricatures and hysterical disgust. By her own admission, this onslaught caused her to consider suicide on numerous occasions. Bill Clinton has never been forced to atone for his sins, but Lewinsky—at the time a young, vulnerable intern who in no way, shape or form could be considered to have had the upper hand in their relationship—has spent a lifetime living with them. The unfairness of this can best be summed up by the comments of Australian journalist Paul Bongiorno, who in 2016 replied to a tweet announcing a telemovie about Monica Lewinsky with the wholly unnecessary comment: 'The actress not ugly enough.'

Whoever the woman might be, if she attempts to enter public life on her own terms and to lead in accordance with her own compass, she'll be targeted for destruction. Look at the appalling response to the historic election of Alexandra Ocasio-Cortez. In 2018, Ocasio-Cortez unseated a ten term incumbent to win the Democratic Party's primary election for the 14th congressional district. She went on to win a seat on Congress in the 2018 mid-terms, becoming the youngest woman ever (at twenty-nine) to make that claim. A proud socialist, she has been subjected to some of the most horrific attacks made on women (and women of colour in particular) who dare to assert themselves as leaders in any capacity, with everything from her intelligence to even her choice of clothing used as a means of discrediting her ability to lead. Because she fights back (with aplomb, I might add), she's treated like a sullen, petulant child – and let me tell you, it's astonishing how frequently grown women are undermined and infantilised simply for the act of standing up for ourselves.

Ocasio-Cortez was one of a record-breaking number of women who put themselves forward for (and won) battles in the 2018 mid-terms. Their presence is undoubtedly agitating the mostly white, mostly male systems of governance that have dominated colonial American politics for centuries. And still, they are overlooked and dismissed from both sides of politics. Despite the extraordinary success Stacey Abrams achieved in the 2018 Georgia gubernatorial election, she received a skerrick of the breathless accolades given to Beto O'Rourke following his narrow loss to Ted Cruz in Texas. Far fewer people discussed Abrams as a potential candidate for the 2020 presidential race, almost certainly because Abrams is both black and a woman and being both of these things apparently renders your political impact invisible to large swathes of the public.

But, we are told repeatedly, *it should all be about merit.*

Bullshit.

It's so easy for lazy people to believe that those privileged most by gender, race, sexuality and class are somehow judged separately from the benefits these attributes bring. Our culture doesn't view women (or people of colour, or disabled people, or gender diverse people, or anyone who isn't a white man, basically) as being inherently meritorious. Imagine—just *imagine*—what the public's reaction would be if the majority of politicians elected to government were women. If the majority of newspaper columnists, TV commentators and CEOs were chicks. Think of the outcry if our talkback radio stations (which are currently wall-to-wall white men, because 'no one wants to listen to women' on the wireless) were suddenly overrun by bloody sheilas.

Merit? No, that wouldn't be merit. That would be 'cultural Marxism'. That would herald the start of matriarchy and the end of the world. It would be a witch-led conspiracy. Women? Running things? UNFAIR.

In fact, the 'merit' argument is little more than a convenient retort to anyone who tries to point out the workings of the deeply flawed systems we live in. It's telling that those who defend the merit system often present themselves (as Trump has done most egregiously) as supporters of women's rights.

If you believe that women are as capable of performing in positions of responsibility as men, it logically follows that we shouldn't see these structures of power being dominated by men. On the other hand, if you defend the current and historical imbalance of power as being due to nothing more than the application of 'merit', it doesn't matter how loudly you profess your feminist credentials—what you quite obviously believe is that white, middle-class, heterosexual men who have always held all the power are the only ones capable of doing so. It means you inherently think these people are *better* than everyone else.

You can't have it both ways.

■

But maybe it's just because so many men find it difficult to even listen to women in the first place. During the 2017 US Senate testimony hearings, Senator Kamala Harris was not only repeatedly interrupted and spoken over by her colleagues, Republican senators John McCain and Richard Burr, she was also later referred to as 'hysterical' by a Trump campaign adviser speaking on CNN.

The treatment of Harris prompted an outpouring of support from women, many of whom shared similar stories of workplace indignation at the hands of sexist colleagues.

There is a tendency for serious dialogue to downplay or outright discard discussions that refer to practices like 'mansplaining' and 'manteruppting'. But while the portmanteaus might seem a little juvenile to some, these twin phenomena are real (and are especially pronounced for women of colour, like Kamala Harris, who must confront the dual aggressions of misogyny and racism). Women aren't exaggerating when we complain of being frequently interrupted, undermined or condescended to. Nor is our awareness of this a fabrication born out of paranoia or some kind of feminine sensitivity. As Susan Chira wrote in the *New York Times* in 2017, gender disparity in the influential realms of America's high-powered industries remains starkly in favour of men. Just over 93 percent and four-fifths of Fortune 500 chief executive officers and board members, respectively, are men, both undeniably significant figures even for people like me who believe that feminism's goal must extend well and truly beyond the success of a small number of privileged (mostly white) women within a capitalist patriarchy.

That this happens in the private sphere is a given, but men's use of it as a silencing tactic in the public realm too is well documented. Joanna Richards is a PhD candidate at the University of Canberra's Institute for Governance and Policy Analysis. In her thesis (published in 2016 and aptly titled *Let Her Finish*), Richards examined the rate and type of interruptions across ten Australian Senate Estimates Committee hearings over the span of a decade, and included an analysis of the interruptions made both by and to male and female witnesses. She found that more than two-thirds of the interruptions that *specifically questioned the speaker's authority and credibility were directed towards women.*

The gendered component of interruptions isn't limited purely to the people most likely to be interrupted—it is also influenced by the environment in which the interruptions are taking place. Richards determined that Australia's Senate Committee hearings featured a male:female ratio of 71 to 29 percent (a split that appears to be reflected across most industries that represent power and influence). Interestingly, Richards found that in this environment men were only slightly more likely than women to be the ones doing the interrupting but that women were disproportionately targeted by those interruptions. When women were the ones interrupting, it was more likely to be classified as a 'positive' or 'defensive' interruption, either to agree with or affirm what someone else was saying or to defend someone already being interrupted by another speaker. Meanwhile, almost 75 percent of men's interruptions were 'negatively trying to take power or take the floor from another speaker'. Additionally, the Senate chair was far more likely to let male interrupters off lightly, while women were 2.5 times more likely than their male colleagues to be called words like 'emotional' and 'unreasonable'.

Men account for approximately 80 percent of US Congress. These hyper masculine environments allow for rampant sexism to be absorbed into corporate and political cultures and executed as standard practice, and the motivation for it goes right back to cultural anxiety about women getting the vote. These are deeply held belief systems, and they are insidiously upheld and reasserted by men banding together across political divides to protect what they perceive to be their rightful territory. Depressingly, Richards' *Let Her Finish* found that drastically uneven gender splits were still currently the *best-case scenario* for the treatment of women operating in these spaces—because the more even the gender ratio became, the more likely men were to try to reassert their dominance and, as Richards put it, 're-masculinise the environment'.

The question often asked, then, is what can women do to change this situation? How can we modify our behaviour in order to deflect the territorialism of men more comfortable with negotiating leadership from people who look like them? But why must we be the ones to navigate a solution to discrimination enacted not by us but against us? Other research shows that women who speak up more assertively are considered less likeable. We are conditioned instead to become what former Australian news anchor Tracey Spicer calls 'the glue in men's conversations' rather than equal participants in our own right.

Some women take to this role with gusto. In America, the stable of young, blonde, white Stepford wives who are trotted out on Fox News demonstrate just how toxic (and intoxicating) this is. They know which side their bread is buttered on, and they'll do everything they can to stop it from suddenly flipping over and landing smack-bang on the floor. Public figures like Christina Hoff Sommers, Ann Coulter and Candace Owens simper and suck up to men everywhere, determined to assure them that they're 'not like other girls'. 'Official Women' like this are frequently used as a counterpoint to the claim of persistent bias and sexism in public life. Ugly, brutish misogynists who loathe opinionated women convince themselves they're the least sexist people they know, because they just love reading 'sensible', 'smart' and 'respectable' women like Hoff Sommers. But it's easy to support the 'other' when these women are eagerly reinforcing everything you believe about your own superiority.

None of this is new. We shouldn't be shocked when accomplished women like Ocasio-Cortez, Abrams and Harris are treated as either less capable of assuming knowledge or more in need of being put in their place. Women are often told that we need to 'work harder' if we want to ascend career ladders (usually by men who've had to do significantly less to make it a lot farther). But that's because it's easy to keep making it a problem of our lack of adaptability or dynamism. How can we expect to challenge systems when we're being sabotaged and condescended to at every turn?

Our voices are not annoying and unwelcome and, despite popular opinion, we don't actually 'talk too much'. It is the system, not the women, that needs to be interrupted.

■

Manhood is never seen as an identity marker, particularly when it comes to leadership. Instead, masculinity is treated like a feature of leadership rather than a complex system in which certain people operate and are given benefit within. Conversely, womanhood is seen as a barrier to overcome, if not distance yourself from entirely. If you're a woman and you're seen to support fellow women, you're accused of participating in some kind of gender-based conspiracy, witches gathering under the full moon to hex all of mankind and take over the world. But because hypocrisy and shifting goalposts are so effective in keeping marginalised groups in line, it's also true that if you speak out against a (conservative) woman you'll be roasted for 'betraying the sisterhood'. We're damned if we do and damned if we don't.

Think about the pearl clutching that happened after American comedian Michelle Wolf delivered a blistering set at the White

House Correspondents' Dinner in 2018. Wolf *eviscerated* members of the Trump administration, some of whom were sitting mere feet away from her. Unsurprisingly, Donald Trump didn't show up for the second year running, because there aren't enough Twitter rants in the world to help the leader of the free world come to terms with people making jokes about him. Or, as Wolf put it, 'I would drag him here myself, but it turns out that the President of the United States is the one pussy you're not allowed to grab.' Savage, but also true.

This was just the first in a long line of brazen jokes at the expense of those complicit in the trash fire that is America's political governance right now. At thirty-two years old, Wolf observed, she was officially 'ten years too young to *host* this event, and twenty years too old for Roy Moore'. She went right to the very edge with a joke about abortion, and then gloated: 'It's 2018 and I'm a woman, so you cannot shut me up—unless you have Michael Cohen wire me $130,000.' She criticised Ivanka Trump for being 'as helpful to women as an empty box of tampons' and she just straight up called Kellyanne Conway a liar.

But, strangely, the most controversial joke of the night seems to have been one about Sarah Huckabee Sanders' 'perfect smoky eye'. Wolf set it up brilliantly, telling Sanders (who remained sitting next to her at the head table for the duration), 'I loved you as Aunt Lydia in *The Handmaid's Tale*. Mike Pence, if you haven't seen it, you would love it.' She then quipped, 'I actually really like Sarah. I think she's very resourceful. She burns facts, and then she uses the ash to create a perfect smoky eye. Maybe she's born with it, maybe it's lies. It's probably lies.'

The fallout was incredible, and only further confirms how people exploit the notion of 'sisterhood' to justify their own sexist critiques of women. MSNBC's Mika Brzezinski tweeted, 'Watching a wife and mother be humiliated on national television for her looks is deplorable.' Maggie Haberman from the *New York Times* tweeted: 'That [Sanders] sat and absorbed intense criticism of her physical appearance, her job performance, and so forth, instead of walking out, on national television, was impressive.'

This revisionism is extremely frustrating. Wolf didn't comment negatively on Sanders' looks at that dinner. That's a fact. The reference to *The Handmaid's Tale* had nothing to do with aesthetics and everything to do with how the terrifying Aunt Lydia represents the female enforcers of male rule in order to carve out some small corner of power within it. (Also, Ann Dowd—the actor who portrays Aunt Lydia in the TV series—isn't ugly. She's over sixty though, and conservatives often confuse those two attributes.)

What really grates here is the abject hypocrisy shown when people (but especially women) behave in ways that conservatives reserve as only acceptable for them. As *New Yorker* writer Emily Nussbaum tweeted, 'The more I think about it, the more impressed I am that Michelle Wolf did such a harsh act WITHOUT insulting any woman's looks. She aimed straight at the white female enforcers & never once suggested that anyone was a bimbo or a dog—like the man they work for surely would have.'

It's enraging to see the same people who otherwise gleefully reduce women to their looks, or who have even cheered on as Trump and his ilk routinely degrade and sexualise women, suddenly pretend that they find such things deplorable. Men like Rush Limbaugh and Piers Morgan lead a stable of similarly privileged bigots who are empowered to spew whatever abusive rhetoric they feel like against women and minorities, with nothing even remotely resembling penance or accountability broached by their employers. Only when it suits them do they pretend to take an interest in women and our rights to be treated like human beings.

The news cycle, particularly the one fed and fostered by social media, works so rapidly that today's furious tweets are tomorrow's distant ephemera. It's what allows the industry to keep men who offend, men who belittle, men who bully and gnash and snarl in their comfortable seats behind their powerful microphones and wide-reaching camera lenses. As management turns a blind eye, offering rudimentary apologies and tepid slaps on wrists, these men continue to cash enormous pay cheques and revel in their own self-importance and invincibility. Their bland apologies, usually offered petulantly and with the standard 'if I've caused you offence' proviso, are meant to be enough; any further demands for accountability are the actions of barking fringe activists trying to destroy free speech. 'Can we just get on with it?' they seem to splutter, as if the public fixation on their inability to do their jobs without breaking formal codes of conduct or defamation laws or defying common sense and decency is unreasonable and distracting.

Much of this spawns from the hyper-patriarchal nature of our country. The Sisterhood is ultimately viewed with suspicion, but being a Man's Man (particularly in Australia) is considered a pretty excellent thing. Man's Men slam back beers, never wear pink and are only allowed to cry when their football team either wins or loses. Whether or not these men exist en masse in reality or just mythology is irrelevant—the stereotype is heralded in the folksy colloquialisms favoured by the likes of Tony Abbott, with his 'good blokes' and 'fair dinkum Aussie' vernacular. Indeed, it was the Howard government, under which Abbott and his conservative policies flourished, that tried unsuccessfully to have 'mateship' included in the preamble of the Australian constitution. Even the preamble's author, Les Murray, didn't agree, arguing that it was 'blokish' and 'not a real word'. When Todd Russell and Brant Webb were rescued from the collapsed Beaconsfield Mine in 2006, then Prime Minister Howard praised the rescue effort as a 'colossal achievement of Australian mateship that has brought from the bowels of the earth two of our countrymen'.

The vision of 'Australian mateship' has always felt distinctly male to me, and I'm not really sure how I'm supposed to fit into it. Perhaps, as with most elements of Australian public life—dominated as it is by white men—I'm expected to just stand at the edge and offer my devotion and approval. Is this how women engage in 'mateship'? By cheering it on, even as it so roundly excludes us? It would appear so, which explains why we're also supposed to appear grateful whenever they throw us a bone.

Make no mistake, this bait-and-switch behaviour is part of a coordinated attack on women that finds leaders and media outlets emboldening the behaviour of people who might otherwise just be shouting into the void. For years News Ltd has run a sustained campaign in Australia with the sole objective of rallying public hatred of feminists and activists of colour, even as they continue to support 'controversial' figures like Milo Yiannopoulos while publishing headlines blaming women for the murderous actions of men. When women (and especially women of colour—remember Tarneen Onus-Williams, the Aboriginal activist who punctuated a blazing speech on Australia's racism at a rally on Invasion Day in 2018 with the battle cry, 'Burn [it] to the ground!' and was harassed by powerful media outlets afterwards calling for her to lose her job) challenge the status quo, the public is unrelenting in their quest to destroy their livelihood, not to mention bombard them with thousands of personally abusive comments and threats.

On Anzac Day in April 2017, activist Yassmin Abdel-Magied was subjected to the most despicable and violent of cultural attacks after she posted a simple seven-word status on Facebook about the tragedy of war: 'Lest. We. Forget. (Manus, Nauru, Syria, Palestine.)'

Unfortunately for Abdel-Magied, others don't consider Anzac Day (that special day on the Australian calendar when our citizens manage to combine the solemn observance of a nation's sacrifice with getting rat-arsed at the pub, pissing in doorways and abusing brown people on the train) to be an appropriate time to 'get political' and discuss the conflicts continuing today that have killed or displaced millions of people.

Abdel-Magied very quickly edited out the second part of her post and offered a genuine apology for causing offence. Despite this, a shit storm of abuse was hurled at her in the following days and weeks. She was hounded by the public, thousands of whom still subject her to vicious insults and threats more than a year later. Conservative politicians sought to make an example of her—presumably because there's no better way to shore up support for your party than by reassuring Australia's most virulent racists that you're on their side when it comes to the migrants. All over Abdel-Magied's public Facebook page and the rest of the internet, you can still read comments telling her she ought to be stoned in the street, that she should be deported, that she is an 'Islamic piece of shit' who should be 'beaten and sodomized', that she should jump off a bridge, that she should kill herself, that she is an 'ugly dog' who should 'get ready to be unemployed', that she is an 'Islamic extremist', that she supports the mutilation of little girls and that, above all, if she doesn't like it here in the land of freedom then she can fuck off.

All that, for a seven-word Facebook reflection that acknowledged the ongoing impact of war on a national day of remembrance. But, then, Abdel-Magied is a woman of colour and a Muslim, and there's perhaps nothing more Astrayan than coming together as a community to unleash racism against both.

The comedian Catherine Deveny (who is white) fared a little better when she shared her criticism of Anzac Day in 2018, though she still received thousands of death and rape threats. After her address was posted online, white nationalists turned up at her house with the intention of harassing her on film. Their supporters jeered: 'It's not illegal to knock on someone's door!' When they discovered she was in the process of reporting the harassment to police, they called her a 'typical feminazi' and a 'pussy'—because apparently women are supposed to just take it when strange men turn up to their house with the intention of abusing them.

Can you *imagine* the reaction if I were to turn up to some bloke's house armed with a camera, harass his teenage child and release his address to the public just because he said something I didn't like online? Christ, I'm called a bully when I just post screenshots of the shit men say to me.

When men and their female foot soldiers use misogyny to enforce the status quo, it's all Voltaire this and Voltaire that and, 'They have a right to speak their opinion!' and, 'Stop playing the gender card!'

But hell, that's probably just my tits talking.

■

The potential for abuse and harm by powerful men closing ranks around one another goes well beyond how women are treated in parliament. The sinews of patriarchy often bind tighter than those of political allegiance or loyalty. Some men simply do not want women working alongside them or above them; it makes them feel like their naturally ordained spaces are being invaded by people whom, outside of being mothers and wives, they don't really understand the point of. And so they make jibes and jeer, the bravado and entitlement growing alongside the gang of merry men willing to join them. They say that women have 'blood coming out of their eyes, blood coming out of their wherever'. They use words like 'shrill', 'shriek', 'hysterical' and 'banshee'. They talk about how a woman looks old and haggard, or how she's ugly, or the way she looks in her clothes. They compare her unfavourably with women who keep to their place, praising the latter for 'knowing how to act like a woman' and being 'refreshing'. They gather together to laugh at those women who dare to try to storm their play-forts, codifying their male supremacy and reinforcing who's really in charge. Those with the most power assemble to swing their dicks around (because there will always, *always* be cis men who care about such things). If it's a social occasion, they'll surround themselves with beautiful young women who are paid (not much) to be there, but whom they can pretend are there because they want to be.

In January 2018, an exposé was published into London's Presidents Club charity dinner, an annual fundraiser that for thirty-three years has brought together some of the city's richest and most powerful men to raise money for causes such as the Great Ormond Street Hospital. As per reporter Madison Marriage's article in the *Financial Times*, 'It is for men only. A black tie evening. Thursday's event was attended by 360 figures from British business, politics and finance and the entertainment included 130 specially hired hostesses.'

The hostesses in question were required to be 'tall, thin and pretty'. They were told their phones would be locked away for the evening, and warned they may have to put up with 'annoying men'. Marriage wrote: 'The hostess brief was simple: keep this mix of British and foreign businessmen, the odd lord, politicians, oligarchs, property tycoons, film producers, financiers, and chief executives happy—and fetch drinks when required.' In a brochure provided to guests, there was a full-page warning that 'no attendees or staff should be sexually harassed'. Still, multiple hostesses reported having been groped, with one woman saying a guest had exposed his penis to her and another saying a guest asked if she was a 'prostitute'.

'By midnight,' Marriage wrote, 'one society figure who the [*Financial Times*] has not yet been able to contact was confronting at least one hostess directly. "You look far too sober," he told her. Filling her glass with champagne, he grabbed her by the waist, pulled her in against his stomach and declared: "I want you to down that glass, rip off your knickers and dance on that table."'

To be clear, these weren't lads out on the town. These were powerful men who operate at the most elite levels of society. Of course, none of those whose names were publicised in connection with the event can remember seeing a thing. It's just amazing how many of them 'left early'.

The sense of being connected to something larger and purposeful—in this case, raising significant amounts of money for genuinely worthy causes—is what enables men in positions of power to claim rewards for their 'good deeds'. If you're donating $400,000 to a children's hospital, don't you deserve to have scantily clad women who are half your age and being paid a pittance drape themselves over you and flatter your ego? Don't you deserve to have other men *see* how powerful you are?

In May 2018, the *New York Times* reported on a 2013 trip to Costa Rica taken by the management team of the NFL's Washington Redskins and their cheerleading squad. (Please note that 'Redskins' is a racial slur, and from this point I will be referring to them as 'the Washington team'.) The trip was ostensibly for a 'calendar shoot'—so why did the Washington team's officials collect the women's passports when they arrived at the Costa Rican resort where they were booked to stay? Oh, sorry, I meant the *adults-only* resort, where the women were asked to pose topless and/or in nothing but body paint for the benefit of the spectators the team management had invited along. As *The Times* reported,

> A contingent of sponsors and FedEx Field suite holders—all men—were granted up-close access to the photo shoots.
>
> One evening, at the end of a 14-hour day that included posing and dance practices, the squad's director told nine of the thirty-six cheerleaders that their work was not done. They had a special assignment for the night. Some of the male sponsors had picked them to be personal escorts at a nightclub.

Those who spoke to *The Times* said they weren't required to have sex with the sponsors (imagine!), but the expectation they 'go as sex symbols to please male sponsors' shouldn't have been considered part of their job. This job, it should be noted, was not well remunerated. In fact, they were only paid transportation costs, meals and lodging. Also worthy of note: the five cheerleaders who spoke to *The Times* did so on condition of anonymity, because 'they were required to sign confidentiality agreements when they joined the team'. Men retain power for themselves and actively work together to keep women out of it, but they double down on that inequality by turning these spaces into playgrounds for men to peacock their sexual appetites and prowess to one another. It's telling that when Barnaby Joyce's affair with Vikki Campion was revealed, politicians from both sides of the aisle argued for his 'right to privacy'. The same courtesy was not extended to Cheryl Kernot when she, as an Australian Democrat, had a consensual sexual relationship with Labor's Gareth Evans and news of this was revealed after she left government. You could argue these two situations are incomparable, because the latter especially involved not just infidelity but also a party switch (Kernot moved from the Australian Democrats to the ALP in the midst of the five-year affair). Still, think about the different treatment Kernot received to Evans. When it entered the public domain, West Australian MP Don Randall sneered that she 'had the morals of an alley cat on heat'. In May 2018, Kernot told journalist Julia Baird that she's still questioned by journalists about the matter, even though decades have passed; Evans, meanwhile, has received an Order of Australia.

In 2013, news broke that a fundraising dinner for the LNP's Mal Brough had included a menu item described as 'Julia Gillard Kentucky Fried Quail: Small breast, huge thighs and a big red box'. At the time, Julia Gillard was the prime minister, and had been recently accused by Abbott of 'playing the politics of division'.

Senior members of the LNP rushed to distance themselves from the event, with the restaurant's owner, Joe Richards, ultimately claiming responsibility. It had been a 'private joke' between Richards and his son, he said, which raises the question of exactly what kind of masculine values were being instilled in that household.

In the fallout, it was made clear that anyone who kicked up a fuss—chicks, basically—was overreacting and falsely crying sexism. You know, 'playing the gender card'. It's a curious accusation that is levelled whenever women complain about entrenched inequality. Rather than listening to our experiences of exclusion and ridicule, men (and their supportive female enforcers of patriarchy) squawk about some mythical card that allows them to deflect any responsibility for their actions. It isn't that the world is sexist and that they benefit enormously from this discrimination—it's that women can't handle jokes. Throughout her leadership, Gillard was referred to as 'deliberately barren', accused of having the mining industry 'pussy-whipped' and queried on talkback radio about whether or not her long-term partner was gay. She dealt with all that *and* managed to pass an extraordinary number of pieces of legislation, even while fronting a minority government. Yet she's still sneered at for being 'the most ineffective Prime Minister this country's ever had!' and apparently that's why women suck as leaders.

It's easy to think of toxic male bonding and abusive, harmful behaviour happening either on the fringes of society or among people who lack influence and power. But the truth is, power is where this all stems from. Men showcasing their importance and claiming their rightful spoils, particularly so when they think no one's watching. In London, it might be a spot of groping and harassment at a charity auction with women who are not explicitly employed as escorts and sex workers (and certainly not paid for that). Sporting codes all over the world shield their golden-goose players from consequences, providing them with 'entertainment' that essentially translates to the provision of women as commodities. Men in business mentor and promote each other, citing babies as the reason women have to be kept down in the storeroom. Politically, there are still far too many men who'd prefer to retire to the billiards room to drink brandy, smoke cigars and play at being Masters of the Universe, even while they coordinate to make laws that govern women's bodies and deny us basic autonomy over our medical, reproductive and economic rights.

The message that this sends in adult life is as simple as if it were scrawled across the doorway of a treehouse: No Girls Allowed.

■

In 2016, as Trump's election victory was being declared, young white men attending a function at Sydney University (one of the country's most prestigious tertiary institutions) began chanting, 'Grab 'em by the pussy! That's how we do it!'

I know these men—or I know their type, at least. They are the ones who flock to feminist pages to mock our hysteria, who call us angry (and sometimes suggest it's because we are unrapeable), who taunt us with 'jokes' about sexual assault and domestic violence. They then insist, angrily, that women are too sensitive, that we criminalise male behaviour and tar all men with the brush that's painted the bad ones. They are the ones who hate women both publicly and privately, and yet assert that feminism's greatest crime is that we hate men. By the time I crawled out of bed that November morning, they had already begun flooding my Facebook page, crowing about how Trump's election would bring an end to 'feminazis'. They're barely out of adolescence, but they already believe that the world belongs to them. Why shouldn't they? Everywhere they look, they're reminded that they were born to rule.

For them, Trump's victory sent a clear message: you can do and say whatever you like to harm whomever you want, because you're the boss. Grab 'em by the pussy. They'll let you do it, and even if they don't no one will hold you to account for it. You were just having a joke. You can't help it if they overreacted and got hysterical. This is why women are unsuited to lead. They can't keep the sand out of their vaginas.

Those young men didn't believe women were lying about the times they said Trump assaulted them. They had even seen Trump admit to it himself. But they just don't care, because caring about things like the dignity and autonomy of women would mean they might not be able to behave exactly as they please at all times. Every time a Kavanaugh is confirmed and rewarded by a system that is designed by men, run by men, for men, it sends another very strong message about how men as a class will always be protected. They can grab 'em by the pussy all they like. They can assault women in closed bedrooms and nothing will happen. They can scream and spit at women who anger them, and no one will accuse them of hysteria only defend their righteous outrage while saying *we should all be very scared for our sons, it's a witch hunt these days*. Meanwhile, they can go on mocking the survivors of sexual assault eagerly and to much uproarious laughter, because this is apparently what powerful men do openly now and isn't it great they no longer have to hide their amazing comedy from the

PC police? They can do all this because the power and potential of privileged white men is still valued far more highly than the lives, bodies and autonomy of women, and any attempt to change this system will vigorously opposed.

We *should* all be deeply scared for our sons. Because the world we live in is telling them that as long as they're white and went to the right schools, it's okay to be criminals, rapists and assholes. Hell, you might even get to run the country one day.

It is good to be the king.

—10—

IT'S JUST A JOKE

The debate about 'rape jokes' (are they appropriate, is it okay to laugh at them, should they be defended) is decades old, but it's first major showing in the post-internet world can be traced back to 2012, when the set of a moderately well-known comedian at a Los Angeles comedy club spawned a viral Tumblr post, an outpouring of Hot Takes™ and a visible example of what it looks like when men close ranks around each other.

It began in July of that year, when a woman who remains anonymous turned up at the Laugh Factory in Hollywood. She was there to see Dane Cook, but stuck around after his set to watch a comic named Daniel Tosh perform. It was the first time she'd heard of him, but who doesn't love to laugh? At a factory of laughs, no less!

What the woman didn't know is that Tosh—who also hosted *Tosh.0*, a TV show on Comedy Central—is a big fan of jokes about rape. So committed is he to exploring the hilarity of rape that his catalogue of jokes about it even includes one involving his sister. Classy guy.

According to a Tumblr post published afterwards on *Cookies For Breakfast*, Tosh's set included a series of 'very generalizing, declarative statements' about rape jokes being universally hilarious. Presumably agitated by the blazing arrogance of a young white man deciding that the traumatic experiences of one-third of the world's women makes for excellent 'material' to advance his generic, lowest-common-denominator comedy career, the young woman called out, 'Actually, rape jokes are never funny!'

Now, everyone knows that if you heckle a comedian then they're going to turn what they hope is their razor-sharp wit on you. Disrupting the flow of someone's set is a faux pas that doesn't usually go down well, especially when the comedian's being called out for being a jerk. But Tosh's response was low even by the already low standards set for male comics who consider the trauma of everyone who isn't them to be their personal playground.

'Wouldn't it be funny if that girl got raped by, like, five guys right now?' he replied, pointing at her. 'Like right now? What if a bunch of guys just raped her?'

Yeah! Wouldn't that be TOTALLY FUNNY? That would really show her! Who does that bitch think she is, coming into a comedy club and thinking she has any right to tell the comedian—the EXPERT!—what is and isn't funny?! Jesus Christ, you'd think she'd actually been fucking raped or something.

Oh. Hmm.

I don't know whether or not the woman targeted by Tosh had a history that included sexual violence. My guess would be . . . probably? I mean, most women have had some kind of experience in which a man has pushed against the boundaries of her consent, if not smashed through them entirely. Sexual violence isn't always the central villain in our stories but it sure is a common enough backdrop for a lot of them. The thing is, even if she hadn't been assaulted in the way Tosh thought fit to joke about before inviting his audience to laugh at the thought of her being gang-raped, she almost definitely knows someone who has been. A woman doesn't need to have been raped herself to object to the use of rape as a cheap punchline by a comedian who is statistically far less likely than her ever to be subjected to such a violation.

After the woman posted her story to Tumblr, a number of people took to social media to condemn Tosh's behaviour. In a rare display of humility, he offered what he called a sincere apology, saying, 'The point i was making before i was heckled is there are awful things in the world but you can still make jokes about them. #deadbabies.'

But there were a number of mid- to high-profile comics who not only felt that Tosh shouldn't have had to apologise at all but who came out swinging in his defence. Dane Cook, the comedian the woman had originally bought tickets to see, tweeted: 'If you journey through this life easily offended by other people's words I think it's best for everyone if you just kill yourself.' Doug Stanhope tweeted to Tosh: 'You're hilarious. If you ever apologize to a heckler again I will rape you.'

Cute.

Alex Edelman, a stand-up comic from New York, warned against trying to make comedians accountable in the moment, telling *The Guardian*, 'If he actually addresses something you've said in a serious way, then a) he's abandoned his bit and b) he's actually made rape really come into the room.'

There's merit to the first part of this statement; comedians aren't there to debate philosophy or morality with their audience, and artful comedy has a precise and delicate flow. But Edelman's second observation isn't just total bullshit, it also signifies how unqualified he is to be making that kind of commentary. Rape is *already* in the room. It's in the traumatic histories of the people present who've experienced it, which is statistically one in five women and one in twenty men. It's in the way some people will tense up the moment they recognise a rape joke is coming, knotting their hands together and gazing steadfastly into their laps. It's in the glances cast around the room in that moment, as individuals look around to see if they're the only ones who aren't 'getting it' because someone once upon a time or maybe even last week made sure they 'got it' against their will.

Rape is in the room.

It's there with the survivors, but it's also in the room with the people present who've perpetrated it. Because make no mistake, they're there too. They're watching and listening and slapping their knees in spontaneous hilarity, and they're observing all the people around them who are doing exactly the same thing. You think rapists don't go and see comedians? Of course they do. And every time a rapist listens to a roomful of people laugh about something they've done—something they almost certainly don't think is that big a deal—they receive the reassuring message that they're not really so bad. That other people think like them. That other people have done the things they've done. That this is what *all* men are really like and, besides, if it were that big a deal, why would everyone find it so *funny*?

Think about one of Tosh's other big defenders, Louis C.K. During the controversy, he tweeted to Tosh: 'Your show makes me laugh every time I watch it. And you have pretty eyes.' Later, he claimed he'd been watching *Tosh.0* and broke a self-imposed social media detox to let Tosh know how funny he found him, completely unaware that it came in the middle of an online blow-up about the merits of offensive comedy and the people allowed to make it. He clarified his stance on *The Daily Show* with Jon Stewart, saying:

> For me, any joke about anything bad is great, that's how I feel. Any joke about rape, the Holocaust, the Mets—aargh, whatever—any joke about something bad is a positive thing. But now I've read some blogs during this whole thing that made me enlightened at things I didn't know. This woman said how rape is something that polices women's lives, they have a narrow corridor, they can't go out late, they can't go to certain neighborhoods, they can't dress a certain way, because they might—I never—that's part of me now that wasn't before, and I can still enjoy the rape jokes.

C.K. was born in 1967, which means it took him forty-five years to realise that rape is 'something that polices women's lives' and not just a peripheral act of violence that happens to some of us with the same probability and element of surprise as, say, dying in a plane crash or enjoying a Dane Cook movie. I first became aware of the circling threat of rape in women's lives before I'd even started my first period, but men like C.K. get to live for almost five decades before 'some blogs' open his eyes—don't worry though, he can 'still enjoy the rape jokes'.

But should we be surprised? In late 2017, shortly after widespread allegations against movie mogul Harvey Weinstein came to light, spawning the #MeToo and #timesup movements, the *New York Times* published an article under the headline LOUIS C.K. IS ACCUSED BY 5 WOMEN OF SEXUAL MISCONDUCT. The piece addressed longstanding rumours of C.K.'s indecent behaviour, which includes asking shocked female industry colleagues if he could masturbate in front of them (and sometimes proceeding to do it) and also masturbating while on a professional work call with a (female) performer whose boyfriend he had previously worked with.

Shortly after the publication of the story in the *Times*, C.K. issued a statement in which he admitted to the allegations, framing his motivation as arising from the curse of being 'admired'. In fact, in his statement he referred to the admiration people—and women especially—felt for him no less than four times, which was four times more than he mentioned the word 'sorry'. After dodging allegations for years and refusing even to entertain the possibility that there might be any truth to them, as if it were *beneath him* to acknowledge such meaningless, petty distractions, he had the gall to write: 'I learned yesterday the extent to which I left these women who admired me feeling badly about themselves and cautious around other men who would never have put them in that position.'

Like so many men caught with their pants down, what C.K. actually seems contrite about is the fact he was finally forced to own up to his actions. But his response is in keeping with his comments that night on *The Daily Show* (which, incidentally, came only a few months after the rumours of his behaviour were first published on the Gawker media network).

'I've read some blogs during this whole thing that made me enlightened at things I didn't know.'

'I learned yesterday the extent to which I left these women who admired me feeling badly about themselves.'

This whole thing is just such a SURPRISE to me!

Bull-fucking-shit.

Rape. Is. In. The. Room. The fact that men choose to ignore it is on them.

This wilful, arrogant dismissal of the relevance of women's experiences and feelings in the world is at the crux of why 'rape jokes' aren't actually a sacrosanct domain in which men can play at cutely shocking an audience while growing their own reputations. Comedy, like most industries with the potential for great reward and riches, is not only dominated by men but also protected by a network of them who want to maintain it as their own private bachelor pad. The lack of equality in women headlining or MCing comedy rooms, working as television comedy writers or performing on late-night sketch shows isn't because, as Christopher Hitchens fatuously argued in 2007, 'women aren't funny'. It's because structural sexism is alive and well, and if it's a challenge for a straight white man to ascend to the top of Yuk Yuk Mountain, just imagine how much more difficult it is for a woman (and more so for a woman of colour) to even get a look-in.

The efforts women in comedy have made to redress this, which include running women-only rooms or creating female comic networks, usually face opposition of some kind. *All-women comedy nights? But that's* sexist*! It should be about merit!* Or, my personal favourite: JUST IMAGINE THE OUTCRY IF MEN TRIED TO DO THIS!!!!!!!!

Mate, no one ever thinks of comedy bills that feature only men as some kind of weird and aggressive assault on the rights of people everywhere not to have gender equality shoved down their throats. That's because people think there are two kinds of people in the business of making others laugh: comedians, and 'female comedians'.

A few months after the Tosh performance got everyone talking about how bad men are at making jokes, an advertisement for a comedy debate in Melbourne began doing the rounds on social media. Resembling a 1940s film poster, it depicted a man and a woman locked in a violent embrace. The man held both the woman's arms in a vice-like grip as she appeared to be trying to wrestle free, his face and mouth contorted into the expression of someone who looks as if he's yelling. In vintage font, the poster announced:

STATION 59 PRESENTS

THERE'S NOTHING FUNNY ABOUT RAPE

A COMEDY DEBATE

Beneath that, the names of eight men appeared in columns marked *Affirmative* and *Negative*. Eight men, fledgling comics, who had been invited to present funny arguments about why rape might actually be a side-splitting topic, to be judged by a male adjudicator. Sounds promising!

The host of the Station 59 Open Mic night (and coordinator of this 'debate') was a man named Kieran Butler, and he was NOT happy to see the integrity of both himself and his event called into question. In the days and weeks following the release of the poster online, he moved to double and then triple down on his insistence that this was about 'freedom', 'democracy' and the right, as he saw it, to 'play in dangerous territory'. He defended Station 59 as a place where inexperienced comedians could 'fall and test out their material . . . and see whether it will work'. When Station 59 bowed to community pressure and cancelled the debate, Butler responded by planning another one for the following week, this time focusing on the question of whether it was inappropriate to host a rape debate in the first place. (Incidentally, Butler's championing of free speech in relation to public statements falls down somewhat given he's threatened to sue me for defamation twice.)

Remember, when survivors of sexual violence object to their trauma being used as a meeting ground for male comics to 'fall and test out their material', they're accused of enforcing whiny safe space bullshit. But when those same men are given boundaries of human decency, it's considered an assault on their fundamental right to free speech which they naturally feel entitled to test out in the 'safe space' of a supportive comedy room.

The Station 59 fiasco wasn't just about the broader topic of rape and who has the right to make cheeky quips about it. At the time, the community of Melbourne's inner north was still freshly grieving the brutal rape and murder of a local woman by the name of Jill Meagher. The Station 59 poster appeared barely two months after Jill was abducted as she walked home after a night out drinking with friends and colleagues. For a week, the community watched and waited in the hope that she would turn up unharmed, only to fracture a little inside when her body was found in a shallow grave fifty kilometres away from where a man named Adrian Bayley had raped and murdered her, and then loaded her into the back of his car so he could discard her by the side of a lonely stretch of road.

Between Jill's disappearance and the discovery of her body, more than a few news articles appeared questioning whether it had been 'sensible' for her to walk the short distance home that night rather than attempt to get a cab or, even better, accept the offer of a male friend to escort her home. She was characterised as a 'party girl' on a local talkback radio station after they'd gone through her Facebook photographs and found a few images in which she was drinking a beer and looked a bit squiffy. Her abduction, rape and murder prompted some (male) commentators to instruct women on what we needed to do to keep ourselves safe. You know it already. Don't walk home alone. Don't drink too much. Don't talk to strange men. Don't put yourself in a situation where you might force a man to sexually violate you.

But the community itself seemed to be having none of it, which made a refreshing change from the victim-blaming we had been so used to (and would, sadly, come to expect again when the memory of this event dulled a bit). After Jill's body was found, more than 30,000 people marched down Sydney Road, Brunswick, to protest the violence, particularly sexual, that is so routinely inflicted on women. Women especially were furious, and this fury became a galvanising force behind the feminist reawakening that has been happening in Melbourne ever since.

So to have a bunch of poxy, arrogant, entitled *fuckbags* sit there and argue about their right to sweat in a room together while cracking jokes about something that doesn't just (as C.K. found himself 'enlightened' about) 'police women's lives' but actually sometimes fucking *ends* them was too much to be borne.

Rape is in the room. It has always been in the room. Until we fundamentally change the dynamics of gender inequality, misogyny, violence and male entitlement, it will always be in the room. If you don't realise that, you have no business standing in front of an audience and using it as a lazy punchline for a bad joke. And if the person most likely to laugh the loudest at your 'provocative' comedy about the sexual violation of another human being is a fucking rapist, then you really have to ask yourself what point it is you're trying to make and whose side you're really on.

■

In 2014, the comedian and feminist writer Lindy West wrote a blog post detailing the year-long battle she'd had with a handful of male comics in Seattle who had taken umbrage at her suggestion that misogyny remained a problem in the comedy scene. Specifically, West was concerned about the entitlement many male comics feel when it comes to making jokes about rape.

In what has now become about as predictable as the daily Twitter storms issued by Donald 'stable genius' Trump, some of these men (and their friends and fans) responded to West by subjecting her to a maelstrom of online harassment. Women have come to expect this when we dare use our voices in public (and especially when we speak into the toxic void of the internet), but familiarity with the methods does not erase the exhaustion that they induce. For the crime of suggesting misogyny might remain a troubling bedfellow of some people working in her industry, West received numerous rape threats, dehumanising jokes about her appearance and weight, and general threats of violence—all things that women are also pompously instructed to ignore, as if complaining about them is a sign not only of weakness but also of hypersensitivity.

Again, note the ironic hypocrisy here: women are abused as fragile widdle babeez for not viewing violence they may actually have experienced as a solid basis for a laugh-a-thon, but men who respond by threatening them with that same violence are heroic freedom fighters defending their inalienable right to scale the cliffs of indecency that others are too afraid to go near. They didn't want to send that rape threat but you *forced* them to when you turned butthurt feminazi on them. And isn't forcing someone to send a rape threat kind of just as bad as forcing someone to do sex? Think about it.

Here's where things get especially ridiculous. One of the comedians who targeted West (in her bestselling memoir *Shrill*, she gives him the pseudonym 'Dave', so we'll go with that) was challenged by West's husband over a comment Dave made in which he said he would love to see West fall down a flight of stairs. In the ensuing email conversation, West's husband told Dave that he would love to talk about it in person.

Dave's response was to take a knife and a gun to the local comedy club in which the trio would all be appearing—'just in case'. In a Facebook post, he wrote: 'I had a switchblade on me, a 9mm in my trunk and I was ready for anything. I know that sounds insane but I've had a wayward past and like I said any time another man threatens me, I take it seriously.'

Just think about that line, and then think about it in the context of a society that insists women just brush off threats, abuse and 'jokes' that draw on centuries of misogyny and specifically gendered violence.

Any time another man threatens me, I take it seriously.

Women, you see, are not allowed to interpret men's actions as threatening because this hurts men's feelings. We are not allowed to 'take seriously' the words and vague intimations of men who make us feel uncomfortable, because not only is that casting aspersions on his intentions, it's also besmirching all men by painting them as rapists, woman-beaters and *misogynists*. And it isn't just the misogynistic banter of comedians we aren't allowed to object to. We're also ridiculed and frequently abused for speaking out against comments made by our male friends, our family members, the public figures who infiltrate our visual and audio landscapes, the men with whom we go to school or work and the men we are entreated to ignore online, sometimes even in spaces we are in charge of monitoring.

Imagine, for a moment, the incandescent outrage a woman would provoke if she announced on the internet that she had taken a gun to a public venue because a man she'd argued with had said he wanted to see her soon and 'any time a man threatens me, I take it seriously'. Think of all the different kinds of ways she'd be denounced as a 'lunatic'. The ridicule that would be heaped on her for being a paranoid, terrified 'fembot', a woman who was so *insane* that she genuinely believed she was *under threat from men who had used their words to threaten her!*

Women are offered up as bodies to be torn apart when we so much as *quip* about men being something other than perfect gods with perfect intentions. When I wrote a private joke in a friend and fellow feminist writer's book riffing on assumptions about homicidal feminist misandry, an international tabloid media outlet published an article claiming, with zero irony, that I had written a 'sick note' to a 'fan'* encouraging her to 'kill men'. Tweets that I've written in what's clearly satirical jest (no, I don't think 'all men must die'—just the annoying ones) have been painstakingly collected and turned into collages that are then posted incessantly

* The journalist responsible knew that the 'fan' in question was a friend of mine, because they previously sat next to each other *when they worked at the same media outlet*. A photograph of the ironic inscription had been posted on her private Instagram account months before, and then mysteriously 'discovered' by her former colleague immediately after I announced I had signed a contract to write this book. Curiously, she was never contacted for a quote and her relationship to me was never qualified for the website's audience.

in response to any argument I make about the very real, very serious problem of men's violence against women—a violence that destroys women's mental health, damages our bodies and psyches, and sometimes, all too fucking often in fact, robs us of our lives.

We might begin our feminist lives as wide-eyed naifs with earnest and gently expressed views about equality, but we quickly learn that advocating for women's liberation from a system of oppression that disenfranchises, abuses and humiliates us on a daily basis is *exactly the same thing* as calling for all men's hearts to be ripped out through their throats and taken to the town square to be displayed on a series of spikes that spell out LET THIS BE A WARNING, FUCKERS. If we don't direct the majority of our feminist attention into making sure men feel adequately respected and in no way, shape or form implicated in what we're discussing, then we're treated like pariahs whose only use for (cis) men is in harvesting their testicles for food during the long, cold winter. (Which, to be fair, is kind of my only use for men. JUST KIDDING! They're also good at opening jars.)

Women are not shown the same leniency as men or given the same benefit of the doubt when it comes to the comedic observations *we* make about the world. Our 'sensitivities' are treated as evidence of our incapacity to participate in a grown-up sphere, even as the men angrily lashing out against them are framed as ideological defenders of free speech and the open exchange of ideas.

There are only so many times you can be told your objection to the ritual abuse and oppression of women is really just an unnecessary and mean attack on men before you decide *fuck it* and agree with whatever nonsense they decide to throw at you. After all, that's where my sun cannon joke came from. After a man lost his job for abusing me online, someone hissed at me on Twitter, 'You won't stop until all the men in the world are fired.' I replied, 'I won't stop until all the men in the world are fired . . . into the sun!'

Reader, you'd be surprised by how many people seem to genuinely believe I'm building a death cannon in the desert.

None of this is to say that comedy can never invoke horrible topics or touch on issues that emphatically make people's lives worse. Contrary to how it may seem, I don't believe that jokes about the subject of rape are universally terrible or in poor taste. Comedy can be an extremely effective tool when used to subvert stereotypes and ideas that abound in a rape *culture*. For example, one of the funniest jokes I know involves a woman whose boyfriend has asked her to explore a rape fantasy as part of their sex life. Despite her hesitation, her friends urge her to go along with it because it's something he really wants—and besides, it's not like he's actually going to *do* it. So she agrees and they plan for him to stage a break-in at their house the following evening.

At the appointed time, he pushes through the back door and into a house submerged in darkness. Suddenly, the kitchen light flips on to reveal the woman standing there with a gun pointed directly at him. She tells him to get out of her house and warns him that if he ever dares to come back, she won't hesitate to pull the trigger.

When she tells her friends about it the next day, they're aghast. 'But why would you do that?' they ask.

'Well,' she replies, 'that's *my* rape fantasy.'

Somehow, I don't think Tosh and co. would like that one too much.

■

But if it's crude misogyny and reprehensible dialogue about women you're after, there is no shortage of examples to be found in some of the men-only Facebook groups that operate 'in secret' in countries all over the world. In Australia, the most famous of these is *Blokes Advice*. At one point boasting over 300,000 members, the group has frequently found itself in the news with the exposure of its general vibe of enthusiastic jokes about violence against women (often referred to in these groups as '2 holes'), rape and the circulation of image-based abuse (otherwise known as 'revenge porn').

You know, just a bunch of blokes hanging out and doing what blokes apparently do.

Some time in 2016 or 2017, I started sharing screencaps of posts that people had been sending me (and a whole bunch of these came from dudes who were disgusted by the behaviour they witnessed on BA so, you know, #notallmen). Hooley dooley, the backlash was intense. It turns out that men who frequent pages like *Blokes Advice* (and *Yeah The Boys*, and *Brothers Unite*, and *Angry Men With Raging Boners For Misogyny And Chronically Fragile Egos*—okay, I made that last one up too) do not like it when people—namely, women and especially me—signal boost their comedy to the rest of the world. The abuse rolls in like a storm, except instead of crashes of thunder and electricity that lights up the sky, it's just a constant rumble of words like *slut*, *whore*, *bitch* and *cunt* and photoshopped images of my head on top of a pig's body. Given the overflow of memes and collages that spew forth from these groups, I should at least be reassured that some men are bucking patriarchal notions of masculinity by being super into crafting.

Occasionally, amid the spray of insults, some members of *Blokes Advice* will try to explain what it is I'm not getting about a community that enjoys trading images of women with black eyes and split lips captioned with punchlines like: 'I said make me a sandwich!'

'It's dark humour,' they say. 'It's meant to release tension.'

Or: 'What happened to freedom of speech?!'

And: 'It's not real, you fucking retard!* It's not like the blokes laughing at it are really gonna go out and do it! Stop demonising men!'

Oh, right, because men never rape women—I FORGOT.

There are a few things wrong with this argument, but let's start with the most obvious: your nominal freedom of speech doesn't mean that people have to agree with you. It doesn't mean they have to smile sweetly and laugh politely when you tell jokes that align you with the perpetrators of deeply traumatising crimes like rape and paedophilia. It doesn't mean your colleagues or employer have to accept your passions as representative of company diversity ('Tanisha from Accounts is a child of Sri Lankan migrants while Damien over in Sales really loves coming up with one-liners about beating women)'. And, perhaps most pertinently, people are allowed to find you gross and threatening according to the nature of the free speech you choose to defend.

When feminists talk about rape culture, we don't mean a culture in which men are being given comprehensive government-sanctioned instructions on how to rape women and get away

* I've quoted this insult a few times in this book, but I wasn't sure if I should at first because it's such an ugly, ableist word. In the end, I decided it was important to show that this kind of hate speech is as much a part of the vocabulary of these young men as words like 'cunt', 'whore', 'bitch' and 'slut'. We should be just as disgusted by the widespread use of ableism as we are by misogyny, and identifying its practice is one of the first steps.

with it. We mean a culture in which the criminal activity of rape is minimised and normalised through dismissive attitudes, victim-blaming, the defence of 'boys being boys' and, yes, the use of sexually violent imagery and disrespect for consent as a vehicle for laughter. There are exceptions, but the overwhelming majority of rape is perpetrated by men against women. So when men sit around trying to outdo each other with how 'savage' their rape comedy can be, their female acquaintances (particularly those who have been raped) are well within their rights to decide those men aren't safe for them to be around.

This matters not just because rape is real but because *rapists* are real. They have real lives with real friends, real jobs and real families. And they walk among us.

In 2015, the circus performer and comedian Adrienne Truscott began touring her phenomenal (and phenomenally successful) show *Asking For It: A one-lady rape about comedy*. In it, she launches an excoriating attack on rape culture and the famous men who've abused their positions to, well, abuse women. Men like Bill Cosby, Daniel Tosh and Woody Allen. The first time I saw it, I didn't know whether to laugh hysterically or cry. Some women in the audience did both.

Afterwards, Adrienne and I had a couple of beers outside and talked about the content. She told me about the time she sat in a college class listening to her tutor share some statistics on sexual violence. To a roomful of bored or impassive students, he reiterated the statistic that one in five women will experience sexual violence in their lifetimes.

'Don't you care about this?' he asked his students. 'Don't you have anything to say about it?!'

'I've got something to say,' Adrienne declared, looking around the room. 'I wanna know which one of y'all raped us.'

It's a brilliant point, and it's how we should start reframing the dialogue around sexual violence. Discussion that fixates on the victims and survivors only succeeds in erasing the perpetrators. If the majority of perpetrators are known to their victims, it stands to reason that they move in the same communities we do. And if university students in particular are at risk of being sexually assaulted (which they are), then the question is an essential one to ask: *Which one of you raped us?*

Here's some frightening data for you. In 2002, academics David Lisak and Paul M. Miller published their paper 'Repeat rape and multiple offending among undetected rapists' in the peer-reviewed journal *Violence and Victims*. The pair posed the following four questions to a sample group of 1882 male college students with a median age of 26.5:

> (1) Have you ever been in a situation where you tried, but for various reasons did not succeed, in having sexual intercourse with an adult by using or threatening to use physical force (twisting their arm, holding them down etc.) if they did not cooperate?
> (2) Have you ever had sexual intercourse with someone, even though they did not want to, because they were too intoxicated (on alcohol or drugs) to resist your sexual advances (e.g. removing their clothes)?
> (3) Have you ever had sexual intercourse with an adult when they didn't want to because you used or threatened to use physical force (twisting their arm; holding them down etc.) if they didn't cooperate?

(4) Have you ever had oral sex with an adult when they didn't want to because you used or threatened to use physical force (twisting their arm; holding them down etc.) if they didn't cooperate?

Of the 1882 students, 120 admitted to rape or attempting to rape. A third of these (44) admitted to only one assault, but the remaining 76 outed themselves as repeat offenders who were collectively responsible for 439 rapes or attempted rapes—an average of 5.8 each.

Lisak and Miller also confirmed their theory that rapists were responsible for more violence generally, particularly violence involving an intimate partner, the physical or sexual abuse of a child and sexual assaults other than attempted or completed rape. Repeat rapists were more likely to be violent overall, accounting for 28 percent of the reported violence (more than 1000 out of almost 4000 incidents) across the entire 1882-man sample.

In 2009, Stephanie McWhorter conducted a similar longitudinal study that involved a sample of 1146 newly enlisted men in the US Navy, tracing their behaviour back to the age of fourteen. Of this sample, 144 men (13 percent) admitted to attempting or completing a rape. However, once again the much larger sample of men within this group of rapists (71 percent) admitted to being repeat offenders, clocking an average of 6.36 assaults each. Together, they were responsible for just over 800 rapes.

Across both studies, the majority of admitted rapes involved intoxication of the victim. A quarter involved force and approximately one-sixth were a combination of the two. Crucially, McWhorter's research indicated that men who grow up to be rapists are likely to start in adolescence.

In 2014, researchers Sarah Edwards, Kathryn A. Bradshaw and Verlin B. Hinsz published a study out of North Dakota titled 'Denying rape but endorsing forceful intercourse: Exploring differences among responders'. The study was limited in terms of numbers and demographics (only seventy-three participants had their answers analysed, and these men were all white and heterosexual), but it appears to correlate with the findings of Lisak, Miller and McWhorter. Rather than querying criminality, the study looked at the language of intention. Specifically, what are the circumstances in which men would cop to rape?

The findings were bleak but unsurprising. A third of participants admitted they would rape a woman if they could guarantee it would remain a secret and they would suffer no consequences. However, they would only admit this *when it wasn't called rape*. Instead, the question was framed as 'intentions to force a woman into sexual intercourse'. A smaller percentage—13.6 to be precise—were willing to admit the same when it was explicitly referred to as rape. Researchers found that men who admitted freely to rape intentions had 'angry and unfriendly' attitudes towards women, such as thinking women were manipulative or deceitful (both of which are feminine traits insisted on by some of the more vigorously misogynistic men who find their home in groups like *Blokes Advice*). The men who admitted to intentions of force were only marginally better, displaying attitudes to the researchers that indicated a 'callous sexism' towards women.

These aren't definitive studies, but they provide us with a good starting point for assessing not just the attitude of rapists in our society but also how they are formed. Sexism is not peripheral to the crime of rape—it is *central*. And making light of violence while elevating the superiority and hypermasculinity of men encourages the perpetrators hiding within those communities to believe that they're in the right. Some might argue that three studies aren't enough to form a definitive picture of sexual violence, and they're probably right. But they help to illustrate part of the broader problem. Even within this relatively small sample of research studies, there were still more than 1200 incidents in which a human being was subjected to rape or attempted rape. The sample might be insignificant, but the trauma endured by those 1200 people isn't—and yes, we should be disturbed by it.

When we talk about rape, no matter what the context might be, we have to assume that we're also talking TO rapists. Most rapists don't fall into the category of Alleyway Attacker. Most rapists probably wouldn't even consider themselves rapists so much as opportunists. And I've got a news flash for you—a Facebook group of 300,000 men definitely has rapists in it. When these men see their online pals in groups like *Blokes Advice* and *Yeah The Boys* sitting around and laughing heartily at sexual violence, rape and violence against women, what does it confirm to them about the validity of their own behaviour? When they see men brainstorming increasingly violent and 'hilarious' ways to humiliate and degrade women, talking about '2 holes', 'whores' and 'c—s', what do they think about how other men express misogyny? When sons hear their fathers make these same jokes, what does it tell them about masculinity and the kinds of men they should be—the kind of men that it's *okay* to be?

I'll tell you what they don't think. They don't think, 'There's something wrong with me.'

I can yell all this until the cows come home (on time, please—we know what happens to girls who stay out too late), but the critique of misogynist humour as a bonding mechanism always results in spirited declarations of all the supposed good these kinds of groups do. *Blokes Advice* in particular is often defended as providing a safe space for men struggling with depression to reach out and get support. No one could fault men seeking help for the mental health issues that traditional notions of masculinity have instructed they repress, but that shouldn't come at the expense of decency and respect for women. Believe it or not, feminists welcome men deconstructing the shame inflicted on them for having feelings. What we object to is the cavalier dismissal of women's mental health alongside it. Survivors of rape and domestic violence experience an elevated risk of PTSD, depression and anxiety. Why should they respect a space that claims on the one hand to be saving the lives of sad men while doing it at the expense of women's own sanity and wellbeing? There's nothing wrong with a masculinity that forms bonds between men and challenges harmful ideas around stoicism and fragility—but that masculinity becomes toxic the moment it relies on misogyny as a means for that connection to occur.

These attitudes aren't excusable. Some of the men who indulge in them so gleefully may just be childish and ignorant, but there are others who harbour a genuine hatred of women. It's impossible for women to know which is which, so the only logical approach is for us to treat all of them with suspicion. And yet, this self-preservation is consistently treated as more offensive and dangerous than the behaviour that spawned it in the first place. Why are women expected to laugh at jokes that make light not just of the violence we are at greater risk of experiencing but that many of us have already experienced? And why is it that the men who are so loud about women needing to relax and stop taking everything so personally are the ones so catastrophically incapable of self-reflection and humility?

Laughing at sexual violence isn't a harmless activity, nor should it be excused because 'well, at least men are chatting about their feelings'. The fact is, you don't know whether the person who loves to ponder the ways he might 'humorously' rape a woman is just a terrible comedian or a serial offender. But given the force with which women are condescendingly advised to practise a more sensible awareness of our safety, can you really blame us for viewing with deep suspicion and fear the men who bond with one another over jokes about harming us?

Until we develop a fail-safe way to identify sexual predators, all we have to go on is people's behaviour. If you don't want to be seen as a potential rapist, maybe the first step would be to stop minimising the criminal action of rape because you think it's an easy way to get a cheap laugh.

■

We aren't powerless against these forces. One of the practical measures we can take is to exercise our rights as consumers to oppose the use of violence and even just basic sexism to sell products. We don't have to put up with it, and we have more power to create change than we might imagine. Think about the protest movement against Wicked Campers, a business that had long held the dubious reputation of being Australia's most feral transport hire company. Popular among backpackers and people who don't mind looking like total cockspanners in public, the fleet was infamous for boasting slogans like 'In every princess there is a little slut who wants to try it just once' and 'Nice legs . . . what time do they open?'.

The Advertising Standards Bureau had handed down rulings on Wicked Campers before, but they were essentially impossible to enforce. But at the start of 2017, after a long and sustained public campaign against the company, the Queensland state government passed legislation that would 'ban offensive and indecent advertisements' on vans and vehicles. The new legislation didn't explicitly target Wicked Campers, but it did ensure that companies like them who refused to comply with ASB rulings within fourteen days would risk having their vehicles deregistered. It was the first time legislative measures had been taken to combat the rampant sexism skeezing its way around the country, and it was seen as a huge win for campaigners who'd fought to have the vehicles removed from circulation.

Sometimes, just having the conversations can be a good place to start, not only for the people struggling to find the funny but also the people angrily defending it. Figuring out who or what a joke's punchline is aimed at isn't just about showing off your progressive credentials—it's also about learning how to tell smarter jokes.

When a company like Wicked Campers puts a van on the road with the slogan 'Fat girls are harder to kidnap' or 'I can already imagine the gaffer tape on your mouth', the question has to be asked: what's the joke supposed to be? In a country that bears the legacy of Anita Cobby (a twenty-six-year-old nurse who, in 1986, was kidnapped by a carful of men who then gang-raped, tortured and murdered her before abandoning her body in a paddock), not to mention the Ivan Milat backpacker murders, what could possibly be funny about the image of someone restrained against their will in the back of a van? In a world where women are abducted, bundled into vehicles and then imprisoned in rape dungeons for years on end, who looks at a white van and thinks, *Let's brighten up this wagon with some light-hearted one-liners about rape*!

If you have to explain the joke, it's either not as funny as you think it is or you've picked the wrong audience. But if you *can't* explain the joke in reasonable terms—and by that I mean provide an actual argument for how the joke fits together and what truths about society it draws on rather than just scream *but it's funny!*—then perhaps you've misjudged its right to sit in the humour oeuvre.

The kinds of misogynist 'jokes' scrawled across Wicked Campers' vans or shared in groups boasting tens of thousands of members or told at the pub or on university lawns or around family dinner tables or private political functions or in male dominated comedy rooms and which are then defended by the (mostly) men who angrily defend their right to find them funny cannot be divorced from the reality of men's violence against women, because this violence is happening every minute of every day. And if you're joking not just about people over whom you have power but also about the violent, degrading practices to which that power ensures you yourself will never be subjected, you are not laughing at or creating clever comedy. You are revelling in your own privilege, and perpetuating the normalisation of violence against people who have less social and political capital than you.

And we are right to consider you a risk to our safety.

■

In *Writing the Male Character* (1982), the Canadian novelist Margaret Atwood recounts the time she asked a male friend why men feel threatened by women:

'I mean,' I said, 'men are bigger, most of the time, they can run faster, strangle better, and they have on average a lot more money and power.'

'They're afraid women will laugh at them,' he said. 'Undercut their world view.'

Later, she posed the same question to women in a poetry seminar she was giving: 'Why do women feel threatened by men?'

'They're afraid of being killed,' came the reply.

–11–

ASKING FOR IT

'You don't know me, but you've been inside me.'

So wrote the survivor at the centre of yet another college-based sexual assault, in a powerful victim impact statement that briefly shone a spotlight on the issue of rape culture for a global audience. Within days of it being published by *Buzzfeed*, the woman's statement had been shared more than twelve million times. It was blistering, precise and devastating.

For fellow survivors, her words were all too familiar.

The woman was addressing a young man named Brock Turner, who was charged in 2015 with the felony assault of her as she lay unconscious outside a Stanford University party. During the assault, Turner removed her clothes and digitally penetrated her with such force that she was left with 'significant trauma' to her genitalia. Later, the woman's impact statement would reveal that the medical examiners had found a mixture of debris, including pine needles, in her vagina.

There were witnesses to the crime: two Swedish graduate students riding past on their bicycles interrupted the assault after realising the young woman lying beneath Turner was unconscious. Turner tried to flee, but the Swedes held him down until the police arrived.

During the course of the subsequent trial, Turner's family and friends described him in glowing terms as a young man whose real crime was that he had consumed too much alcohol. A letter of support from Turner's father lamented the young man's lack of appetite since the trial began, imploring the judge not to punish him for what amounted to 'twenty minutes of action'. Media outlets couldn't resist mentioning Turner's status as a champion swimmer, their stories illustrated by photographs of the young white man smiling. In news cycle time, it took an entire ice age for media to publish his mugshot (a move that has as much to do with white supremacist culture as it does rape culture—think of the photographs these same outlets choose to publish of the young black men murdered by police officers in the United States).

Once convicted of felony assault, Turner faced a maximum sentence of fourteen years in prison. But Judge Aaron Persky offered the view that a young man like Turner—white, athletic and 'from a good family'—wouldn't fare well in federal prison. Instead, he was sentenced to six months in the Santa Clara county jail. He was out in three.

This is what rape culture looks like.

■

Whenever I write or speak about rape culture, I'm invariably challenged by young men questioning its very existence.

'Rape happens, does not make it a rape "culture" though,' one young man wrote to me recently. 'People don't support rapists, we punish them. Therefore it is not our "culture".'

No amount of evidence would convince him otherwise—not the statistics on rape convictions, which show that fewer than 1 percent of all cases brought to police result in a guilty verdict, nor the daily examples of language used to minimise rape and its impact on survivors, nor even the numerous high-profile cases that demonstrate just how readily people lend their support to men accused of rape.

A few years ago, I delivered a lecture on sexual violence to a group of around a hundred students at a university. I took great care to define 'rape culture' not as a system that enthusiastically and brazenly teaches people how to rape but one that instead minimises the perceived impact of sexual violence by teaching society that there are always extenuating circumstances. *She went home with him. She gave him mixed signals. She was drinking. She was flirting. She was dressed like she wanted it. She didn't say no or fight back. She's done it before. What was he supposed to do?*

During my talk, I carefully went over the details of the Turner trial, including the fact that his swimming record was frequently mentioned in articles covering the assault charges and that his status as a young white man with a privileged upbringing earned him special consideration when it came to sentencing.

When I'd finished speaking and called for questions, a young man put his hand up.

'How can you claim we live in a rape culture?' he demanded. 'No one is teaching anyone else to rape! Everybody hates rape! Rapists get, like, really long sentences!'

Reader, there aren't enough #facepalms in the world.

It seems to be young men especially who live in this fantasy land where 'everyone' is universally opposed to rape, no ifs, ands or buts. I'm probably reading too much into it (because I *am* a hysterical, man-hating banshee, after all), but it's almost as if men are socialised with a completely different set of rules and expectations when it comes to understanding the role that sexual violence plays in our society. Weird, right?

Rape culture doesn't refer to a system in which sexual violence is being overtly encouraged or taught. Rather, it characterises a society in which the impact of sexual violence is not only minimised but the definition of what constitutes 'real' sexual assault is considered up for public debate and scrutiny. It enforces and codifies the language of victim-blaming and perpetrator-excusing. It very carefully provides an array of caveats and explanations for why the ordinary boys and men who comprise the majority of perpetrators of sexual violence (as opposed to the more popular view of the Alleyway Monsters) are not really to blame for their actions. In terms of how 'culture' is conceived in this concept, it's better to think of it as less the yoghurt itself and more the fermentation process that creates the perfect conditions for the yoghurt to exist.

A function of rape culture is that it works especially hard to provide excuses for the rich young white men whose careers and futures are treated with more respect than the bodies of the women they assault (particularly when those bodies belong to women of colour, sex workers, working-class women, disabled women or any combination of those characteristics). The other young men who question my stance on this issue no doubt genuinely believe that 'everybody hates rapists'—but that's because rape culture has succeeded in convincing the general population that rapists never look like men you know and, therefore, the men you know can never actually be rapists.

Supporters (conscious or otherwise) of rape culture are extremely invested in maintaining the fiction about what properly defines a rapist. A rapist isn't the man you work with or the one you drink beers with at the pub. He isn't the man you train with at the gym or the one you play football with on the weekend. He isn't the nice young lad who lives in a college dorm while studying engineering. A rapist isn't married with children, nor does he have parents or siblings or a network of people who've known him all his life. He isn't the bloke who fixes your car, the one who holds the door open for stragglers, the man who sells you vegies at the greengrocer or that nice guy who reads the weather on the evening news. He isn't your brother, your son, your boyfriend or your husband. He's certainly never wealthy or even from a moderate middle-class background, and his class—especially when combined with white skin—protects his actions from ever being likened to those of a *real* rapist.

Real rapists, as everyone knows, are those antisocial, itinerant Shadow Men who live in the walls and bear no resemblance to other men at all. Real rapists exhibit openly misogynistic attitudes, which is how you can tell the difference between them and men whose misogyny is cloaked in more complex contradictions, the men who are 'really good blokes' who, at worst, have 'just made a mistake' and at best are being hounded by vengeful women after fame and money.

Listen, it would certainly be a lot easier if rapists were easy to identify by the five-pronged tail growing out of their butts. If we could clock rapists in both public and private spaces, we could better protect ourselves from their choices. Unfortunately, life isn't that simple. Rapists aren't accompanied by the piercing smell of rotten eggs, nor is their skin covered in thorns. Rapists do indeed look just like everyone else.

Why, some of them probably even look like men you know.

■

If you don't think you need to be worried about the lessons young men are learning about entitlement, sex and coded male bonding, then allow me to demonstrate to you in meticulous detail why you're wrong.

Towards the end of March 2018, as the international cricketing world twisted itself into knots over evidence of ball tampering by the Australians (not the first time men from this country have been caught fiddling with their balls, to be honest), a far more damning example of male entitlement in team sports was coming to its judiciary conclusion in Ireland. Unlike the manipulation of an inanimate object, this incident involved the alleged sexual assault of a young woman by two well-known rugby players, the alleged attempted sexual assault of her by one of their teammates and the alleged attempts to obstruct justice for the young woman by a mutual friend of all four men.

Just another day on the elite male sportsmen stage, I guess.

If you have even a passing knowledge of rape culture, you'll be unsurprised to learn that the first of these transgressions (the ball tampering) triggered more anger among the general public than the second—because *obviously* being caught cheating in the world's most boring game is a far greater crime than colluding with your mates to sexually degrade and violate 'some slag' at a party.

But let's back up a little.

The complaint relates to events that took place in the early hours of 28 June 2016. Ulster rugby players Paddy Jackson, Stuart Olding and Blane McIlroy and their friend Rory Harrison had been out drinking in Belfast. After spending a few hours in the VIP area at Ollie's nightclub in the Merchant Hotel, at 2.30 am they decided to head back to Jackson's house to continue partying. They were accompanied by four young women.

At 5 am, one of these young women—we'll call her Jane Doe—was escorted home in a taxi by Harrison. According to later courtroom testimony given by the taxi driver, she was 'crying and sobbing throughout the journey' and 'definitely seemed very upset'. The driver recalls that Harrison appeared to be comforting the woman while speaking 'in code' on the phone with an unnamed person. As the driver told the court, 'I recall him saying to the person on the phone, "She is with me now, she is not good, I will call you in the morning."'

What transpired between 2.30 and 5 am on the morning of 28 June would later become the subject of a jury trial with four defendants: Jackson, facing one charge each of sexual assault and rape; Olding, one charge of rape (with a second charge of sexual assault having been dropped earlier); McIlroy, one charge of exposure; and Harrison, one charge of perverting the course of justice and withholding information.

So, what happened?

THE PARTY

(Readers are advised the following account contains graphic descriptions of rape and sexual assault.)

In a transcript of a WhatsApp conversation presented to the court, Jane Doe is shown texting her friend the next day saying she'd had the 'worst night ever' and had been 'raped by 3 Ulster fucking scum'. In a series of messages, she alleges Jackson followed her into a bedroom when she went to get her bag. She says he came up behind her and 'the next thing I'm bent over the bed'. Her friend asked, 'Were there more than one?', to which Jane Doe replied, 'Two and then a third tried to get involved. I was crying.'

During the eventual trial, the prosecution argued that while Jackson vaginally raped Jane Doe, Olding entered the room and proceeded to orally rape her. Jane Doe told the court the alleged assault only ended after a third man, McIlroy, entered the room with his penis in his hand and said, 'You fucked the other guys, why won't you fuck me?'

'It was at that point that my fight instinct kicked in,' she told the eight men and three women sitting on the jury.

After this, Harrison (the one later charged with perverting the course of justice) escorted Jane Doe home in a taxi, her sobbing on his shoulder. Phone records later showed that the person he'd been overheard speaking with on the phone was McIlroy. A few minutes after this call, CCTV footage at Jane Doe's home shows Harrison walking her to the front door and giving her a hug. Shortly afterwards, he sent her a message saying, 'Keep the chin up you wonderful young woman.'

'Thank you so much for leaving me home,' Jane Doe replied. 'I really appreciate it Rory, you've been far too kind.'

THE AFTERMATH

The next day, Harrison held two concurrent conversations over WhatsApp—one with McIlroy, and one with Jane Doe.

At 12.01 pm, Harrison messaged Jane Doe and asked, 'Feeling better today?'

She replied fourteen minutes later, at 12.15 pm, saying, 'To be honest no, I know you must be mates with those guys but I don't like them and what happened was not consensual which is why I was so upset. Again, thank you for taking me home. That was really appreciated.'

He replied, 'Jesus. I'm not sure what to say.'

Meanwhile, Harrison—whom Jane Doe had earlier described to her friend as 'a really nice guy'—was corresponding with McIlroy simultaneously.

McIlroy, 12.03 pm (responding to a message that had been deleted and was unable to be retrieved by police): 'Really, fuck sake, did you calm her, where does she live?'

Harrison, 12.03 pm: 'Mate no jokes she was in hysterics, wasn't going to end well.'

Harrison, 12.03 pm (in a message that was deleted and then recovered by police): 'Aye, just threw her home then went back to mine.'

Earlier that morning, Jane Doe had summarised her physical distress in a text to her friend: 'I have bruising on my inner thighs. I feel like I've got bruising literally on my fanny. They were so rough I've got my period a week earlier.' (During the trial, she said that Jackson had at one point tried to fit his entire hand into her vagina. A medical examination conducted shortly after the alleged rape confirmed she had sustained a vaginal tear and that this was likely responsible for the bleeding she had confused with her period. Meanwhile, photographs deemed inadmissible as evidence because they might 'prejudice the jury' showed spots of blood on Jackson's bed. Jackson's defence successfully argued that the photographs should be disallowed because they showed additional bloodstains that didn't belong to Jane Doe. Jackson declined to explain where they came from.)

As her injuries were being detailed to a friend who was now urging her to go to a rape crisis centre and consider reporting the incident to the police, Jackson et al were describing a very different night on their own private messaging services.

Responding to a message from a friend asking, 'How was she?', Olding replied, 'She was very, very loose.' He told the friend (later revealed to be fellow Ulster teammate Craig Gilroy) that they had spent the previous evening at 'Cutters, Ollies, then after-party'.

Gilroy replied, 'Any sluts get fucked?'

'Precious secrets,' came the response.

Shortly after, Olding boasted in a group chat that included the four men that 'there was a bit of spit roasting [when a woman is penetrated vaginally and orally at the same time] going on last night fellas'. Jackson replied almost immediately, saying, 'There was a lot of spit roast last night.' Olding described it as being 'like a merry go round at the carnival'. A man not present during the alleged assault posted, 'Why are we all such legends?', to which McIlroy replied, 'I know it's ridiculous.'

Two days later, McIlroy bragged in another WhatsApp message, 'Pumped a girl with Jacko on Monday. Roasted her. Then another on Tuesday night.'

Shortly afterwards, an official complaint of rape was made by Jane Doe, and Jackson was advised to get a solicitor. McIlroy texted Harrison and asked, 'Do Paddy and Stu have a lawyer and stuff. [sic] When do you reckon they'll be released . . . do his parents know?'

Harrison replied, 'No idea—they didn't tell me anything. If not my dad will know who to get on to.'

McIlroy: 'Do you know who this girl even is, this is ridiculous, surely it's all just gonna get dropped?'

Harrison: [replies with Jane Doe's real name.]

McIlroy: 'What age, what school?'

Harrison: 'Hopefully it'll be thrown out, Just a silly girl who's been [sic] done something then regretted it. She's causing so much trouble for the lads.'

She's causing so much trouble for the lads.

The Trial

Jane Doe hadn't wanted to go to the police. When her friend advised her to file a report, Doe's response was incredulous. 'I'm not going up against Ulster rugby,' she said. 'Yea, because that'll work.' She later explained her change of mind to the court, saying, 'The more I thought about it, rape is a game of power and control. They rely on your silence. The only way you take the power back is when you actually do something about it. I may be preventing it happening to someone else.' She went on, 'It could so easily have been my friends outside Ollie's. It could have been my sister outside. [Reporting it] was the best decision I made.'

Unfortunately, it appears her fears of 'going up against Ulster rugby' were well founded. During the course of a trial in which each of the four accused had access to top-notch legal representation (and in which four different defendants meant four separate cross-examinations of the complainant), Jane Doe was grilled about what QC Brendan Kelly (representing Jackson) called her 'inconsistent accounts' of the night in question. He suggested she was after any celebrity, pointing to CCTV footage in which she was shown briefly (and barely) interacting with two other popular sporting figures outside Ollie's nightclub. She dismissed this as absurd.

Upon hearing that Jane Doe had experienced a 'freeze response' (widely recognised by medical professionals as common in situations where extreme trauma is occurring, from sexual assaults to military attacks), Kelly pressed: 'What does frozen mean? Is it one of the lies? Is it a lie deployed to explain what happened?' He argued that Jane Doe was 'fixated' with Jackson, and that she had lied about being raped because she was scared her friends would find out she'd had 'group sex' with Jackson and Olding. Requesting that Jane Doe's clothing from the night of the party be shown to the jury, Kelly suggested the bloodstains found on her underwear were the result of bleeding that had taken place before the alleged assault. This was categorically rejected by Jane Doe, who pointed again to medical confirmation that she had suffered an internal tear.

Kelly cross-examined her for three days straight.

Frank O'Donoghue, acting for Olding, focused on many of the same points as Kelly during his cross-examination but asked why Doe had made a claim of vaginal rape against his client. He reminded the jury that Olding was charged with one count of oral rape. Jane Doe reminded O'Donoghue that by the time of her medical examination, she hadn't slept for thirty hours and was in a state of emotional distress. Additionally, she said there were points at which both men were behind her and so she couldn't be sure which of them was penetrating her vaginally. (The jury later learned that Olding had initially been charged with one count of vaginal rape, but that this had been dropped by the Public Prosecution Service.)

Cross-examination by Gavan Duffy QC, the lawyer acting for Harrison, repeated the claim by Kelly that Jane Doe had been 'staring' at Jackson that night and had followed him upstairs. 'He could well be right about that,' she replied, 'but he is also sitting in the dock.'

Like Kelly, McIlroy's lawyer Arthur Harvey QC grilled Jane Doe about the so-called 'inconsistencies' in her account. She had told a doctor during her initial medical examination that McIlroy had entered the room before lowering his trousers, but to the court she said he came in already naked.

'You go into shutdown,' she responded. 'It's incredibly hard to state what happened until you've actually processed it.'

'You've said this before,' Harvey replied, criticising her use of the second-person 'you'. 'It's almost as if you're repeating something you've read rather than your personal experience.'

'I'm not going to argue with you over grammar,' she snapped back. 'You're not putting words in my mouth.'

Later, one of Jane Doe's friends gave evidence for the prosecution. Asked why her friend had been so reluctant to go to the police, she replied, 'Because of what's happening in this room. It's daunting, quite horrible and you get blamed. It's a distressing process.'

By the time she was allowed to leave the stand, Jane Doe had endured eight days of cross-examination, leading some members of the public to argue that it looked like the alleged victim of rape was the one being put on trial. Her name, used numerous times in a courtroom accessible to members of the public, was quickly leaked on an online message forum. She was accused (as women always are) of trying to 'destroy the lives of decent young men'. Harrison had claimed in his own testimony that he hadn't believed her when she told him the events of the night weren't consensual, and had decided her complaint was motivated by regret. She was upset when he dropped her home, but he assumed this was because Jackson had 'rejected' her. Hell hath no fury etc.

One of the prevailing problems in deciding the outcome of rape and sexual assault trials lies in the baggage that the people charged with making that decision bring with them. *What was she wearing? How much had she been drinking? Had she been kissing him? Was she flirting with other men? Had she had sex before? She wanted it, didn't she? What did she expect?* These are all questions that are asked routinely of rape complainants, whether or not they ultimately end up taking their case to trial. Women are expected to be the gatekeepers of sex; if we fail in our duty to do this, we are then held responsible for the actions of the men who breach the borders. How could they be expected to refrain when it was all just laid out there for them? When she made it so *easy* for them by being there? And look at how she was dressed, with her tits out and her short skirt and all that lipstick she had on. She was practically *begging* for it, dolled up like that. Why would she bother to make herself look so attractive if she didn't want to attract someone? A bloke can't be blamed for giving her what she wanted, just because she woke up regretting it the next day.

This is also a significant reason why the stories of rape complainants can change during the reporting process. It isn't just that confusion and trauma muddle their recollection, although this is an important factor. It's that women who live in the world are all implicitly aware of the requirement that we conform to a brief. When it's not uncommon to hear people sneer of complainants that 'she didn't act like a rape victim afterwards', it stands to reason that people reporting assaults will try to circumvent that accusation by acting as much like they think a rape victim 'should' act in order to be believed.

In the book *Eggshell Skull*, Bri Lee documents her time working as a judge's associate in the District Court of Queensland, attending trials and sentencing hearings for sexual crimes against both adults and children in metropolitan Brisbane and regional Queensland towns. Entering the legal industry as an idealistic young graduate, Lee rapidly became disenchanted as she witnessed the system's inability to deliver justice to the complainants in cases such as these.

'All the problems associated with the difficulties women face in trying to access justice stem from the fact that the system wasn't set up to hear them or acknowledge their experiences,' she told me in an email. 'Juries expect "evidence" of sex crimes to be clearly damning CCTV footage or 100% accurate DNA samples. In the vast majority of cases the only evidence is witness testimony, and it's very easy for a barrister to cross-examine a witness until she's crying and second-guessing herself, or stumbling over her answers. It feels to me like we'll forever be playing catch-up.'

Women are still denied any kind of acknowledgment of authority when it comes to defining the impact of things that are done to us. It's men (and young men of privilege and power in particular, whose 'promising futures' loom large when determining the outcomes of rape trials) who are given the right to decide if a woman has consented, even if they never asked for consent and every action they took leading up to and beyond the moment they penetrated someone indicated they didn't care if consent was present anyway.

But it's the fervent belief in male entitlement that forms the foundation of rape culture—entitlement to women's bodies, to power, to protection and, at last, to vindication. It isn't enough that men in a rape culture are so often acquitted of sexual crimes against women. The injury that's been done (apparently) to their *reputations* and personal pride has to be avenged. How is the vengeance delivered? By the ritual character destruction and ostracisation of the women who've tried to hold them to account.

This is certainly true of the treatment of Jane Doe in Belfast, both at the hands of the lawyers engaged to act for the male defendants and the members of the public determined to punish her for daring to bring a case against them. Lee's point about the system being inherently set against women's interests is an important one. At a fundamental level, there is the question of whether or not women's interests or positions are even understood as existing *separately to how men conceive of them.* One of the most revealing aspects of the Ulster rape case came for me in the form of an early message sent from Jane Doe to her friend, explaining why she couldn't possibly have consented to sexual activity. She said, 'Like I hadn't even shaved my legs. Had only tanned the bottom of them and my arms. I wasn't up or ready for fucking anything.'

All too often, sexual behaviour and 'provocation' is judged through the lens of male desire, and this carries over into the courtroom. She is dressed in a certain way that pleases him, ergo she wants him to be pleased. But this fails to take into account the comprehensive conditioning women are subjected to throughout our lives that gives primacy to our appearance and ability to conform to conventional standards of beauty but also instils shame in us about the ways we fail to uphold it. As someone who has grown up aware of how appearance forms one of the most powerful currencies for women, it makes total sense to me that another woman would put it in these terms. That yes, a woman may put time and effort into her outward appearance in order to fulfil the obligations expected of her (and receive a reward of positive male attention)—but that a much clearer indicator of whether or not *she* intends to have sex that night is if she has coiffed and polished and smoothed the bits of her body that will be seen and touched and, crucially, *judged* by the male gaze and all its spurious demands the moment her clothes come off.

Jane Doe may have consented to a party that night. She may even have consented to a kiss. But I believe her when she says she didn't consent to being 'spit roasted' by two men, one of whom 'allegedly' inflicted a vaginal tear that caused her underwear to be soaked through with blood.

The jury disagreed. On 28 March, after a nine-week trial, it took eight men and three women just three hours and forty minutes to return a unanimous verdict of not guilty for all four men and their respective charges.

■

After the acquittal of the four men in Belfast, a fierce public debate about rape culture and the legal system ensued. Feminist groups of course argued eloquently against the practice of victim-blaming, the interrogation of rape survivors and the coddling of privileged men protected from the consequences of their actions by their status and a 'boys will be boys' attitude. Those with a different opinion screeched into the void about how 'lying sluts' and 'fame-hungry bitches' needed to be punished for 'trying to ruin the lives of decent young lads' who'd done nothing wrong, guvnor. Among the most frustrating comments were those that insisted these young men had been 'found innocent', and therefore deserved some kind of compensation in the form of payment from their accuser or even a prison sentence handed down to her.

There's no such thing as a verdict of 'innocent' in a court of law. Prosecutors are asked to prove their case beyond a reasonable doubt, and a judge or jury is called upon to decide if that has been accomplished. A verdict of not guilty means that, in the eyes of the judge or jury, the prosecution has failed to prove their case beyond a reasonable doubt.

This is hard enough to do when dealing with crimes untainted by centuries of patriarchal supremacy and misogynist viewpoints. But when you're talking about rape trials in particular, it's impossible to expect that a typical jury of twelve average people has been protected their entire lives from the impact of the rape culture we all live in. If victim-blaming attitudes run rampant in members of the public (and we have ample evidence to demonstrate that this is the case), it's naive at best to believe that members of a jury are immune to the same preconceived ideas about women's behaviour and the right of men to 'make mistakes'—mistakes perhaps even some men selected for jury duty have secretly made themselves.

And yet, so often it's the complainants in rape and sexual assault cases who are treated as if they were the ones on trial—first by the police officers they need to convince of the veracity of their claims, then by the defence lawyers engaged to tear apart their characters, and finally by the members of the public who eagerly seize the opportunity to indulge in a spot of good old-fashioned Scarlet

Lettering. As the blogger and writer Glosswitch noted in the UK's *Independent* newspaper on 28 March 2018, 'The response is disappointing but not necessarily surprising. After all, who has really been on trial here? Whose guilt, morally if not legally, have we really been trying to prove? Watching the trial progress, it seemed to me the question was never "are these men rapists?", but always "is this woman a liar?"'

Claims too that women do 'this sort of thing' for fame or money or even (perhaps especially) revenge are also ludicrous. Who would invite the kind of 'fame' that sees thousands (if not millions) of people dissect your sex life, your looks, your motivation and even your right to be treated like a human being? Where are the piles of money that are supposed to be the big payday for women who come forward with allegations of rape? And who would willingly submit themselves to nine weeks of an exhausting trial, eight days of brutal cross-examination and a potential lifetime of people calling them names like 'lying whore' and 'evil bitch' just because they've crafted the world's most irrational revenge scheme? Ditto the obnoxious claim that trials like these are pursued because of 'regret'—as if anyone would expose themselves to slut-shaming, ridicule, anger, victim-blaming and potentially even violence because they had too much to drink one night and woke up feeling the cringe.

If you want to talk about evidence beyond a reasonable doubt, those claims simply do not stack up.

■

(Aboriginal and Torres Strait Islander readers are advised that the following contains the names of Indigenous people who have died.)

But the odds are stacked even further against the victims and survivors of sexual assaults if they also happen to be women of colour. In 2011, an Aboriginal woman named Lynette Daley was killed on a beach in northern New South Wales. The facts of the case are among the most horrific I've ever seen. Adrian Attwater and Paul Maris, the two men Lynette was with, raped her so violently that she sustained a blunt force trauma to her genital and uterine area, causing her to bleed to death. In an inquest later, a forensic pathologist described her injuries as 'more severe than those which occur in even precipitous childbirth'.

It took hours for Attwater and Maris to call the police that day. In the interim, they set to work covering up the evidence of their crime. Attwater dragged Lynette's body into the ocean to try to wash off the blood while Maris burned all her clothes and the blood-soaked mattress on which she had been killed. When the police arrived, Attwater tried to claim she'd had a seizure while swimming naked in the ocean. They had burned her clothes and the mattress, they said, because 'they stank'.

There's no lens through which you can look at this case and see anything other than a repulsive, deliberately violent attack meted out by two men who raped and killed a woman and then tried to aggressively hide the evidence. On the recording of his phone call to triple zero, Attwater can be heard saying, 'What a good fucking Australia Day, fuck sake, fucking hell you bloody bitch.'

And yet, despite the overwhelming case against them, the NSW Director of Public Prosecutions declined to prosecute the pair not once *but twice*, claiming there was 'insufficient evidence'. It wasn't until May 2016, when *Four Corners* released their report 'Callous Disregard', that the DPP was prompted to charge both

Attwater and Maris. Five years had passed since the pair had brutally murdered Lynette on Ten Mile Beach.

Incredibly, both Attwater and Maris claimed that the rape had been consensual. When questioned by police about how such 'group sex' unfolded, Attwater replied, 'These things happen . . . girls will be girls, boys will be boys.'

Boys will be boys.

It took a jury just thirty-two minutes to convict Attwater and Maris of one count each of aggravated sexual assault. Attwater was also found guilty of manslaughter, while Maris was found guilty of hindering the discovery of evidence. In December 2017, they were sentenced to a minimum of fourteen years and three months for Attwater and at least six years and nine months for Maris.

It had taken almost six years for Lynette's family to secure justice.

But the infuriating reality is that this isn't uncommon for Aboriginal people in a country that has consistently meted out violence against them from the very start of colonisation, more than two hundred years ago. As Celeste Liddle wrote for the *Sydney Morning Herald* in 2016 ('Think our justice system isn't racist? Compare Lynette Daley's case with the kids at Don Dale'):

> It is significantly easier for Aboriginal people to be imprisoned than it is for them to seek justice through the exact same system . . . The imprisonment rates of Aboriginal women have doubled in the past decade, accounting for almost all the increase noted in the female prison population over that time. A reasonable portion of these incarcerated Aboriginal women have also been victims of crime, such as domestic violence. Some may have reported these instances, others probably

> didn't . . . [but] what confidence are Aboriginal women supposed to have that our cases will be handled fairly and correctly? How do we know we won't end up being victimised by the justice system as well?

Lynette Daley was denied justice for so long precisely because she was an Aboriginal woman, and the system makes a point of looking away even as it pushes them through the cracks.

■

'No one dreams of their first time being in an alleyway with someone whose name they can't even remember. No one wants that.'

In 2013, a man named Luke Lazarus led a young woman named Saxon Mullins away from a dance floor and into the alleyway behind his father's nightclub. He ignored her repeated protestations that she wanted to go back inside, while attempting to pull down her stockings and underwear. Saxon resisted by pulling them back up. He then commanded her to turn away from him, ordering: 'Put your fucking hands on the wall.' She complied. He tried to penetrate her, but had difficulty because (as he allegedly put it) she was 'tight'. After Saxon told Lazarus she was a virgin, he directed her to get on all fours and 'arch' her back.

'I just did it,' she told the ABC's *Four Corners* program in 2018. 'At that point I was just kind of in [sic] autopilot a little bit. I just wanted to go. And this was the quickest way I thought I could leave. I just thought, "Just do what he says and then you can go."'

Lazarus then anally penetrated Saxon. It was less than ten minutes since they had first met.

The next day, Saxon presented to the Northern Sydney Sexual Assault Service, where the examining doctor discovered a number of 'painful grazes' around the entrance to her anus.

Across town, Lazarus was texting a friend. 'I honestly have zero recollection of calling you, was a sick night,' he said. 'Took a chick's virginity, lol.'

'Bahahaha. Nice popping [those] cherries. Tight?' his friend replied.

'So tight,' said Lazarus. 'It's a pretty gross story. Tell ya later.'

Two years later, Lazarus was convicted of having sexual intercourse with Saxon Mullins without her consent. He served eleven months of a three-year prison sentence before successfully appealing his conviction. The judge in his appeal accepted that Saxon hadn't consented, but didn't agree it was clear that Lazarus had known this. During both trials, Lazarus was given glowing character references by numerous prominent members of his community, including the mayor for Waverley. He was described as 'a nice guy' who respected women and had 'lots of female friends'.

This question of consent continues to stump both those inside the legal system and those commentating from the sidelines. Consent is a language that has many thousand more words than just 'yes' and 'no', but it's these two that everyone fixates on when determining the strength of a rape complaint. *Perhaps she didn't say yes—but she didn't say no, either.* It's a thought process that overwhelmingly favours the men most likely to be accused of rape, and the degree to which it will be used to protect them varies according to how much prestige and status their privilege affords them.

In 2014, the journalist Anna Krien published a blistering exploration of the off-field antics of Australia's football codes.

Night Games took an uncompromising look at the toxic masculinity that permeates a world in which players are considered both gladiators and kings. Marching to war on the battlefields of football stadiums and cheered on by crowds thirsty for blood, these 'heroes' duke it out for the pleasure of an audience of thousands. Their commitment and sacrifice at the altar of Football is treated with reverence, and because of this they're given leave to indulge in the spoils of war once the final whistle sounds.

And what are the spoils?

Footy sluts. Star fuckers. Strays. Lying skanks.

These are the terms that have been used to describe women who've made allegations of sexual assault against AFL players over the years, dozens and dozens of whom have been accused and yet only one of whom has ever been convicted. In almost every case, public opinion has been overwhelmingly on the side of the players. Because boys will be boys, right? She was asking for it, she kissed him, she invited him in, she sat on his couch, she lay on his bed, she'd had sex with his friend, she was there, she was there, she was there.

I mean, what's a red-blooded man supposed to do? She was practically *begging* for it.

In *Night Games*, Krien documents a criminal trial involving a young man accused of raping a woman after the 2010 AFL Grand Final. The man himself was not a footballer, but he was present at a celebration party alongside Collingwood players Dayne Beams and John McCarthy. After having consensual sex with the man she'd been dating, the young woman said she felt 'compelled' to have sex with Beams while a number of other men, including McCarthy, were present in the room. Neither Beams nor McCarthy were charged by Victoria Police, but when news broke the next day that two Collingwood players were being implicated in a sexual assault there was no shortage of supporters lining up to condemn the woman as either hopelessly naive or a liar. Former AFL player Peter 'Spida' Everitt took a break from aimlessly scratching his balls to tweet, 'Yet another alleged girl, making alleged allegations, after she awoke with an alleged hangover and, I take it, an alleged guilty conscience.' He followed this up with the truly ground-breaking, 'Girls!! When will you learn! At 3am when you are blind drunk & you decide to go home with a guy IT'S NOT FOR A CUP OF MILO! Allegedly.'

Got that, ya bunch of stupid bloody slappers? Stop asking blokes to fix you up with a nice drink when you walk into their homes, because you're not there for hospitality—you're there to be raped. *Allegedly.*

This idea that women give up any right to their own bodies the moment they cross the threshold of a man's house (or his bedroom) is more widespread than people think. *What did she expect?* is often asked of women who report being sexually assaulted after having even the barest interaction with men, as if it's not a revolting indictment on society—and masculinity especially—to have women walking around assuming that men are just waiting for an opportunity to rape them. Mind you, the phrase itself is a nice companion to the other high-rotation response that's given whenever feminists talk about rape culture and the risks posed by it to women's safety, which is: *Why do you hate men and assume they're all rapists?*

Rape apologists! Can't live with them, can't blast them into the far reaches of the universe and enjoy the thought of their empty carcasses floating through the cold and barren emptiness of space until the end of time.

But, then, why would the motivations of women (beyond 'knowing what to expect') possibly be considered relevant in a rape trial? All that really matters, it seems, is whether or not the men accused of sexual assault have decided for themselves that their alleged victim was consenting. Unlike the women (and it is usually women) who are effectively put on trial and forced to prove they didn't consent to being 'spit roasted', filmed, shared among friends, penetrated while they were unconscious or asleep, or any other of the degrading acts that survivors of sexual assault have been subjected to over the years, it seems the men being accused (and it is usually men) are required only to say 'it was consensual' as a defence and they will have people falling over themselves to agree.

In a column published in the *Irish Independent* on 31 March 2018, following the handing down of the verdicts in Belfast, journalist Ewan McKenna wrote:

> There's still a startling number of men happy to hide behind the boys-will-be-boys and she-was-asking-for-it undertones. It makes you wonder what goes on in the mind of a person who celebrates a rape trial verdict as if a victory for their gender and as if vindication for acts that shouldn't ever have taken place?

It's a question I've wrestled with numerous times over the last few years, and one that I consider central to the challenges being confronted by this book. There are always people willing to defend men accused of rape by arguing that consent was in place, even though their conviction is based on nothing other than the say-so of the man involved. A gang rape becomes group sex, the rape of an unconscious woman a case of 'next-day regret'—and the truth is whatever the man being defended by the public and/or his immediate community says it is.

But here's a question. Why does 'consent'—in the eyes of the stalwart defenders of these accused rapists—always look like anything from women giving in, to women being ambushed by numerous men and placed in an untenable situation? How can people still be so uneducated about the importance and necessity of an *ongoing* consent that their belief an initial 'yes' was secured allows them to happily ignore the objectively horrifying acts of degradation and disrespect that came afterwards?

Like, why aren't people more concerned about the *kind* of sex a lot of young men seem to be pursuing and the methods with which they choose to pursue it? Call me crazy, but I just feel that taking turns on a woman and high-fiving each other over it then sharing the recorded footage around school or uni or the locker room as evidence of what a loose slut she is might not be the healthiest expression of masculinity, and as such is probably not worthy of a robust and spirited defence.

In 2002, the Cronulla Sharks (a rugby league team from New South Wales) was involved in an alleged sexual assault involving a nineteen-year-old woman in Christchurch, New Zealand. The woman (later given the pseudonym 'Clare' in the *Four Corners* investigative report 'Code of Silence' about sexual assault in Australian football codes, aired on 11 May 2009 (and tell me, why is it that the public broadcaster repeatedly appears better at prosecuting rapists than the Office for Public Prosecutions?)) went into a hotel room with two of the Cronulla rugby players, only to have a further twelve (a mixture of players and team staff members) come in afterwards. Six of the men had sex with her.

Others just watched and masturbated. Clare told *Four Corners* that her eyes were shut for most of it but 'when I opened my eyes there was just a long line at the end of the bed'.

She consented!

Clare filed a report with police five days later, but no charges were laid. Later, she was diagnosed with PTSD. By the time of the *Four Corners* investigation, she had attempted to take her own life several times.

She consented!

Matthew 'Matty' Johns was the captain of the Cronulla Sharks in 2002 and one of the two men who originally accompanied Clare into that hotel room. He told *Four Corners* that he had followed her to the car park after the alleged assault and apologised for the presence of the other men, some of whom had, as one man admitted to journalist Sarah Ferguson, climbed through the bathroom window and commando crawled across the floor.

She consented!

In 2009, when 'Code of Silence' was due to be broadcast, Matty Johns issued a pre-emptive public apology on Channel Nine's *The Footy Show*, the panel discussion program he had been employed by for at least the previous seven years. Referring to the report, he said, 'Um, for me personally it has put my family through enormous anguish and embarrassment and has once again, and for that I'm just, can't say sorry enough.'

'Alright, mate, well said,' his co-host Paul 'Fatty' Vautin replied. 'Alright, let's get on with the show.'

After the report was broadcast, and it became apparent that the issue wasn't just going to disappear, Johns participated in a softball sit-down interview with Channel Nine's Tracy Grimshaw.

He reiterated his regret for causing embarrassment to his wife and family, but affirmed that in his view Clare had been 'a willing participant' and that his only crime was that of 'infidelity' and 'absolute stupidity'.

Johns had more than his fair share of supporters, but the exposure didn't sit well with the bigwigs at Nine. Johns agreed to leave his hosting role on *The Footy Show*, a move that prompted an even bigger backlash against Clare. 'He's innocent!' fans screamed. 'Why did she go into the bloody hotel room?!' and 'Why did it take her so long to make a report?!' and 'There were no charges laid, so nothing bloody happened!' Some people argued it was a puritanical response to 'group sex', and that all this was a massive beat-up because 'she bloody well CONSENTED!'

How do we know that she consented? Because Johns said so. And if a man says sex was consensual, nothing a woman says to the contrary will ever be enough to convince people determined to protect his reputation and preserve his entitlement.

But the question of *who's* consenting and to what is key, as is the question of how that consent is settled on.

Consider the case of Ched Evans. In 2012, the English footballer was convicted for the 2011 rape of a nineteen-year-old woman at a hotel in North Wales. Evans was released after serving half of a five-year sentence, and he proceeded to pursue an appeal. That appeal was granted and a retrial ordered in which a legal exemption allowed for the jury to hear 'evidence' of his victim's previous sexual history. This formed part of a defence campaign that also included the private offer of £50,000 as a 'reward' for information that would help clear the millionaire's name, paid twice to a man who had previously given evidence that supported the woman's claims.

The inclusion of new testimony by two men (both of whom were known to the footballer) who claimed to have had sex with the victim during a similar time period was vehemently opposed by everyone from advocacy groups to the former solicitor general, Vera Baird, but the three presiding justices called it a 'rare case' in which it would be appropriate to allow 'forensic examination' of the woman's sexual behaviour. The testimony of these men included Very Important Facts about their supposed time with her, including that she had asked to be 'fucked harder' and had favoured a particular sexual position—both things that Evans claims were features of his encounter with her but that were also by this stage a matter of public record.

She consented!

Never forget that a woman's right to say no to sexual contact disintegrates each time she invokes her right to say yes.

The prosecution in both trials argued that the woman had been too drunk to give consent but, intoxication aside, the circumstances surrounding the allegations that led to Evans' initial conviction should be considered sobering even for those people determined to find every caveat they can to excuse sexual coercion and violence. On the night in question, Evans had been out in Rhyl with a group of friends that included his teammate, Clayton McDonald. It was McDonald who picked up the woman in a takeaway shop and brought her back to his hotel room—a room that had been booked and paid for by Evans. On the way, McDonald contacted Evans to let him know he had 'got a bird'. Evans then made his way to the hotel, used the fact that he had made and paid for the booking to access a key from the hotel reception and then let himself into the room.

The lights were out.

During the retrial, prosecutor Simon Medland QC said, 'I'm going to suggest that she did not even know it was you [having sex with her].'

Evans rejected this proposition, claiming, 'I would not hurt a girl, I would not do anything to harm a girl.' He claimed that his entry prompted McDonald to ask the woman, 'Can my friend join in?' to which she replied, 'Yes.'

And yet, he also acknowledged during his account that he'd lied in order to get the room key, that he exchanged no words at all with her before, during or after they had what he claimed was consensual sex and that he left the hotel via a fire escape rather than through the lobby.

She consented!

Key witness testimony for the prosecution during the retrial came from a hotel receptionist who claimed to have heard 'noises of people having sex' from the room in question. The court was told he'd heard 'a male voice saying from behind the door quite loudly and forcefully: "Are you gonna suck that cock or what?"' He heard no reply from the woman, and the same male voice said, 'No?' in an 'enquiring tone'. He also recalled seeing two young men standing suspiciously close to the window outside the room in which the alleged rape took place.

Oh yeah—according to evidence offered during the retrial, Evans' younger brother and another man were watching through the window and 'trying to film what was happening'.

She consented!

As with the first trial, the prosecution's case hinged on the inability of an inebriated woman to properly consent to sex. The jury disagreed, ultimately deciding that Evans' knowledge of this lack of consent couldn't be assured and therefore he couldn't reasonably be convicted of rape.

It took the jury just under three hours to settle on a verdict of not guilty.

The woman, whose name was leaked on social media during the trial, has been forced in the aftermath to move home and change her identity. She continues to be harassed to this day.

There are more stories like this, more examples of men colluding with each other to sexually abuse and degrade women as part of a fun group activity, all the while claiming everything's above board. In all of them, consent and dialogue about what can be expected to happen is something apparently only valued between the men or boys involved, while respect for the women present is basically non-existent.

If you don't think this might be a problem for the young men you know, think again. This is *exactly* a problem that all parents of young men should be worrying about. In no particular order, reflect on the following . . .

In 2012, an unconscious girl was carried from party to party by fellow high school peers in Steubenville, Ohio. She was raped, urinated on and then left on her front lawn. The incident was filmed and posted to social media, and later bragged about. The two young ringleaders, Trent Mays and Ma'lik Richmond—self-proclaimed members of a 'rape crew'—were tried and sentenced to one and two years, respectively, in juvenile detention. Numerous media outlets expressed concern for the loss of the two football stars' 'promising futures', while editorials bizarrely concluded that this was not a clear demonstration of the need for greater sexual respect or understanding around consent, but rather a lesson for young people to be more careful about their use of social media.

Many people in the tight-knit community blamed the victim for ruining her attackers' lives and destroying their college prospects.

In Auckland, New Zealand, similar teenage use of social media revealed a group of young boys calling themselves the 'Roast Busters'. The boys bragged about plying girls with alcohol and raping them while they were incapacitated. When the story broke, it was revealed that one of the boys was the son of a local police officer; according to complainants and reports, the police had been aware of the Roast Busters' operation for at least two years, and nothing was done to stop them. On being caught, one of the boys wrote in a public comment on Facebook that he had used this as a 'learning opportunity' and apologised to the girls—the girls who were raped by his gang—who had been 'effected [sic] by this whole ridiculousness'.

In Missouri, fourteen-year-old Daisy Coleman was plied with alcohol and then allegedly raped by a seventeen-year-old school peer. Her thirteen-year-old friend was also allegedly raped by a fellow peer. Video footage was recorded and then later passed around at school. Following the assault, Daisy was dumped on her front lawn in the freezing cold, where she spent three hours in a semi-conscious state before her mother found her. But although initial investigations found there was a case to answer, the investigation was later dropped. Daisy and her brother were bullied at school, her mother was fired from her job and the Coleman family was forced to leave town.

In Texas, news broke that a cheerleader had been kicked off her cheerleading team because she refused to cheer for the sports player who raped her. In this instance, the occurrence of the rape had been corroborated by at least three witnesses, two of whom broke into the room to try to stop it and later chased the perpetrators. When the girl returned to school the following week, it was to a chilly reception; some of the students had gone so far as to paint two of the perpetrators' numbers on their faces to protest their removal from the football team. Again, the victim was vilified by her community and called a slut. Anonymous letters were sent to her house blaming her for ruining the lives of 'nice respectable boys'. The fact that she had been drinking was used as evidence of her complicity. According to one former friend, sympathy waned because she didn't 'act like a rape victim'.

We can also look to Texas for perhaps one of the most egregious forms of assault (and subsequent victim blaming), where an eleven-year-old girl of colour was gang-raped by eighteen teenage boys and young men ranging in age from early adolescence to twenty-seven. She had been lured to a secluded trailer and then threatened. In what should now no longer be a surprise, video footage was taken on mobile phones and later reported to a teacher by a peer who had seen it passed around at school. There's categorically no question of this being a sexual assault against *a child*—but in a subsequent *New York Times* editorial, the victim was described as having 'dressed older'. The same editorial published quotes from neighbours who blamed the girl's mother for letting her wander around by herself and who railed against the effect of the incident on the assailants. One community member was quoted as saying, 'It's just destroyed our community. These young boys have to live with this for the rest of their lives.'

The system lets down all women, but it lets down women of colour most of all.

She consented!

She consented!

She consented!

Let's be very clear about something. The 'consent' that's really in play in situations like this is that agreed on by men pursuing sexual activity with each other. The woman is never a part of those conversations. She is only meant to facilitate the planned outcome of them.

This is not what consent looks like. If there are multiple people in a room and you are discussing the terms of engagement with everyone but the person whose consent matters most of all, you are acting with conscious duplicity. If you craft a plan with your friends to spring sex on an unsuspecting participant at the last minute, to corner them and give them no other option but to say yes, you are making that choice for a reason. If you don't make even the most basic of attempts to have a conversation with the person who you will later claim was 'definitely a willing participant', you are revealing your callous disregard for their right to say no. Young male rugby players texting each other (as McIlroy did to Jackson) asking, 'Any chance of a threesome?' and then deciding to walk in anyway isn't what 'seeking consent' looks like. One man telling another 'I've got a bird' and that other man then surprising her fifteen minutes later in a dark room isn't how sex should work. A rugby team feeling confident enough to burst into a room occupied by two of their teammates and a nineteen-year-old girl and then line up to take their turn indicates to me that this was a frighteningly well-practised activity. Teenage boys dehumanising and humiliating their female peers as part of a sex act is scary, but so too is the fever with which their communities will rush to shield them from the consequences of their actions.

As a society, we have to ask ourselves why it is that we refuse to challenge boys on this behaviour and work instead to offer them every excuse in the world to make that behaviour just a standard part of their life education. Why are we so afraid to look at that murky space between how the law defines guilt and lack of guilt, and commit to treating as intolerable some of the things that we find there?

She consented!

No, she didn't.

Not fighting back isn't the same as consenting. Relenting isn't consenting. Giving in out of self-preservation isn't consenting.

Are people so afraid of challenging male entitlement that they would risk their young boys becoming rapists rather than speak to them about what enthusiastic consent and good, healthy sex looks like? Please, I implore you, have these conversations with your sons. You should *want* them to make different choices from the ones constantly being modelled to them as 'boys being boys'.

In her closing statements to *Four Corners*, Saxon reminded everyone what consent truly looks like.

'All you need to say is, "Do you want to be here?"' she explained. 'And very clearly, "Do you want to have sex with me?" And if it's not an enthusiastic "yes", then it's not enough. If it's not an enthusiastic "yes", it's a "no". That's it. And then, you're committing a crime.'

Enthusiastic consent. Unlike facing down a legal system written by men and invested in men's interests, it's really not that fucking hard to master.

■

Committing to radically challenging the rape culture we live in isn't just about creating better outcomes for boys. It's also about recognising the significant impact this culture has on girls. In 2016, a searing first-person account of abuse and its aftermath appeared on the news and media website *Inquisitr.* In a piece titled 'One Woman's Collision with Rape Culture on the Path to Greatness', journalist Caitlin Johnstone recounted the testimony of a young female swimmer whose career was thwarted because of the sexual trauma inflicted on her by one of her male teammates. Over the course of a few weeks, the teenaged swimmer was continually harassed and physically assaulted by him. She recalls him pinning down her body with his in a hotel room after an out-of-town swim meet; pressing her up against a car and forcing a kiss on her; even pulling her bathing suit down to the laughter of other teammates, until one of them urged him to stop before telling her not to cry because 'it's not a big deal'.

The young woman's complaints were downplayed, first by her friend and then by her coach. The latter told her, 'don't make waves here' because 'we need to keep the team together'. Her performances in the pool grew worse. She placed badly at nationals. She started to miss more and more practices, until one day she just quit.

Commenting on Brock Turner's case on one of my Facebook posts, a woman named Louisa Curry sharply observed, 'I see a pattern emerging in rape culture that suggests women have a past, while men have a potential.' As a community, we are urged to think of the futures of these young boys and men, to see their crimes not as conscious choices but simply the unfortunate outcomes of living in a world in which girls continue to be temptresses and jezebels and boys continue to be boys. It is not choice that undoes these young men, but circumstance. We might now call it the Brock Turner treatment, though of course it's a practice that precedes the handing down of a paltry six-month prison sentence to a rapist who knows how to swim good. Like Turner, the Steubenville rapists were also spoken of in terms of their 'promising' futures. Roman Polanksi, who drugged and raped a thirteen-year-old girl more than forty years ago and then fled America after pleading guilty, has been defended by hundreds of his industry peers; his 'art' is not only heralded but supported, consumed and financially rewarded. Schoolboys in Australia are routinely excused as having just done 'what boys do' when they perpetrate acts of violence against their female peers, like stealing their intimate photographs and sharing them in repulsive, predatory networks.

And yet, what of the promising futures of these girls and women? The world is awash with women who would have bloomed into something magnificent had they not, as Caitlin Johnstone put it, 'collided with rape culture'. But this collision does occur, and it continues to do so at alarming levels because we are yet to reach a point where the promising futures of young girls are considered every bit as important and precious as the promising futures of young boys.

It is not the job of women to dutifully absorb the collisions men force on their lives. These acts of harm and violence are not casual mistakes men should be forgiven for making on their ascent to the top. They are the barriers that can so easily prevent women from living up to the potential they once had.

In her interview with Johnstone, the anonymous swimmer issued a call to arms.

> What I am proposing here is that we make women a big deal.
>
> I want to know how many other women who were destined to win a medal at the Olympics didn't because someone took the wind out of her sails, robbed her of her spirit, and removed her drive for greatness. I want to know how many women

out there didn't compose that song, or write that screenplay, or publish that book. I want to know how many women didn't finish that degree, or get to hang that painting in an art gallery.

I want to know what this world could be like if women got to be really fucking big deals.

When people talk about rape and consent, who is it that they choose to make 'a big deal' in that equation? Almost inevitably, it turns out to be the boys and men who perpetrate violence within a rape culture and are supported at every turn to escape the consequences. And when young boys see these conversations being had, when they see members of the public, their fathers, their uncles, their teachers, famous men they admire and perhaps have aspirations to one day be, like, talking about 'liars' and 'sluts' who stitch up good blokes because they woke up with a case of buyer's remorse and, besides, *she consented*, then what they hear yet again is that men are the ones entitled to decide the terms of reference for sexual interaction, and 'indiscretions' are mistakes all young men are entitled to make at least once on their journey through life. As the complainant at the centre of the Turner rape trial wrote in her victim impact statement, 'We should not create a culture that suggests we learn that rape is wrong through trial and error.'

We should be focusing instead on making a world in which women get to be considered just as big a fucking deal as men. But that world should also be one in which the scope of what a 'big deal' means for men isn't confined to restrictive, toxic ideals of masculinity that cause nothing but harm.

It is essential that we give boys *something better* than the excuses so routinely offered to them and that we demand more from them than the laziness these stereotypes reinforce. Women's bodies are still being used as the conduit for men's reckoning with each other. What does it say about certain expressions of masculinity that colluding in the assault of women—even just by way of intentional sexual trickery—can be used as a pathway to male bonding? And what does it say about us as a society that we make it so easy for this to not only happen, but to be rigorously defended as an essential part of their laddish identities?

Boys will be boys.

These are challenges that we must take on as a society if we want to prevent our daughters' lives being derailed by rape. But these are also the realities we must face if we want to prevent our sons being the ones who rape them.

For the sake of them all, we need to fix this now.

—12—

WITCH HUNT

> People's lives are being shattered and destroyed by a mere allegation. Some are true and some are false. Some are old and some are new. There is no recovery for someone falsely accused—life and career are gone. Is there no such thing any longer as Due Process?

So tweeted President Donald Trump at the start of 2018. His tweet was in response to the resignation of White House Staff Secretary, Rob Porter, who had been accused by at least two women of spousal abuse beginning at least as far back as 2003. One of those women, Jennifer Willoughby, filed for an emergency protection order against him in 2010. In a blog post written in April 2017, Willoughby described the abuse she alleged she suffered in her marriage to Porter, saying, 'The first time he called me a "fucking bitch" was on our honeymoon. (I found out years later he had kicked his first wife on theirs.) . . . He belittled my intelligence and destroyed my confidence . . . in my home, the abuse was insidious. The threats were personal. The terror was real.'

More than a decade earlier, Porter's first wife, Colbie Holderness, had taken photographs of a black eye she says Porter inflicted on her when they were holidaying in Florence. Over the subsequent years, she spoke to family, friends, clergy and even the FBI about the abuse. In fact, the FBI spoke to both Willoughby and Holderness about Porter when the Trump Administration took office, because White House staff members all require security clearance. That it was proving difficult for Porter to obtain his was apparently not considered an issue by the people he ultimately ended up working for. After the allegations were made public (but before Porter resigned), the White House Chief of Staff, John Kelly, said in a statement, 'He is a friend, a confidante and a trusted professional. I am proud to serve alongside him.' He went further, calling Porter 'a man of true integrity and honour and I can't say enough good things about him'.

After Porter's resignation, Trump—who repeatedly claimed throughout his presidential campaign that 'nobody respects women more than Donald Trump'—told reporters, 'He . . . says he's innocent. And I think you have to remember that . . . we absolutely wish him well, he did a very good job when he was at the White House.'

These attitudes are not uncommon. Far from the accepted belief that unfounded allegations will ruin a man's career—that indeed, as Trump tweeted, 'there is no recovery for someone falsely accused'—the exact opposite is true. Men's careers recover all the time following accusations of abuse and/or sexual violence against women. Hell, men's careers recover following *convictions* for these things. Male power has always been valued and protected more than women's bodies, no matter what level of abuse they may have been accused of. As Dahlia Lithwick wrote of Porter in a piece for *Slate* on 8 February 2018, 'Taken together, all the grown-ups in the room protected, privileged, and covered for Rob Porter despite everything they knew about his pattern of abuse, because his career was important to them.'

In the wake of #MeToo, paranoia about women organising to 'take down men' has been at an all-time high. The idea that feminists began organising decades ago to quietly stage the world's slowest moving coup against men is laughable, but it seems this is still far easier for some people to believe than the alternative: that women have suffered sexual assault, harassment and physical abuse as a matter of course throughout history, and that men have largely been supported to get away with it.

So, here is an incomplete list of men who have either been accused or convicted of various crimes against women and a description of the impact these accusations had on their careers. I make no judgments either way about the truth of these allegations. I have just tried to lay the circumstances out as they occurred.

Please note: I understand this list could be significantly longer, but I have chosen a selection that I feel adequately represents the issue.

Casey Affleck: In 2010, two of Affleck's former colleagues filed civil lawsuits against him after working with him on the set of *I'm Still Here*. One of the women alleged Affleck had made 'unwanted and unwelcome sexual advances' at work, while the other said the actor had snuck into her bed, caressed her back and then later verbally attacked her for refusing his advances. The civil suits came to the public's attention in 2016, while Affleck was on the publicity trail for his role in *Manchester by the Sea*. Affleck went on to win ten major awards, including an Oscar, Golden Globe and BAFTA for Best Actor. At the time of writing, he has two movies and a TV miniseries in production.

Roger Ailes: Ailes died in 2017, but his twenty-year career at Fox News (part of which was spent as the network's chairman) was plagued by allegations of sexual harassment. At least four female journalists went public in 2016 with stories about their former boss, whose alleged harassment had been well known to network executives over the previous two decades. Ailes resigned from Fox News and went on to become a key media adviser on Donald Trump's presidential campaign, helping the candidate to prepare for the first of his presidential debates with Hillary Clinton.

Woody Allen: In 1992, Allen was publicly accused of molesting his adopted daughter, Dylan Farrow. The allegations were repeated over the years, including by Dylan herself in 2017. In addition, Mariel Hemingway (who made her film debut in 1979 as the girlfriend of Allen's character in *Manhattan*—she was sixteen, he was forty-four) revealed in 2015 that she was subjected to unwanted romantic attention from Allen after the movie's completion. Despite this, Allen has never had difficulty attracting A-list stars to appear in his movies (although more are turning their backs on him now that #MeToo has become so prominent). In 1996, he received a Lifetime Achievement Award from the Directors Guild of America, and in 2014, he was honoured with the Cecil B. DeMille award at the Golden Globes.

Alec Baldwin: In 2007, Baldwin left a voicemail message on his daughter's phone in which he referred to her as a 'rude, thoughtless pig' without 'brains or decency'. Ireland Baldwin was eleven years old at the time. In 2017, Baldwin admitted he had bullied women in the past and behaved in 'a very sexist way'. Baldwin made the comments at the Paley Center for Media, where he was being honoured for his 'distinguished career and supportive efforts for the organization's educational initiatives'. In 2018, Baldwin published a series of tweets in which he defended Woody Allen and inferred that Dylan Farrow was a liar.

Dayne Beams: In 2010, the AFL player was questioned by police over sexual assault allegations following that year's grand final. No charges were laid. In 2018, he stepped down as captain of the Brisbane Lions after his father's death.

Nathan Bock: In 2009, when Bock played AFL for the Adelaide Crows, he admitted to assaulting his girlfriend outside a city nightclub. He was put on 'indefinite suspension' by club officials, but the suspension was lifted one week later when the team was due to play Geelong. In round 17 of that year, he was awarded the Showdown Medal for the player judged 'best on ground' in the game played between the Crows and Port Power. Less than a year later, the newly formed Gold Coast Suns lured him to Queensland with the offer of a significantly higher salary package. In 2011, he received a two-match suspension for leaking information to a friend and two family members that assisted them in bet placing, meaning his punishment for hurting the gambling industry was twice what he received for hurting a woman. After his retirement, he moved into a coaching role.

Marlon Brando: In the 1972 movie *Last Tango In Paris*, Bernardo Bertolucci and Marlon Brando conspired to film a graphic rape scene without the knowledge or consent of the lead actress, Maria Schneider. Although Schneider wasn't actually raped by Brando, the scene itself wasn't in the script and it was deliberately kept from her. Bertolucci said he and Brando had come up with the idea the morning before shooting, and hadn't told Schneider because the director 'wanted her reaction as a girl, not as an actress'. Schneider was nineteen at the time; Brando was forty-eight. In 1999, *Time* magazine named him as one of its 100 Most Important People of the Century. In 2005, *Forbes* revealed he was one of the highest-earning deceased celebrities of that year.

Richard Branson: In October 2017, a woman named Antonia Jenae named Branson in a #MeToo post as having 'motorboated' her (that is to say, buried his face between her breasts and rapidly shook it back and forth) without her consent during a private party in 2010 on his property, Necker Island. Jenae was a back-up singer for Joss Stone, and said that Branson had earlier asked her to show him her breasts. Stone has confirmed she recalls the incident. In 2018, as Branson's company Virgin Galactic continued testing rocket flights with the eventual plan to take tourists into space, it was estimated the mogul had a net worth of US$5 billion.

Josh Brolin: In 2004, the actor was charged with spousal battery after his wife of four months, the actress Diane Lane, called police and said he had hit her. She later declined to press charges. In 2009, he was nominated for an Academy Award.

Chris Brown: The night before the 2009 Grammys ceremony, Brown assaulted his then girlfriend, Rihanna, in an attack that left the superstar with a split lip, facial bruises and a black eye. Brown pled guilty to felony assault and was put on five years' probation and sentenced to six months of community service (which he didn't complete). Both Brown and Rihanna had been due to perform at the awards ceremony. It appeared that Brown was blacklisted for a while, but in 2012 he was invited to perform at the ceremony once again to stage his 'comeback'. This was the same year he was awarded Best R&B album for his record, *F.A.M.E.* He has been nominated numerous times since. In the intervening years, he's faced other allegations of violence against women, including punching one woman in the face in a Las Vegas nightclub and threatening another with a gun. In 2017, he released a documentary called *Chris Brown: Welcome to My Life* in which he appears to blame Rihanna for his attack against her. His net worth is approximately US$30 million.

Kobe Bryant: In 2003, the NBA star was arrested in connection with a sexual assault complaint filed by a nineteen-year-old woman. The woman alleged Bryant had raped her in the room of a hotel in which she worked. He told police he'd had sex with the woman but claimed it was consensual. In late 2004, the case was dropped, but Bryant released a statement reading: 'Although I truly believe this encounter between us was consensual, I recognize now that she did not and does not view this incident the same way I did . . . I now understand how she feels that she did not consent to this encounter.' Although Bryant lost some sponsorship deals at the time, most of them were resumed a couple of years later. In 2007, CNN estimated his endorsement deals to be worth approximately

US$16 million a year. In 2018, after he'd retired from professional sports, he won an Academy Award for his work on an animated short called *Dear Basketball.* That same year, ESPN announced they would be launching a new show with Bryant at the helm.

Don Burke: In 2017, a Fairfax investigation revealed the former television presenter had faced a slew of sexual harassment allegations during his years in the Australian television industry, including that he commented frequently on the size of women's vaginas and what sexual positions they favoured. Despite numerous women reporting his behaviour to network executives at the time, Burke remained in his role for years. He has denied all allegations, saying only that he was a perfectionist.

Louis C.K.: Rumours of the comedian's treatment of women (principally, masturbating in front of them without their consent) had always been ignored or denied by him. However, a 2017 article in the *New York Times* forced him to confess to the longstanding allegations against him. Louis C.K.'s career did suffer following the article's publication; but not for long. In March 2018, an article appeared in the *Hollywood Reporter* canvassing opinions from fellow comedians as to how the disgraced comic could return to the stage. 'I don't think people want this to be a life sentence,' said Comedy Cellar owner Noam Dworman. Louis Faranda, executive talent producer for the comedy club Carolines, predicted C.K. would be back 'within a year, making fun of his mistakes'. And indeed he was, appearing unexpectedly (and unapologetically) at the Comedy Cellar less than a year after his disgrace. His first set included a rape joke.

Bertrand Cantat: In 2003, the former frontman of French rock band Noir Désir was convicted of murdering the French actress Marie Trintignant after fatally beating her in a hotel room. He served four years in prison for the crime. In 2007, as he prepared to release his first album since leaving prison, he called it 'despicable' to have become 'the symbol of violence against women'. In 2017, the French music magazine *Les Inrockuptibles* featured Cantat on the magazine's cover. Cantat was promoting a new album at the time. In 2018, he was booked to play at a series of music festivals around France but withdrew after a public backlash.

Wayne Carey: In 1997, Carey pleaded guilty to indecent assault after grabbing the breast of a woman passing by on a busy Melbourne street. In 2007, Carey was arrested by police in Florida after very publicly glassing his then girlfriend in the face and neck. Two days later, the Nine Network sacked him while 3AW announced it wouldn't be renewing his contract. In 2012, he joined the AFL commentary team at Triple M and was given a role on One HD's short-lived *The Game Plan*. A year later, the Seven Network employed him as a host on a series of *Talking Footy* specials. The following year, he was contracted permanently as a panellist on *Talking Footy* and as a commentator for Friday night AFL games.

Nick Carter: In 2018, the singer and actress Melissa Schuman filed a police report alleging the Backstreet Boy had raped her in 2002. Schuman was a virgin at the time, and claims Carter refused to listen as she repeatedly said no. Carter has claimed that his sexual interactions with Schuman were all consensual. The allegations follow a police report filed against Carter in 2006, alleging he had forced a twenty-year-old woman to perform oral sex on him. In 2012, he performed with the Backstreet Boys on *Late Night with Jimmy Fallon.* In 2015, he was a contestant on *Dancing with the Stars.* He returned in 2017 as a guest judge. That same year, he appeared as a judge on the show *Boy Band.*

Bill Clinton: A number of women have accused the former US president of sexual assault and/or harassment, with the alleged incidents dating back to 1978. In an extensive interview with NBC in 1999, Juanita Broaddrick claimed Clinton raped her in a hotel room when she was a volunteer working on his gubernatorial campaign in Arkansas. Several people back up Broaddrick's claims, including a friend who said she found Broaddrick shortly after the alleged assault. Broaddrick says Clinton attempted to apologise to her in 1991, after she saw him outside a meeting in Little Rock. Since coming forward, Broaddrick has been accused of being a stooge for the right and even of making up the rape story because she didn't want her boyfriend to know she had 'cheated' on him. Clinton served two terms in the White House.

Sean Connery: In 1965, the James Bond star told *Playboy*, 'I don't think there is anything particularly wrong about hitting a woman—although I don't recommend doing it in the same way that you'd hit a man. An openhanded slap is justified—if all other alternatives fail and there has been plenty of warning. If a woman is a bitch, or hysterical, or bloody-minded continually, then I'd do it. I think a man has to be slightly advanced, ahead of the woman.' In 1993, he reportedly told *Vanity Fair*, 'There are women who take it to the wire. That's what they are looking for, the ultimate confrontation. They want a smack.' His first wife, Diane Cilento, has alleged that he verbally and physically abused her during their marriage. In 1999, Connery was declared the Sexiest Man of the Century by *People* magazine. In 2000, he received a knighthood.

David Copperfield: In early 2018, a woman named Brittney Lewis claimed the magician had drugged and assaulted her in 1988, when she was a teenage model. She says she reported the incident to the FBI in 2007, the year that pageant winner Lacey Carroll accused Copperfield of sexually assaulting her in his home in the Bahamas. In 2017, Copperfield earned US$61.5 million.

Bill Cosby: Cosby's career may be well and truly over now, but allegations of sexual assault and rape have been made against the comedian for decades. He has been accused by more than fifty women of charges relating to rape, child sexual abuse, sexual battery and drug-facilitated sexual assault. His alleged crimes date back to 1965 and span a period of more than forty years. Although the allegations were hardly a secret, little attention was paid until until male comedian Hannibal Buress gave voice to them in 2014. That same year, tickets to Cosby's shows reportedly netted almost US$11 million. His net worth in 2018 was estimated to be approximately US$400 million.

Neil deGrasse Tyson: In 2014, Tchiya Amet published a blog post in which she alleged the astrophysicist drugged and raped her in 1984, when they studied together at the University of Texas. She repeated the claims in 2016 and then relinked to the blogpost in 2017 as the #MeToo movement began to take off. In 2015, the US

National Academy of Sciences awarded the Public Welfare Medal to Tyson in recognition of his 'extraordinary role in exciting the public about the wonders of science'.

Johnny Depp: In 2016, Amber Heard filed for divorce from her actor husband and applied for a temporary restraining order against him. She alleged Depp had begun 'obsessing over something that wasn't true' and 'became extremely angry'. She claimed the actor threw a phone at her 'with extreme force', and it connected with her cheek; photographic evidence of a bruise was later tendered. Claims of violence were backed up by friends of Heard, while Depp was publicly supported by the comedian Doug Stanhope, who in a column for *The Wrap* accused Heard of 'blackmailing' Depp. The director Terry Gilliam (who later criticised the #MeToo movement) tweeted a link to the column with the comment, 'Like many of Johnny Depp's friends I'm discovering that Amber is a better actress than I thought.' Heard and Depp eventually settled out of court, with Heard declaring she'd donate the proceeds to charity. Depp continues to represent Dior as their face of Sauvage. In 2017, following news Depp would resume his role as Gellert Grindelwald in *Fantastic Beasts: The Crimes of Grindelwald*, author J.K. Rowling said in a statement, 'Based on our understanding of the circumstances, the filmmakers and I are not only comfortable sticking with our original casting, but genuinely happy to have Johnny playing a major character in the movies.'

Michael Douglas: Journalist and author Susan Braudy has alleged that, when she was in charge of Douglas's New York production office in the late 1980s, he sexually harassed her and once masturbated in her presence. She claims she was asked to sign a confidentiality agreement, and that her employment was terminated shortly after. Her account has been corroborated by friends of hers from the time, including the author Michael Wolff. Douglas has called the story 'a complete lie'. In 2004, Douglas was the recipient of the Cecil B. DeMille award.

Ched Evans: Evans was convicted of rape in 2012, but successfully appealed his conviction on his release from prison (I have expanded on this case in 'Asking for it'). While in prison he had discussions with football officials about the possibility of him returning to his club, Sheffield United, but ultimately he signed with Chesterfield FC just prior to his retrial. In 2017, Sheffield United FC bought him from Chesterfield for half a million pounds and offered him a three-year contract that quadrupled his salary.

Michael Fassbender: In 2010, Sunawin 'Leasi' Andrews filed a restraining order against her former partner, Fassbender, that ordered him to stay at least a hundred yards away from her and her two children. She alleged abuse against the two-time Academy Award nominee that she claimed left her with US$24,000 in medical bills. She also alleged that, on one occasion, Fassbender returned from a night of partying with a friend and the two tried to get into bed with her. She left the room, but in her court filing detailed how, when she returned and tried to wake him the next morning, 'he threw me over a chair and broke my nose'. Following the allegations, Fassbender went on to star in *12 Years A Slave* (for which he received an Academy Award nomination), *X-Men: First Class* and *Alien: Covenant.*

James Franco: In January 2018, allegations emerged claiming Franco had sexually harassed two students at his Studio 4 film school. One of them, Sarah Tither-Kaplan, said she felt Franco created 'exploitative environments for non-celebrity women that he worked with under the guise of giving them opportunities'. By February, the number of accusers of sexual misconduct had risen to six. Shortly afterwards, it was announced that Franco would be returning to his starring role on HBO's *The Deuce.*

Mel Gibson: In 2010, Gibson was caught on tape telling his then wife Oksana Grigorieva that she 'looked like a fucking bitch in heat, and if you get raped by a pack of ni**ers it'll be your fault'. (Gibson had also been captured on tape in 2006 saying, 'Jews are responsible for all the wars in the world.') Shortly after, Grigorieva filed for a restraining order, claiming Gibson had punched her several times, causing injuries that included a broken tooth and a concussion. Gibson denied punching her, but admitted he had slapped her 'one time'. In 2018, Gibson was nominated for Best Director at the Academy Awards.

Alfred Hitchcock: In the early 1960s, the actress Tippi Hedren was under contract to work with the director she claimed subjected her to aggressive sexual advances. After she rejected him, Hitchcock is alleged to have 'acted vengefully toward her on the set and then, when she was unwilling to work with him again, refused to let her work with other directors'. Decades later, Hedren stated publicly, 'All those years ago, it was still the studio kind of situation. Studios were the power. And I was at the end of that, and there was absolutely nothing I could do legally whatsoever.' Hitchcock is widely regarded as being one of cinema's most important and influential auteurs. At the time of his death in 1980, he had a net worth of US$200 million.

Dustin Hoffman: As the #MeToo movement saw allegations emerge against a series of men in Hollywood, Hoffman was accused of having sexually harassed a number of former colleagues and employees, with one allegation dating back to 1984. Kathryn Rossetter claimed the actor had regularly groped her while the pair were performing together in *Death of a Salesman* on Broadway. She also says the actor exposed her body to the stage crew one night. The allegations came shortly after Anna Graham Hunter accused the actor of sexually harassing her when she was a seventeen-year-old intern on the film set of *Death of a Salesman* in 1985. A third woman says Hoffman exposed himself to her in a hotel room when she was a high school student. A fourth accused the actor of digitally penetrating her without her consent while they worked on the 1987 film *Ishtar.* A fifth alleged the same thing, this time while the pair were in a car filled with people. Even Meryl Streep has said Hoffman grabbed her breast the first time they met on the set of *Kramer vs. Kramer.* So far, nine women have alleged sexual misconduct against the actor. It's not yet clear what the impact will be on his career going forward but, throughout the decades this abuse is alleged to have occurred, he continued to win accolades and roles, including two Academy Awards for Best Actor.

Matthew 'Matty' Johns: A 2002 pack sex incident involving Johns and eleven of his teammates was brought to light in the 2009 broadcast of *Four Corners*' 'Code of Silence'. A nineteen-year-old woman was left with PTSD and suicidal ideation after her experience with the Cronulla Sharks (the team captained by Johns). By mutual agreement, Johns resigned from his role on Channel Nine's *The Footy Show* in the wake of the *Four Corners* report. Less than six months later, Nine invited Johns to rejoin its stable, offering an annual contract worth $600,000—more than he'd been on at the time of his resignation. He declined, accepting a deal in 2010 with Nine's network rival Channel Seven. Since 2011, he has co-hosted *The Grill* on Triple M radio. In 2012, he joined Fox Sports Australia, where he has hosted his own show ever since.

R. Kelly: Allegations against the musician span twenty-four years, dating right back to his (illegal) marriage to Aaliyah in 1994, when she was only fifteen. He has been sued numerous times for inappropriate sexual contact with a minor, settling out of court each time. He was at one point charged with creating child exploitation material, but was acquitted on the grounds that the jury couldn't be certain the person featuring opposite him in the video was a minor. In 2017, R. Kelly finished an arena tour and his music appeared on the soundtrack to *Pitch Perfect 3*. He has another tour planned for 2018.

John Kricfalusi: In 2018, two women accused the creator of *Ren & Stimpy* of preying on them when they were minors. Robyn Byrd and Katie Rice both allege Kricfalusi spent a period of time grooming them before sexually abusing them. Byrd was only sixteen when the animator flew her to Los Angeles to be his live-in girlfriend and 'intern'; their 'relationship' was an open secret among his co-workers. His lawyer has acknowledged the existence of this relationship, attributing it to a period of 'emotional and mental illness'. Nickelodeon continues to air *Ren & Stimpy*. Kricfalusi's net worth is estimated at US$10 million.

Matt Lauer: Numerous women have accused the former NBC host of sexual misconduct, including one woman who says Lauer exposed himself to her in his office and then reprimanded her for not performing a sex act on him. After the allegations became public, NBC fired the *Today* show host. But Lauer's misconduct is said to have been widely known for years. Several women said they complained to network executives, but their complaints were ignored. At the time of his dismissal, Lauer was on an annual salary of US$25 million.

Danny Masterson: Multiple women have alleged that US actor Masterson raped them in the early 2000s, with the first police report against him being filed in 2004. In response, the Church of Scientology (of which Masterson is a member) submitted more than fifty affidavits denying the woman's story. In March 2017, long before #MeToo, journalist Tony Ortega revealed the Los Angeles Police Department had been investigating Masterson for 'at least three alleged cases of rape or sodomy of women who were also Scientologists and who claim they were pressured by the Church of Scientology not to contact police or go public with their accusations'. Throughout this time, Masterson was starring in and executive producing the Netflix series *The Ranch*. It was eventually announced in December 2017 that the streaming service would be writing him out of the series.

T.J. Miller: During the early 2000s, the *Silicon Valley* star is alleged to have sexually assaulted and punched a fellow student at George Washington University. The claims were corroborated by a number of people who attended GWU at the time, as well as tested in a student court. In the intervening years, at least three sources in the comedy world confirmed that Miller joked privately about having perpetrated violence against a woman in the past. Some female performers told *The Daily Beast* that they refused to work with Miller because of this. Miller went on to appear in the sitcom *Silicon Valley* and to star in *The Emoji Movie* and *Deadpool* 2. His career has seemingly unravelled after a series of alcohol-related incidents, but a comedy club booker has said of him, 'Maybe he'll do rehab humour for his comeback.'

Roy Moore: In November 2017, nine women came forward to allege sexual misconduct against the US Senate candidate and former Chief Justice of the Supreme Court of Alabama. Three of these women allege Moore sexually assaulted them while they were still minors, with one as young as fourteen at the time. Most of the incidents were alleged to have occurred in the late 1970s, when Moore was an assistant district attorney. Although numerous high-profile Republicans called for Moore to withdraw from his Senate campaign, he was endorsed by none other than President Donald Trump. After initially cutting funds to his campaign, the Republican National Committee later renewed their support of Moore. He lost the election, but shortly after was granted an annual pension of just over US$135,000. In March 2018, it was reported he was seeking US$250,000 in donations to help him fight a lawsuit brought against him by Leigh Corfman, the woman who says he molested her when she was fourteen. At the time of reporting, he had raised little more than US$30,000.

Bill Murray: In 2008, Jennifer Butler filed for divorce from Murray, citing multiple counts of physical violence and a pattern of intimidation. Butler alleged in court documents that the revered actor and comedian punched her in the face during a confrontation in 2007, telling her she was 'lucky he didn't kill her'. The case was widely reported at the time. He went on to star in a number of television and movie projects, including Wes Anderson's *Isle of Dogs* and *Moonrise Kingdom*. In 2017, Murray's net worth was estimated at US$140 million.

Nelly: In February 2018, it was reported that the rapper was being investigated for an alleged sexual assault that occurred in 2017. His accuser claims she was brought into a dressing room by the rapper, who proceeded to masturbate in front of her and try to force her to perform oral sex on him. In 2017, Nelly was accused of rape by a twenty-two-year-old student from the University of Washington. Months later two more women came forward to allege sexual assault against him. In June 2018, Nelly embarked on a tour of the United States, with many of the shows sold out.

Gary Oldman: In 2001, Donya Fiorentino alleged that her ex-husband choked her and beat her with a telephone as their children looked on. She has since called their marriage 'a giant car crash', and said, 'I would rather get eaten by a great white shark than go through [it] again.' Oldman went on to star in numerous films, including the Harry Potter franchise. In 2018, he received the Academy Award for Best Actor for his turn as Winston Churchill in *The Darkest Hour.*

Bill O'Reilly: In January 2017, the top-rating Fox News host settled a sexual harassment suit for US$32 million. Twenty-First Century Fox (headed by Rupert Murdoch) acknowledged at the time they had been aware of the woman's numerous allegations against O'Reilly, which included repeated harassment, the sending of pornographic material to her and a 'nonconsensual sexual relationship'. Prior to this, there had been at least five similar settlements made relating to allegations of sexual abuse by O'Reilly. In February 2017, Twenty-First Century Fox extended his contract by four years, at an annual salary of US$25 million. In October 2017, the *New York Times* reported that Murdoch (along with his sons Lachlan and James) 'made a business calculation to stand by Mr. O'Reilly despite his most recent, and potentially most explosive, harassment dispute', believing that his 'value to the network increased after the departure of another prominent host, Megyn Kelly'. Kelly had left the network after alleging sexual harassment against its CEO, Roger Ailes. In April 2017, O'Reilly's contract was terminated after some of the settlements became public. Details of those settlements included the fact that the women involved were required to turn over any and all evidence they had against O'Reilly, and to discredit the materials as 'counterfeit and forgeries' if they were ever to become public. He was rumoured to have left Fox with a US$25 million severance package. In late 2017, his net worth was reported as hovering somewhere between US$85 and US$100 million.

Sean Penn: In 1988, the actor was alleged to have assaulted his then wife, Madonna. Penn pleaded guilty to a misdemeanour. He went on to win the Academy Award for Best Actor twice, once in 2003 and again in 2008. The wins followed three earlier nominations.

Roman Polanski: In 1977, the auteur was charged with drugging and raping a thirteen-year-old girl (he pled guilty to the lesser charge of unlawful sex with a minor), but soon fled to France, where he has lived since. When Swiss authorities arrested him in 2009 and threatened to return him to the US, thousands of celebrities (including Harvey Weinstein and Woody Allen) became signatories to a petition started by French philosopher Bernard-Henri Lévy calling for his exoneration. Citing Polanski's difficult life as an excuse for his crime, Levy argued, 'It is shameful to throw a 76-year-old man into prison for unlawful sex committed 32 years ago.' In 2002, Polanski won the Cannes Film Festival's Palme d'Or for his movie *The Pianist*, and an Academy Award, BAFTA and César Award for Best Director. In 2009, he received a lifetime achievement award at the Zurich Film Festival.

Terry Richardson: Allegations against the photographer date back to at least 2010, when model Jamie Peck claimed Richardson had asked whether he could 'make tea with her used tampon', took his clothes off and 'aggressively assaulted her'. In 2014, model Anna del Gaizo told *Jezebel* that he had exposed himself and tried to persuade her to perform oral sex on him, while model Sena Cech also alleged sexual abuse against him. They join numerous other women who have alleged sexual misconduct against Richardson over the years. During that same period, Richardson has photographed high-profile celebrities, including Miley Cyrus, Lady Gaga, Beyoncé and even President Barack Obama. In late 2017, almost two decades after the first allegation against Richardson was made, Condé Nast announced they would be severing all contracts with him.

Arnold Schwarzenegger: Five days before the 2003 election in which Schwarzenegger rose to the position of California governor, he was accused by several women of having engaged in sexual harassment over a period of at least twenty-five years. The allegations included claims by three women that Schwarzenegger had groped their breasts, while a fourth said he had grabbed her bottom underneath her skirt. The actor and politician apologised, saying he had 'behaved badly sometimes' while denying some of the claims. He said, 'I've learned my lesson. I think that now I am not representing myself but representing the state of California, it is a totally different ball game.' In 2011, after completing two terms as governor, he returned to acting. He reprised his role as the Terminator in 2015's *Terminator Genisys*. In February 2018, Amazon Studios announced they were developing a new series called *Outrider* that Schwarzenegger will both star in and executive produce. In 2019, he will appear in a new *Terminator* movie.

Ryan Seacrest: In February 2018, Suzie Hardy told *Variety* that she had been sexually harassed for years by her former boss. The single mother, who had worked as Seacrest's personal stylist for *E! News*, said she endured 'unwanted, sexually aggressive touching, groping and attention'. She first reported the alleged harassment in 2013, and was fired shortly afterwards. Seacrest continues to host *Live with Kelly and Ryan* and *American Idol*, and produces *Keeping Up with the Kardashians*. His net worth is estimated at US$380 million.

Charlie Sheen: Charlie Sheen has a long history of allegedly abusing women, including 'accidentally' shooting fiancée Kelly Preston in the arm, throwing chairs at former wife Denise Richards, being sued by a UCLA student for allegedly hitting her in the head after she refused to have sex with him and, in 2009, being arrested for assaulting his wife Brooke Mueller. At the time, he was the highest-paid actor on television, earning US$1.25 million per episode for his role in *Two and a Half Men*. It was only after making disparaging public comments about the show's creator, Chuck Lorre, in 2011 that Sheen's contract was terminated. By the time of his dismissal, his per episode salary had jumped to US$1.8 million. He was hired again to star in the sitcom *Anger Management*, which commanded the highest ad rates the FX network had ever seen.

Bill Shorten: In 2014, it emerged that the Labor leader had been accused of sexual assault back in the 1980s. The alleged victim stated on Facebook: 'In 1985 I joined the ALP. In 86 at the age of 16 I . . . became a delegate for state and national conferences. In 86 I went to a Young Labor camp down near Geelong . . . I was alone . . . at about 4am there was a knock at my door. It was him at the door. He pushed me into a bathroom, up against a towel rail, pulled down my pants and raped me.' After the allegation emerged, Victoria Police confirmed they had investigated a charge of historic sexual assault but were advised by the Office of Public Prosecutions that there was no reasonable prospect of conviction. As such, no criminal charges were pursued. Shorten remains the leader of the ALP at the time of writing. He has always adamantly denied the allegations.

Jeffrey Tambor: In late 2017, American actor Tambor's former assistant Van Barnes alleged that the actor had groped and propositioned her. Tambor denied the allegations, but they were soon followed by new claims from his co-star on *Transparent*, Trace Lysette. He continued to vehemently deny the accusations, expressing disappointment in the decision of Amazon and Jill Soloway (*Transparent*'s creator) to end his employment with the show. Shortly afterwards, it was announced he would be appearing in season five of *Arrested Development*. In a *New York Times* interview with the cast in May 2018, Tambor was defended by some of his male castmates over an incident in which he verbally harassed co-star Jessica Walter on-set, reducing her to tears. Walter had described the incident as being one of the worst she had ever experienced during a career spanning more than six decades.

Robin Thicke: The creator of what has been called an anthem for sexual assault ('Blurred Lines') was accused in 2017 of having been violent towards his former partner, Paula Patton. Patton was granted a temporary restraining order against the musician, and said Thicke had been physically and emotionally abusive. In June 2018, 'Blurred Lines' was certified diamond, having become one of the best-selling singles of all time.

Clarence Thomas: In 1991, Anita Hill testified before US Congress that Thomas, a candidate for the Supreme Court, had engaged in a pattern of sexual harassment while she worked for him at the Department of Education and the Equal Employment Opportunity Commission. Hill, an African-American woman, was decried as a 'liar, a temptress and a race-traitor' who was 'trying to keep a black man off the Supreme Court'. Thomas was ultimately confirmed by the Senate, with a vote of fifty-two in favour, forty-eight opposed. Supreme Court appointments are for life. The annual salary is more than US$250,000.

James Toback: In October 2017, an article appeared in the *Los Angeles Times* citing thirty-eight women alleged to have been subjected to sexual harassment by the award-winning director and writer. Since the article appeared, the number of accusers has risen to more than 200. One of those women, A-list actress Rachel McAdams, says she was twenty-one when Toback sexually harassed her on the pretext of meeting to discuss an audition. When she told her agent the next morning, she recalls her agent getting mad and saying, 'I can't believe he did it again. He did this to one of my other actresses.' In April 2018, it was reported that the LA County District Attorney's Office had declined to press charges against Toback.

Donald Trump: To date, at least sixteen women have alleged sexual harassment and/or assault at the hands of Trump. He has been accused of raping a thirteen-year-old girl. His former wife, Ivana Trump, alleged in divorce proceedings that Trump had raped her during their marriage, though the claims were later recalled after a settlement was reached. In late 2016, shortly before the US election in which Trump was running as the Republican nominee for president, audio footage from 2005 was released in which he can be heard to say, 'You know, I'm automatically attracted to beautiful—I just start kissing them. It's like a magnet. Just kiss. I don't even wait. And when you're a star, they let you do it. You can do anything. Grab 'em by the pussy.' Trump is now the president of the United States of America.

Mike Tyson: In 1992, heavyweight boxer Mike Tyson was handed a six-year prison sentence for raping Desiree Washington, who was eighteen at the time. He was released after three. His first wife, Robin Givens, described life with Tyson as 'torture, pure hell, worse than anything I could possibly have imagined'. He appeared in the 2009 buddy movie *The Hangover* playing a caricature of himself. In 2012, director Spike Lee helped Tyson bring his one-man show *Mike Tyson: Undisputed Truth* to Broadway. In 2013, Tyson's book *Undisputed Truth* made it onto the *New York Times* bestseller list. In 2017, *USA Today* wrote in a positive profile piece that the former boxer turned podcaster had 'reinvented himself and become a sought-after personality just by being himself'. In 2018, he became the face of an ad campaign for Ultra Tune, an Australian car-servicing company.

Lars von Trier: In 2017, singer-songwriter and actress Björk spoke publicly for the first time about the abuse she was allegedly subjected to while filming von Trier's *Dancer in the Dark* (2000). In two separate Facebook posts, Bjork accused the Danish director of having repeatedly sexually harassed her during the course of the production, alleging he even tried to sneak into her room at one point. In 2018, von Trier was welcomed back to the Cannes Film Festival—following a seven-year ban issued in 2011, for comments in which he joked he was a Nazi—to promote his new film. *The House That Jack Built* follows a serial killer over the course of twelve years as he mutilates and tortures women and children. Although a significant number of people walked out during the screening, those who remained gave the film a standing ovation.

Harvey Weinstein: In October 2017, a *New York Times* article detailed allegations of sexual harassment, abuse and assault perpetrated by the powerful Hollywood producer dating back to 1985. The allegations spawned the #timesup movement, and the #MeToo movement founded by civil rights activist Tarana Burke a decade earlier went global. Weinstein's accusers included well-known actresses like Rose McGowan, Angelina Jolie, Gwyneth Paltrow, Annabella Sciorra, Salma Hayek, Lupita Nyong'o, Ashley Judd, Mira Sorvino and Asia Argento, plus dozens and dozens more. Since the initial story broke, more than eighty women have accused the former head of Miramax and The Weinstein Company of abuse. The incidents include at least eighteen allegations of rape. In 2010, former Miramax employee Ivana Lowell wrote about Weinstein's behaviour in her memoir, *Why Not Say What Happened?* He was questioned in 2015 by members of the New York Police Department after model Ambra Gutierrez reported he had touched her inappropriately. Gutierrez worked with the NYPD to record Weinstein admitting to the behaviour. On the audio tape, he can be heard trying to coerce her to accompany him to his hotel room as she repeatedly resists. Against the advice of local police, the Manhattan District Attorney declined to press charges. References and jokes about Weinstein's behaviour towards women—young actresses in particular—date back decades, with Gwyneth Paltrow hinting on the *Late Show with David Letterman* in 1998 that Weinstein will 'coerce you to do a thing or two'. In 2018, Paltrow revealed to *Vanity Fair* that Weinstein had tried to assault her in a hotel room in the late 1990s. She told her boyfriend, Brad Pitt, about it at the time and reports that he 'threatened to kill Harvey' if he ever went near her again. Pitt went on to make numerous movies with Miramax and The

Weinstein Company. Rose McGowan alleges Weinstein raped her during this same period. Lucia Evans, a former actress, alleges Weinstein orally raped her in 2004. In a 2017 article for the *New Yorker*, Ronan Farrow alleges that the previous year Weinstein had hired ex-Mossad agents to collect information on his accusers and the journalists investigating him, and to use this to discredit their claims. Numerous women allege Weinstein threatened to destroy their careers if they spoke out against him or refused to comply with his advances. In December 2017, the director Peter Jackson admitted he blacklisted Mira Sorvino and Ashley Judd after what he called 'a smear campaign by Harvey Weinstein'. Both women had been slated to appear in Jackson's adaptation of *The Lord of the Rings*, but were abruptly dropped from the production. In May 2018, Weinstein was arrested by the NYPD and charged with multiple counts of rape, criminal sex acts, sex abuse and sexual misconduct. Weinstein pleaded not guilty. At the time of writing, he was awaiting trial. His net worth is currently estimated at US$50 million.

EPILOGUE

Dear F_____

My darling boy, the first thing you need to know is that I love you. My love for you is a constantly evolving creature. It has made its home in my heart, but it travels through every part of my body finding new places to set down roots. Every night, I think to myself that it's impossible for me to love you any more than I already do; that my body is so full of love for you that it simply can't fit a shred more in. And every morning I wake up and realise that, just like you, it's grown a little bit more in the dark.

A few hours after you were born, when the chaos of birth was over and our room was quiet and still, I began to drift off to sleep only to be interrupted by a wet, mucous-y cough coming from the bassinette next to my bed. I bolted upright and furiously smashed the call button for the nurse. I lifted you up, still unsure of how to hold you properly, and handed you to the calm man who appeared before me.

Don't worry, he said, gently rubbing your tiny back. *This is normal.*

I felt in that moment just how terrifying it was to have you, the precious person who had placed such primal trust in me. It seemed like life from then on would be lived on the precipice of a cliff, and that if I failed to pay proper attention you could go tumbling over the edge. When we brought you home from the hospital, I lay with you on our bed in the dim glow of the lamplight and thought to myself, *I've made a terrible mistake.* I knew that a huge amount of responsibility lay before me, and I feared I wasn't up to the task.

I hope you know that having you has been the greatest gift of my life.

At first, I didn't know how to have a boy. I know how cruel the world can be to girls, and that this cruelty in turn affects the boys who don't conform to what people expect of them. I knew that no matter what kind of boy you turned out to be (if, indeed, you turned out to be a boy), there was no guarantee you would be treated kindly for it. To be *girlish* as a boy is to be deficient in some way. To do things 'like a girl' is to be embarrassingly lacking in skills and ability, a shameful waste of all the promise your masculinity is supposed to deliver on. The boys perceived to be 'too feminine' by a society terrified of what soft, gentle masculinity might mean are frequently subjected to the twin tyrannies of homophobia and misogyny. We will always provide shelter for you from other people's fear and bigotry, but not every boy is so lucky.

In our house, you'll be just as likely to find princess costumes in your toy box as you will a pirate's hat or a football. You're currently obsessed with trains, but you also like to put them in the seat of your dolly stroller and walk them around the living room. You ballet dance along with Emma Wiggle, and when she says goodbye you lift your hands to your head and copy her as she wishes you a 'bowtiful day'. You may not ever want to wear the dresses we have hanging in your closet, but we want you to know that they are just as legitimate a choice for you as a pair of jeans. I'm prepared (I think) for the moment you might come home from kindy or school and tell me something like 'pink isn't for boys' or that 'girls can't do x, y or z', but it still breaks my heart to know how little time you and your friends have before that lesson will be forced on you. I'm trying to make sure you're strong enough to resist it. I hope I succeed. No matter what happens, I hope that our home will always be a soft place for you to land.

There are other homes out there, battlegrounds with lines drawn around gendered roles and expectations. In such homes, there are daily reminders of what makes a 'real' boy, and they're strictly enforced. These boys live with adults who deny them toys and clothes based on nothing more convincing than the sex they've been assigned at birth. They might have fathers who mock them for liking butterflies and fairies, and mothers who side with those men because they're also afraid of what it means to produce a son who, in their eyes, 'fails' at being a boy. This is where the first lessons of toxic masculinity are learned, and the potential they have to cause lifelong harm cannot be underestimated.

You are lucky, my darling. You have a father who is gentle and kind, who models empathy and compassion. You will never be made to feel ashamed or afraid to cry in front of him. Sharing your emotions isn't a sign of weakness—it's a sign of strength.

You're only little now, and you probably think I have the answers to everything. But by the time you read this, you'll be old enough to realise that I'm just as confused about life as you are. I can only tell you what I've learned along the way.

Here's what I know.

Your kindness and empathy are valuable. You have both these things in spades, and you must hold on to them. If you trust what they tell you, they'll help you to make the right choices.

Power is not gained by taking something from another person. Don't use women as a way to reckon with your own feelings of inadequacy or anger. We are not the conduits for male pain.

Violence is not the way to solve your problems. You'll meet people along the way who think it's normal for boys to scrap with each other, to use their fists to settle disagreements and try to come out the winner. These people are wrong. Violence is ugly and brutal, and you are neither of these things.

We all need to be held sometimes. Homophobia is such a destructive force in men's lives. It teaches you to avoid each other's touch and to shield yourselves from platonic male affection. It's okay to hug another man. It's okay to cry in front of each other. It's okay to say you love each other. Be stronger than the message that tells you sharing basic human emotions with another man makes you somehow less of one.

Respect women. Unless we succeed in radically changing the world in the next twenty years, understand that women have legitimate reasons to be afraid of you sometimes. This isn't a reflection on your behaviour (I hope) but a response to the realities of the world they live in. Instead of getting upset about how it makes you feel, work with them to help make it different.

Enjoy friendships with women. Listen to women when they talk to you about their lives, and recognise that their experiences are just as valid as yours. They don't need you to explain their feelings or rationalise the things they might be talking about. As a white man, there are lots of inequalities you'll be protected from during your life. Seek to expand your understanding of the world and the privilege you have within it, and then be a part of dismantling the system.

Resist other men's attempts to bond with you over the degradation of women. It isn't funny to joke about raping women or beating them. Telling them to 'get back into the kitchen' or 'make a sandwich' is bad comedy, and we've raised you with better teachers than that. I hear these things from boys and men all the time, and I can tell you they're not funny—they're degrading and frightening. Don't align yourself with people who rely on making women feel afraid in order to make themselves feel better. Too many men claim to oppose gendered violence while failing to speak out against it when they see their peers perpetrating it. You can be braver than that.

Seek intimacy. Sex should be a conversation between consenting adults. You are not owed anything by anybody.

Recognise that there is infinite pleasure to be had in making sure your partner or partners are enjoying themselves, and exploring your mutual desires together. They can say no at any stage. So can you.

Embrace sensitivity. Don't let a world that's frightened of soft men succeed in breaking you. We have too many broken men. We need men like you, men whose strength comes from being gentle. Have faith in this.

Remember, your life is no more valuable than anyone else's. But you can live in a way that brings value to everybody.

These are the things I wanted to teach you. I hope I have succeeded.

But all that is in the future. For the time being, yours is a simple life. You wake, you eat, you play and you sleep. We ask you where your foot is and you grab it, smiling. You laugh endlessly, and it is the most beautiful thing I've ever heard. When your friends come to play, you hug them. When you walk together, you reach for their 'ham'. You know how to say *please*. You know how to say *thank you*. You know how to say *sorry*.

You are my son, my sun. I am dazzled by your brightness. You burn me with your beauty. I am at peace in the warmth of your rays.

I want this world to be different for you. I want you to have more choices about the kind of boy you want to be. Boys will be boys, but we have so far collectively failed to let you all be anything other than the most rigid, damaging and reductive form of boy. What if we tried to do things differently? It might require a number of attempts on our part. We may have to return to the drawing board again and again. But if we work at it, if we direct our energies into addressing our mistakes and finding better solutions, we can paint an alternative picture.

Boys will be sensitive. Boys will be soft. Boys will be kind. Boys will be gentle. Boys will respect girls. Boys will be accountable for their actions. Boys will be expressive. Boys will be loving. Boys will be nurturing.

Boys will be different from everything the world has so far told them they have to be in order to be a man.

To my darling son, my light and my life. I will not be the one who hands you the knife and shows you how to carve out the parts of yourself that don't fit. To the sons of my friends, to my nephews. To the boys who want butterflies painted on their cheeks, the boys who twirl in dresses and the boys who always pick the sparkly shoes: we can do this together.

Are you ready?

Love,
Mummy

ACKNOWLEDGMENTS

How do I begin to thank all of the people who helped bring this book to life? It has been a labour of love, tears and heartache in so many ways, and I couldn't possibly have managed without the incredible support of the people who believed in it just as much as I do.

First and foremost, to my formidable publisher Jane Palfreyman at Allen & Unwin. There aren't enough words in the world to thank you for the faith you've shown in me over the last three years. I am so proud to call you a friend and mentor. To work with someone so passionate is a blessing, but to do this in particular with someone who cares as deeply about these issues as I do is truly a gift. Australian publishing is so lucky to have you. To my publishers at Oneworld, thank you thank you thank you for taking a chance on an Australian girl.

To Christa Munns and Ali Lavau, who have worked their magic once again by kindly prodding me to burn the bits that weren't working and to help shape the bits that showed promise into something much better. This book would be a dog's breakfast without you. Thank you to Sarah Baker for her careful proofreading of these pages, and her insightful margin notes! Thank you also to Harriet Wade at Oneworld and Kate Bland – you are perfection.

To my publicist, Louise Cornegé. What can I say? I adore you. In all the brilliant things that have happened in the last couple of years, it seems unfair that I also got to find a wonderful new friend. But I'll take it.

To Tami Rex and Fleur Hamilton: marketing are the unsung heroes behind book sales and us sensitive, highly strung authors thank you from the bottoms of our insecure little hearts.

Thank you to Jacinta di Mase, who is still quite literally the best agent anyone could ask for. I cannot imagine what my life would be like now if I hadn't met with you in that coffee shop all those years ago. I would probably be working in that coffee shop. I love you.

Thank you to my editor at Fairfax, Nat Reilly, who has been so understanding about the weeks I've taken off at the last minute to get this writing done. You rock my world. Thank you for believing in me.

My deepest gratitude to Margot Fink and Nevo Zisin for their work as sensitivity readers on the chapter 'It's a boy', and also to Gala Vanting for her work as a sensitivity reader on the chapter 'We know what boys are like'. Your insights were invaluable and greatly appreciated.

My heartfelt thanks to the following people who all generously permitted me to quote their work throughout this book: Jess Hill, Carina Chocano, Ben Folds and Matt Lubchansky. Some excerpts from this text have also previously appeared in my columns for Fairfax.

Thank you to the women who hold me close: Fyfe, Pop, Swish, Tui, Betho, Maim. You're still the best girl gang out.

Amy Gray, I miss you like a left arm that's been lost in a war. Let's go buy some Motown records soon.

This book literally couldn't have been written without the generous support of those who lent me their quiet houses. To Marieke Hardy and Amelia Chappelow, you are angels. Thank you to Polly for being my writing companion in these times. Thank you also to the legendary Mary Crooks from the Victorian Women's Trust. I can't stress enough how important it is for women (and mothers especially) to be given the gift of space and time to write. It is political, of course, as everything is.

To my crew of mothers, for whom this is all as pressing and important as it is to me. Anais, thank you for being the one to steady the ship when needed. Anna, thank you for paving the way. Karen, thank you for being a sounding board. To Lou, who has shared a carriage with me on the motherhood train from the beginning and whose companionship I would be lost without. My sister and best friend, Charlotte, who has always provided me with a perfect model of compassion, patience and empathy. To all of you, thank you for being so committed to raising boys who will be different. They are lucky to have you, as am I.

To Paige. Simply put, this book wouldn't exist without your care and support for F. Thank you for loving him so dearly, and being someone I can trust wholeheartedly to leave him with. Every page of this book has you written on it.

To my mother, Luciana. I miss you every day.

Thank you to my partner Jesse. The last time I wrote acknowledgments like these out, we were two waiting to become three. Who knows what extraordinary things we did in a past life to deserve the bood but if we don't make any sudden movements, maybe they won't realise they made a mistake. Thank you for being the best, kindest, and softest example of loving masculinity that he could possibly have. I have no fears for him, because he has you.

Finally, to my son. You are the reason. You are the answer.